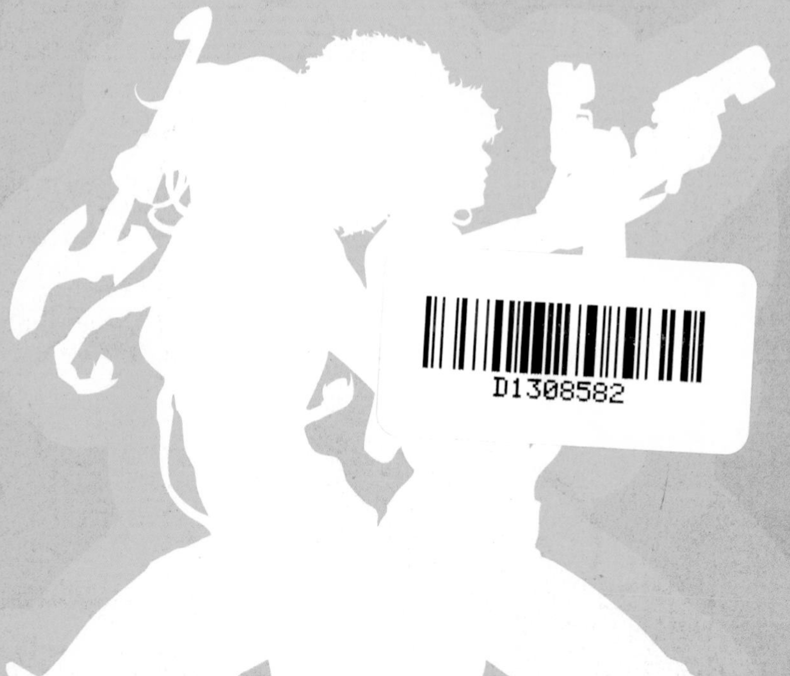

THE FEARLESS DEFENDERS

DOOM MAIDENS

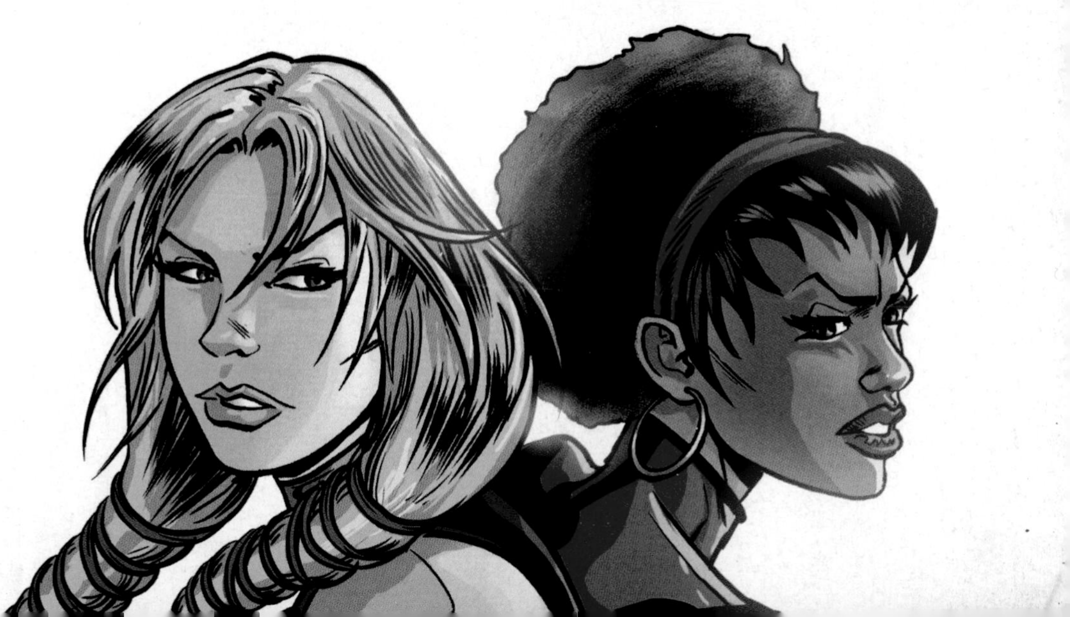

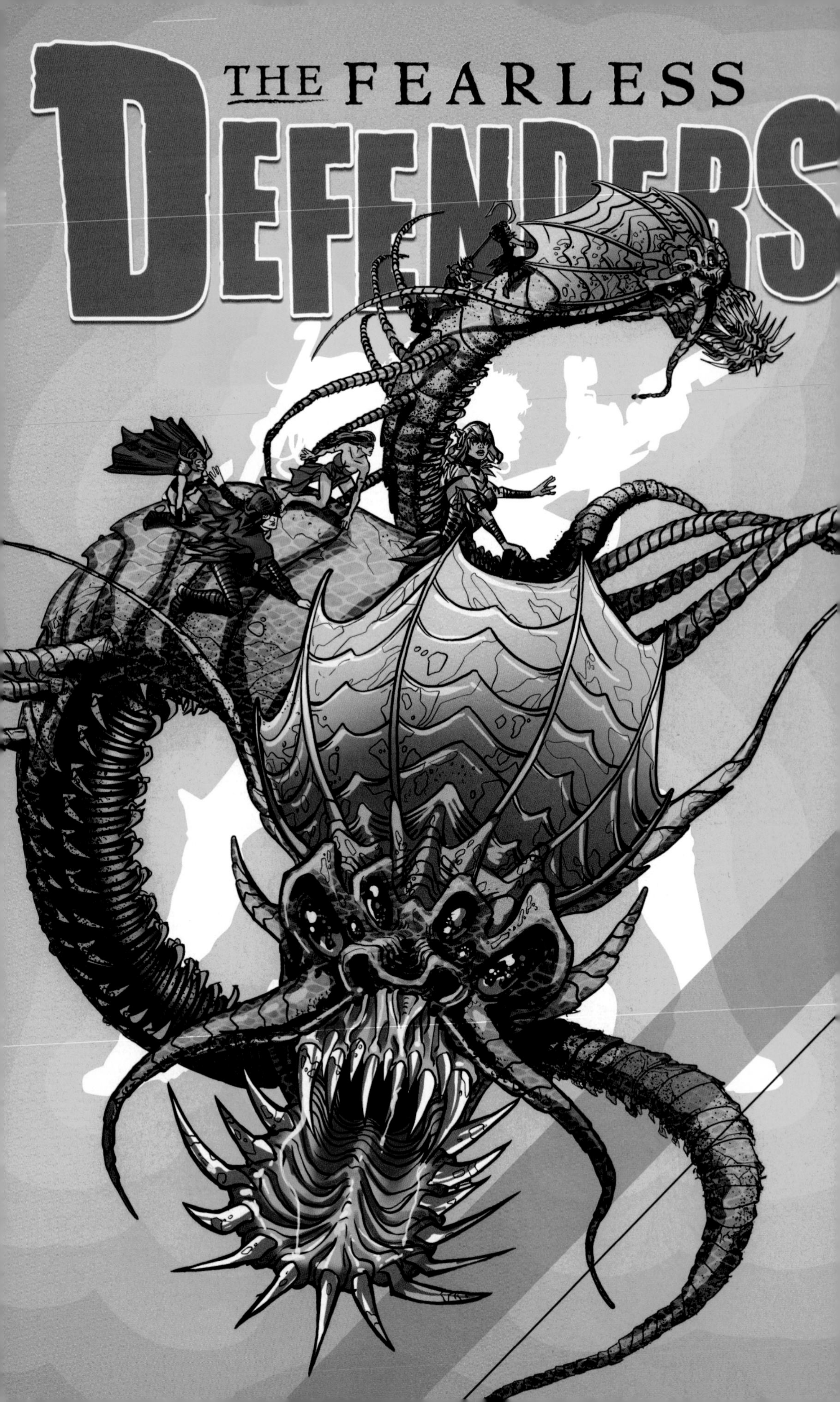

THE FEARLESS
DEFENDERS

DOOM MAIDENS

WRITER
CULLEN BUNN

ARTIST
WILL SLINEY

COLORIST
VERONICA GANDINI

LETTERER
VC'S CLAYTON COWLES

COVER ART
MARK BROOKS

COLLECTION EDITOR
JENNIFER GRÜNWALD
ASSISTANT EDITORS
ALEX STARBUCK
& NELSON RIBEIRO
EDITOR, SPECIAL PROJECTS
MARK D. BEAZLEY
SENIOR EDITOR, SPECIAL PROJECTS
JEFF YOUNGQUIST
SVP OF PRINT & DIGITAL PUBLISHING SALES
DAVID GABRIEL
BOOK DESIGNER
RODOLFO MURAGUCHI

EDITOR IN CHIEF
AXEL ALONSO
CHIEF CREATIVE OFFICER
JOE QUESADA
PUBLISHER
DAN BUCKLEY
EXECUTIVE PRODUCER
ALAN FINE

EDITOR
ELLIE PYLE

EXECUTIVE EDITOR
TOM BREVOORT

FEARLESS DEFENDERS VOL.1: DOOM MAIDENS. Contains material originally published in magazine form as FEARLESS DEFENDERS #1-6. First printing 2013. ISBN# 978-0-7851-6848-5. Published by MARVEL WORLDWIDE, INC., a subsidiary of MARVEL ENTERTAINMENT, LLC. OFFICE OF PUBLICATION: 135 West 50th Street, New York, NY 10020. Copyright © **2013** Marvel Characters, Inc. All rights reserved. All characters featured in this issue and the distinctive names and likenesses thereof, and all related indicia are trademarks of Marvel Characters, Inc. No similarity between any of the names, characters, persons, and/or institutions in this magazine with those of any living or dead person or institution is intended, and any such similarity which may exist is purely coincidental. **Printed in the U.S.A.** ALAN FINE, EVP - Office of the President, Marvel Worldwide, Inc. and EVP & CMO Marvel Characters B.V.; DAN BUCKLEY, Publisher & President - Print, Animation & Digital Divisions; JOE QUESADA, Chief Creative Officer; TOM BREVOORT, SVP of Publishing; DAVID BOGART, SVP of Operations & Procurement, Publishing; C.B. CEBULSKI, SVP of Creator & Content Development; DAVID GABRIEL, SVP of Print & Digital Publishing Sales; JIM O'KEEFE, VP of Operations & Logistics; DAN CARR, Executive Director of Publishing Technology; SUSAN CRESPI, Editorial Operations Manager; ALEX MORALES, Publishing Operations Manager; STAN LEE, Chairman Emeritus. For information regarding advertising in Marvel Comics or on Marvel.com, please contact Niza Disla, Director of Marvel Partnerships, at ndisla@marvel.com. For Marvel subscription inquiries, please call 800-217-9158. **Manufactured between 6/22/2013 and 7/30/2013 by QUAD/GRAPHICS ST. CLOUD, ST. CLOUD, MN, USA.**

10 9 8 7 6 5 4 3 2 1

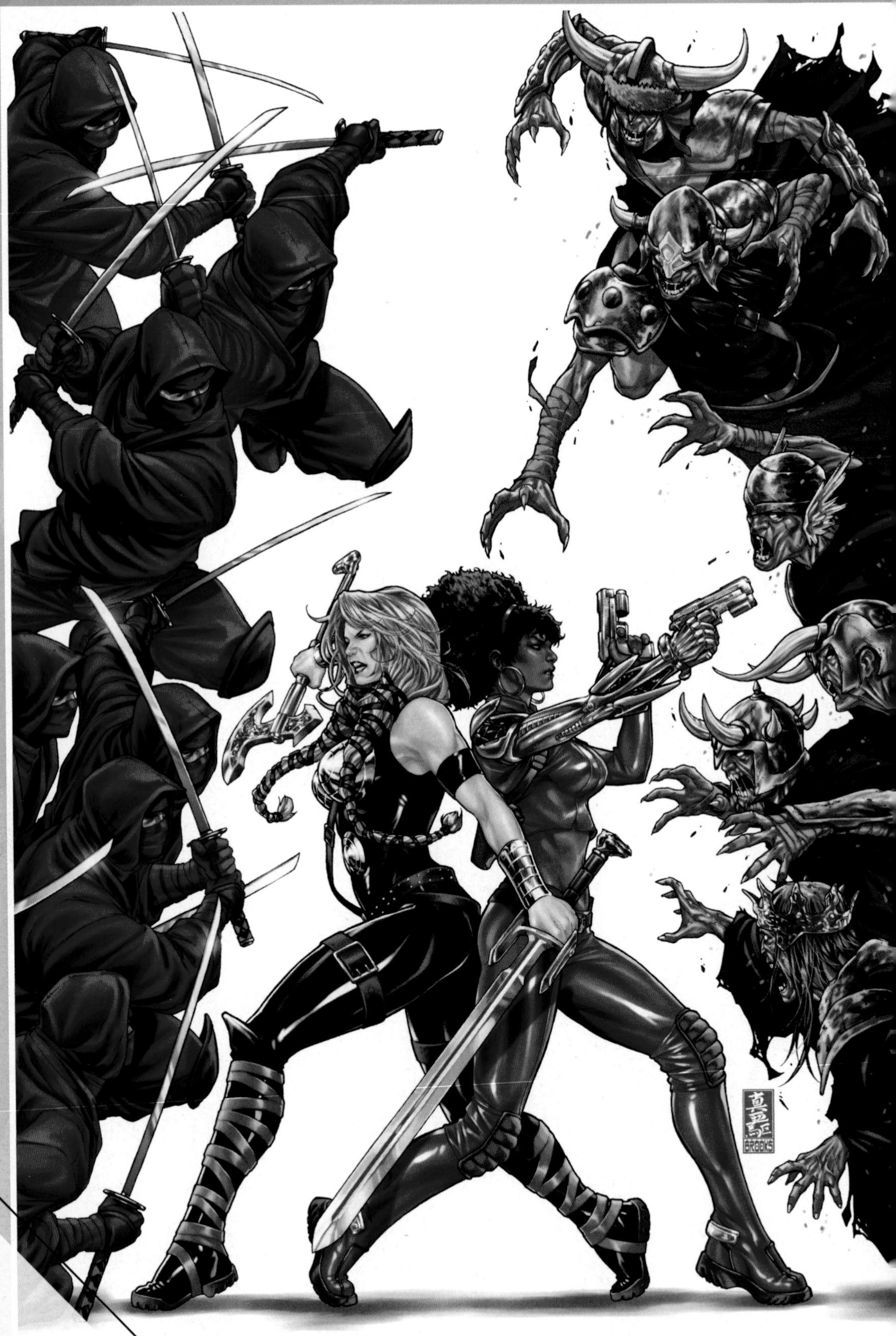
BROOKS

1

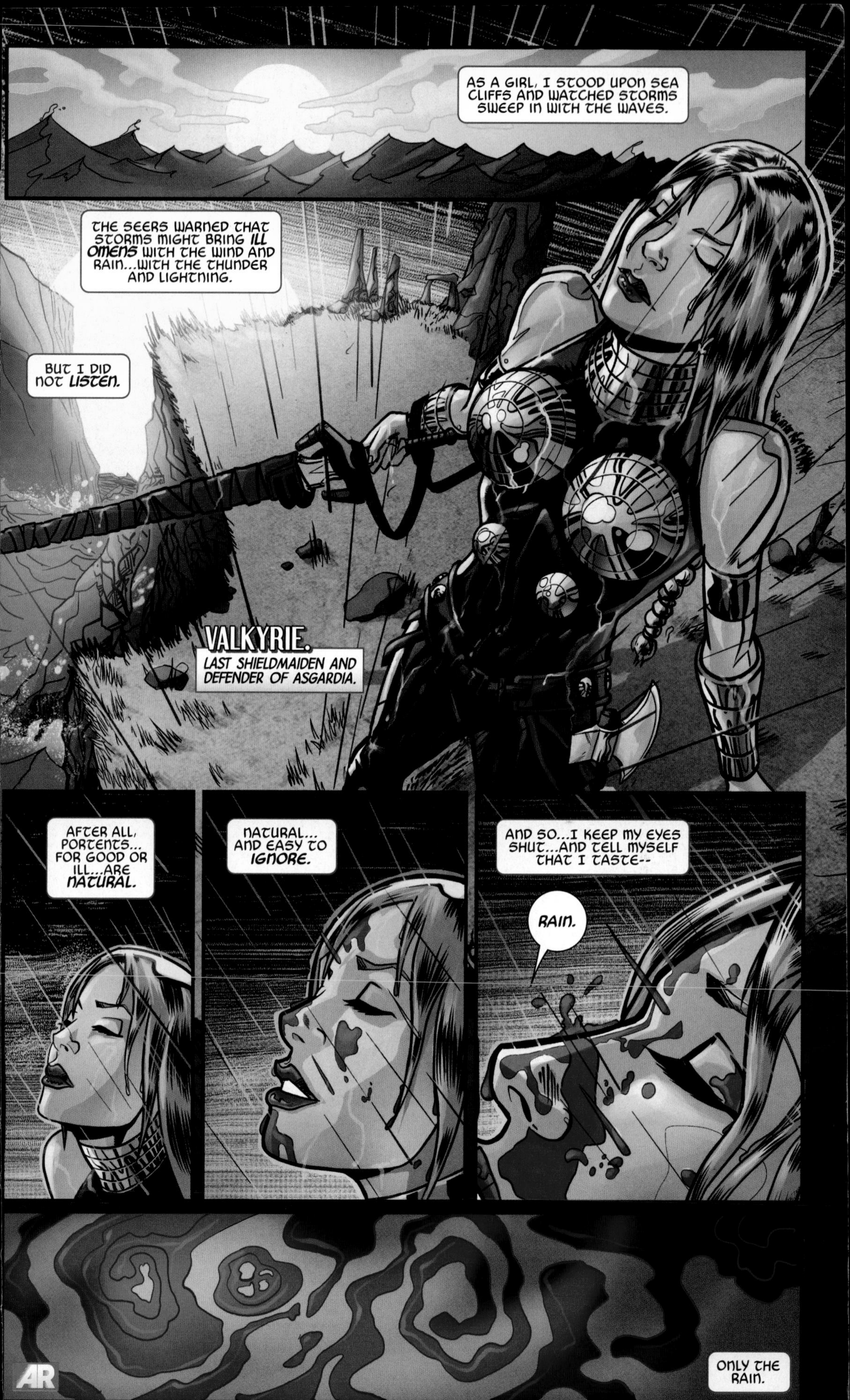

AS A GIRL, I STOOD UPON SEA CLIFFS AND WATCHED STORMS SWEEP IN WITH THE WAVES.
THE SEERS WARNED THAT STORMS MIGHT BRING ILL OMENS WITH THE WIND AND RAIN...WITH THE THUNDER AND LIGHTNING.
BUT I DID NOT LISTEN.
VALKYRIE.
LAST SHIELDMAIDEN AND DEFENDER OF ASGARDIA.
AFTER ALL, PORTENTS... FOR GOOD OR ILL...ARE NATURAL.
NATURAL... AND EASY TO IGNORE.
AND SO...I KEEP MY EYES SHUT...AND TELL MYSELF THAT I TASTE--
RAIN.
ONLY THE RAIN.

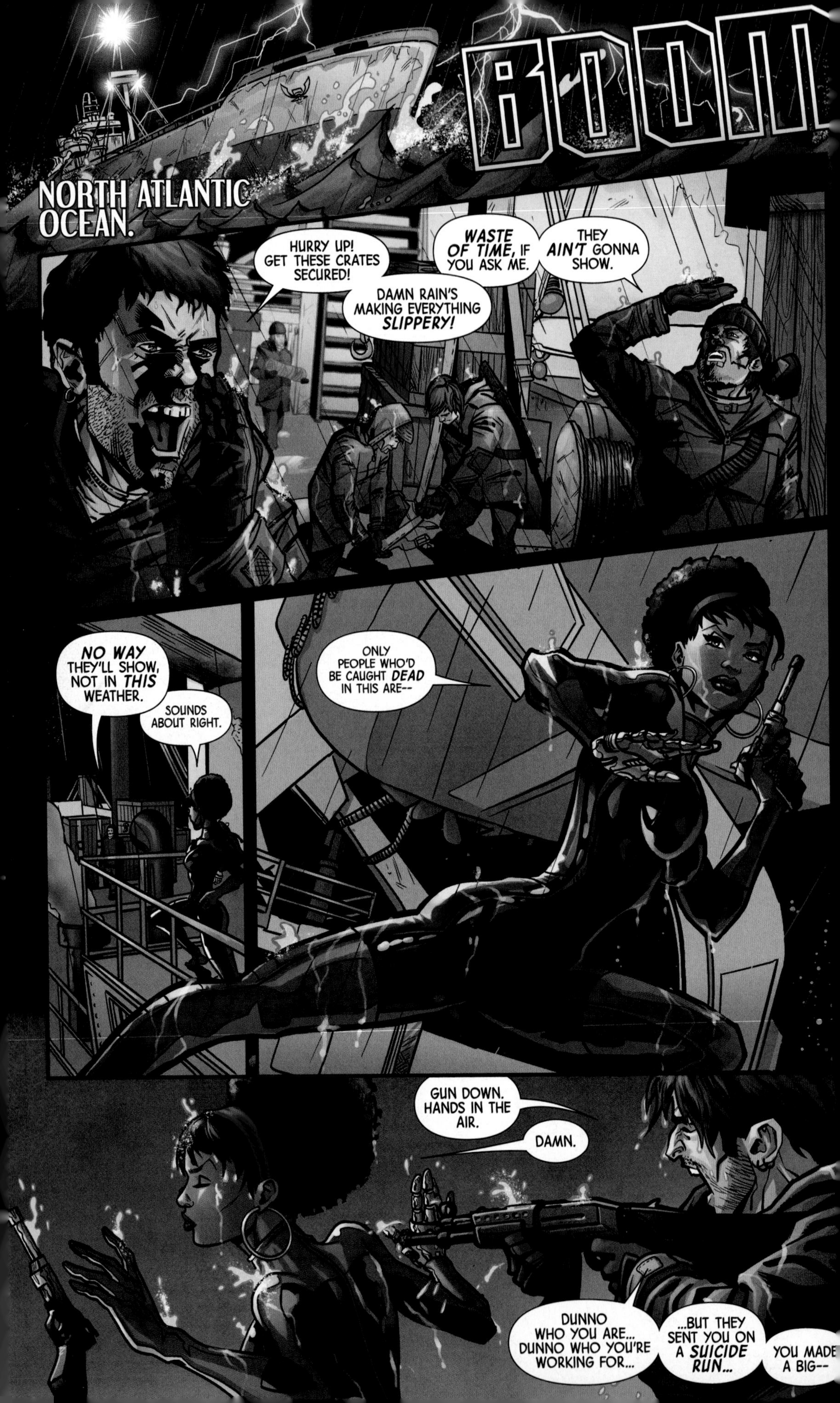
BOOM
NORTH ATLANTIC OCEAN.
HURRY UP! GET THESE CRATES SECURED!
DAMN RAIN'S MAKING EVERYTHING SLIPPERY!
WASTE OF TIME, IF YOU ASK ME.
THEY AIN'T GONNA SHOW.
NO WAY THEY'LL SHOW, NOT IN THIS WEATHER.
SOUNDS ABOUT RIGHT.
ONLY PEOPLE WHO'D BE CAUGHT DEAD IN THIS ARE--
GUN DOWN. HANDS IN THE AIR.
DAMN.
DUNNO WHO YOU ARE... DUNNO WHO YOU'RE WORKING FOR...
...BUT THEY SENT YOU ON A SUICIDE RUN...
YOU MADE A BIG--

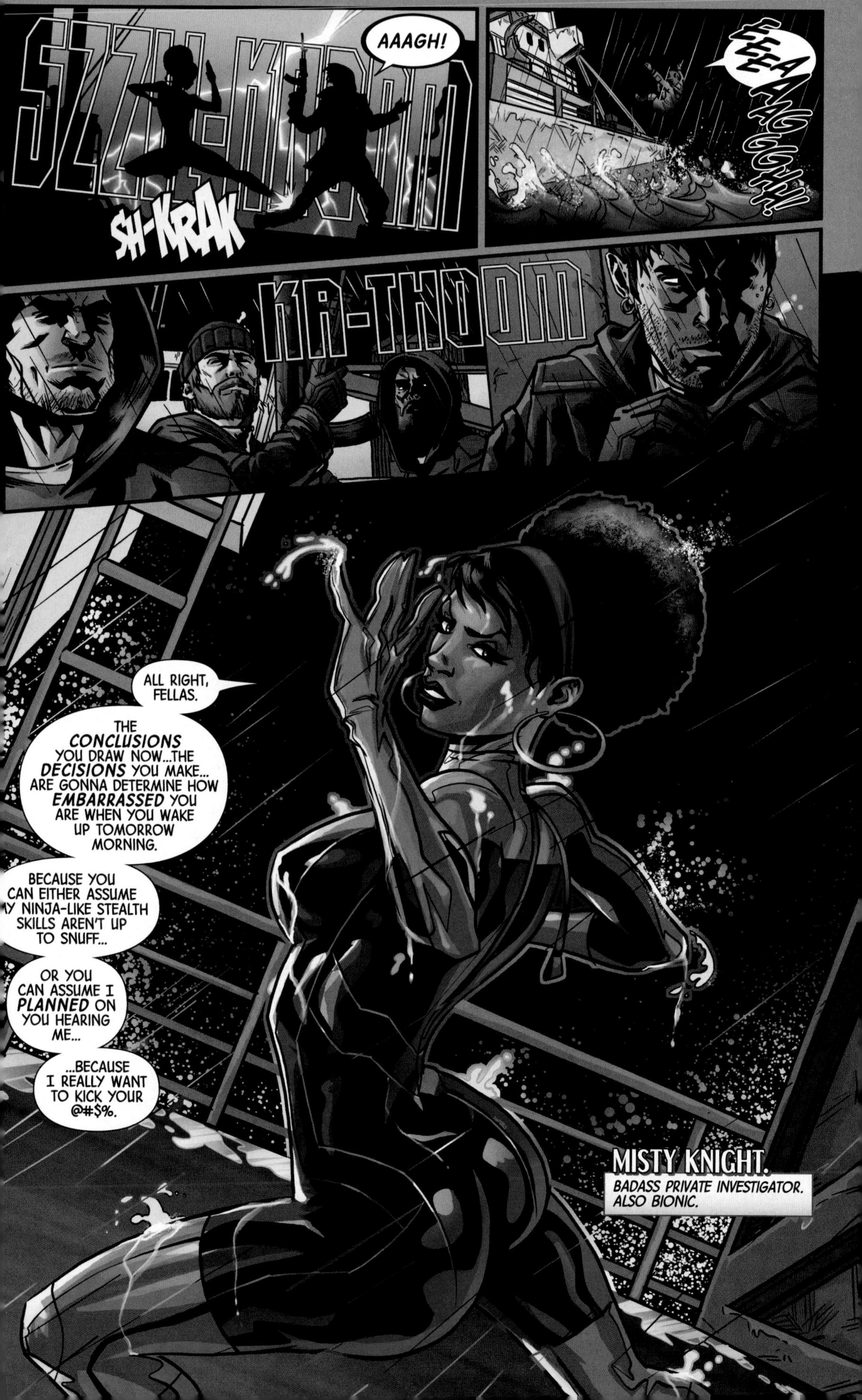
SZZZH-KRAAM
AAAGH!
SH-KRAK
EEEAAAGGGHH!
KR-THOOM
ALL RIGHT, FELLAS.
THE CONCLUSIONS YOU DRAW NOW...THE DECISIONS YOU MAKE... ARE GONNA DETERMINE HOW EMBARRASSED YOU ARE WHEN YOU WAKE UP TOMORROW MORNING.
BECAUSE YOU CAN EITHER ASSUME MY NINJA-LIKE STEALTH SKILLS AREN'T UP TO SNUFF...
OR YOU CAN ASSUME I PLANNED ON YOU HEARING ME...
...BECAUSE I REALLY WANT TO KICK YOUR @#$%.
MISTY KNIGHT.
BADASS PRIVATE INVESTIGATOR. ALSO BIONIC.

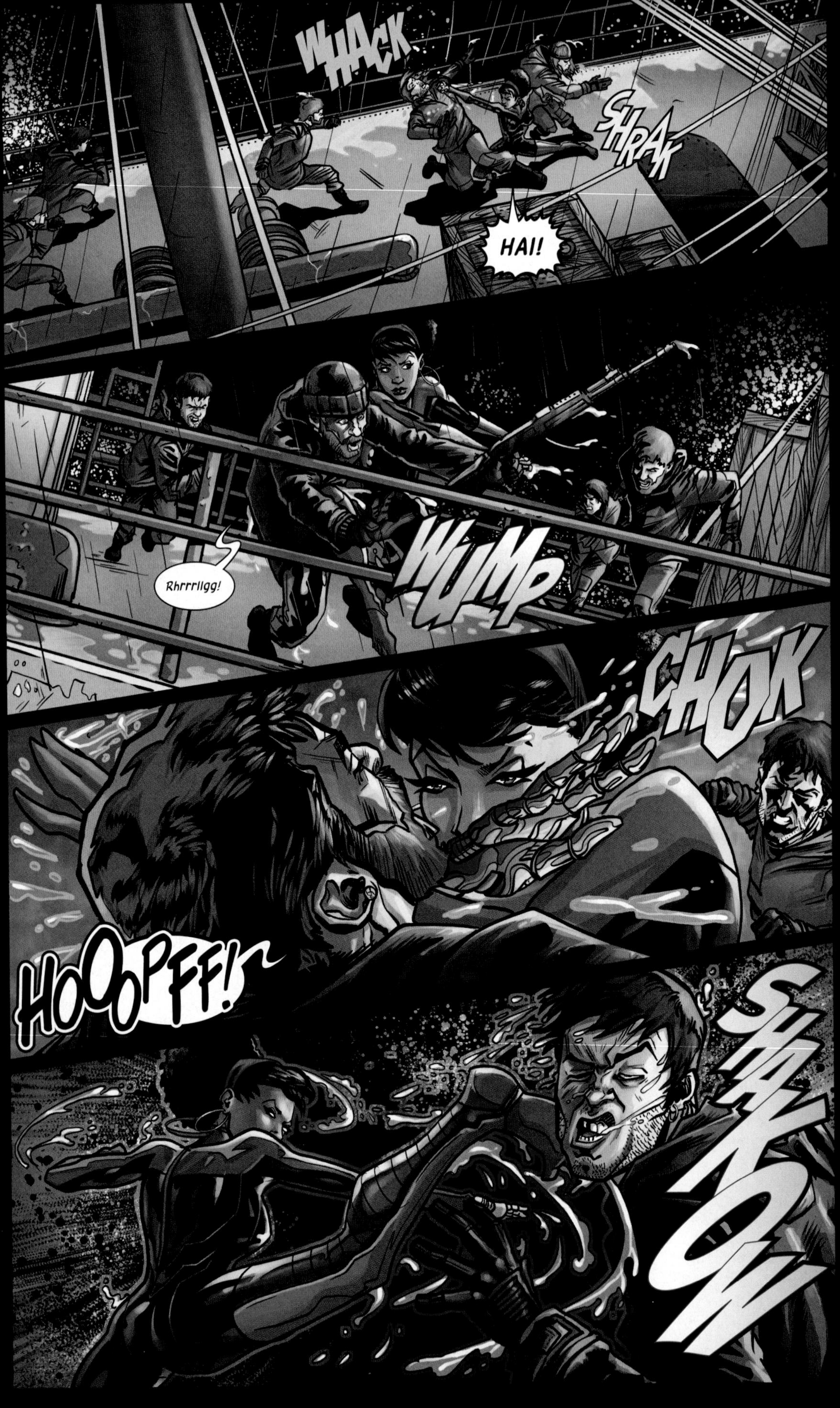
WHACK
SHRAK
HAI!
Rhrrrllgg!
WUMP
CHOK
HOOOPFF!
SHAKOW

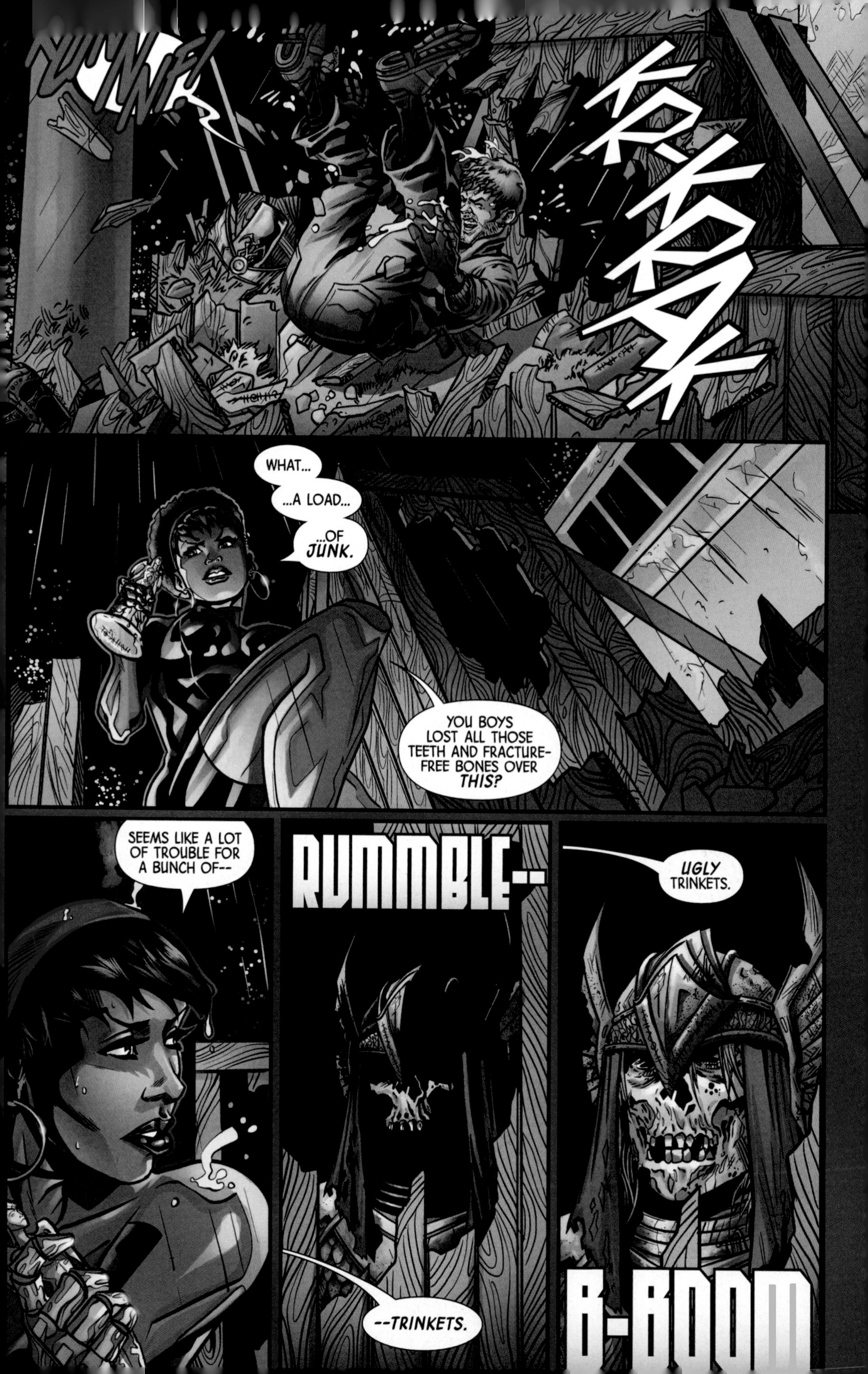
YUUNF!
KR-KRAK
WHAT...
...A LOAD...
...OF JÜNK.
YOU BOYS LOST ALL THOSE TEETH AND FRACTURE-FREE BONES OVER THIS?
SEEMS LIKE A LOT OF TROUBLE FOR A BUNCH OF--
RUMMBLE--
--TRINKETS.
UGLY TRINKETS.
B-BOOM

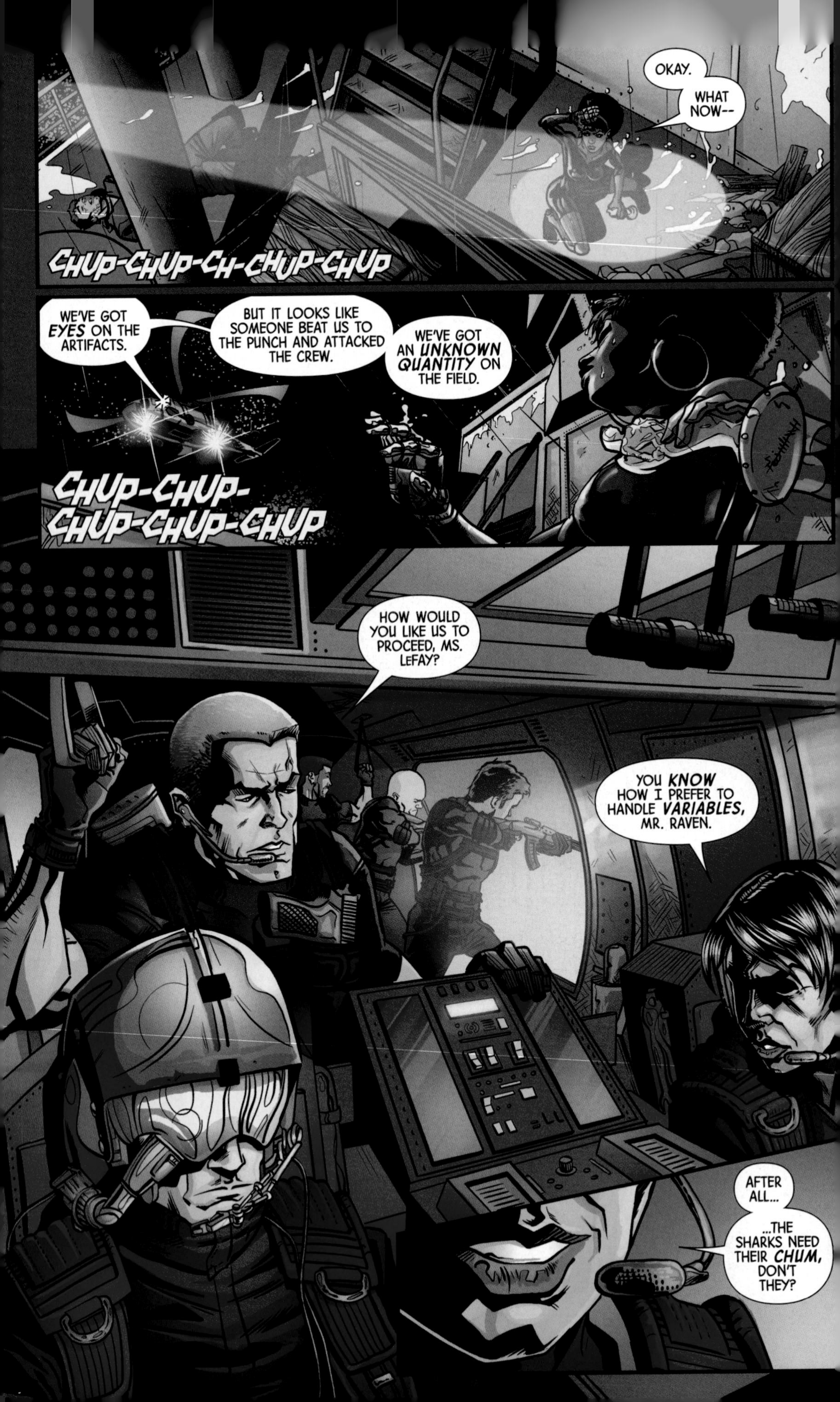
OKAY.
WHAT NOW--
CHUP-CHUP-CH-CHUP-CHUP
WE'VE GOT EYES ON THE ARTIFACTS.
BUT IT LOOKS LIKE SOMEONE BEAT US TO THE PUNCH AND ATTACKED THE CREW.
WE'VE GOT AN UNKNOWN QUANTITY ON THE FIELD.
CHUP-CHUP-CHUP-CHUP-CHUP
HOW WOULD YOU LIKE US TO PROCEED, MS. LeFAY?
YOU KNOW HOW I PREFER TO HANDLE VARIABLES, MR. RAVEN.
AFTER ALL...
...THE SHARKS NEED THEIR CHUM, DON'T THEY?

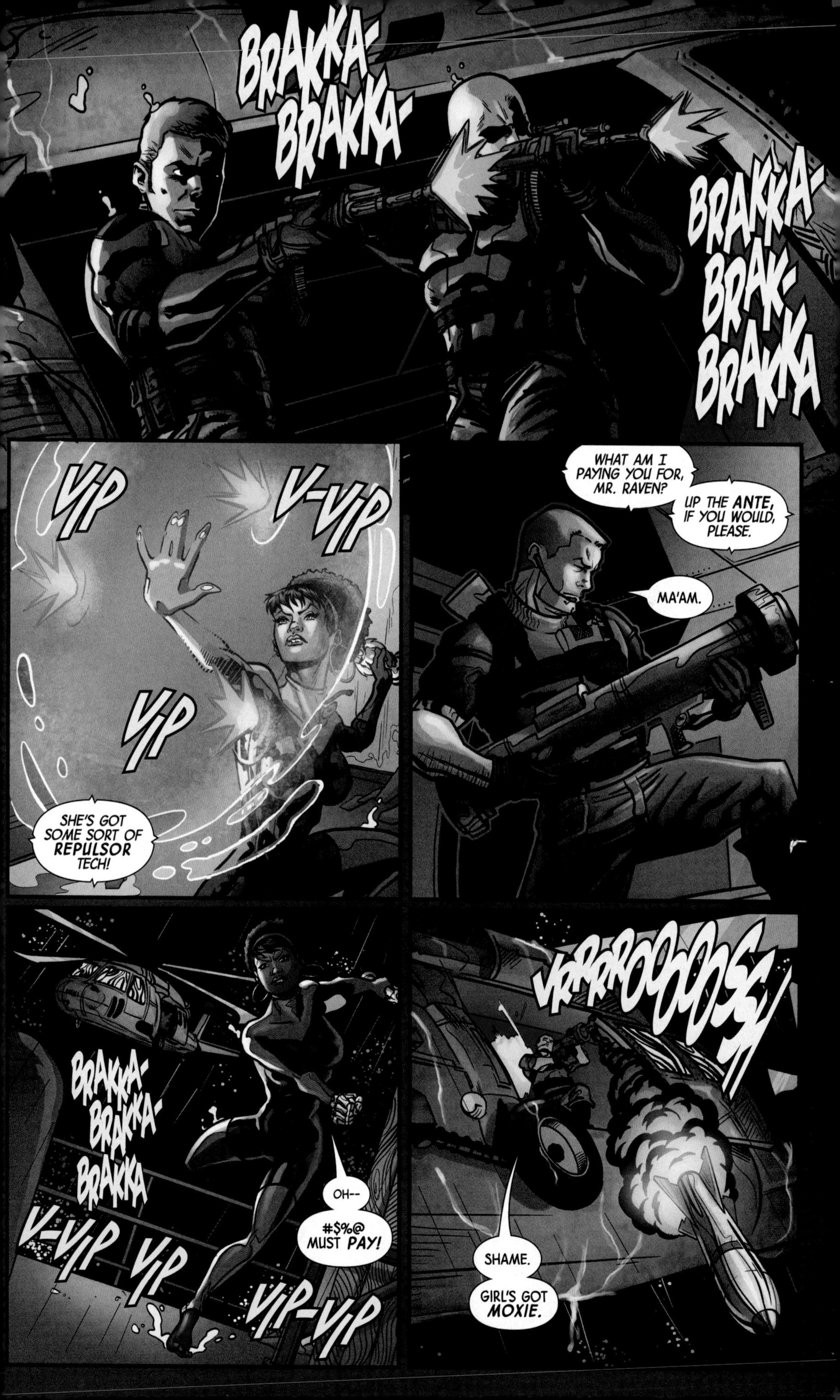
BRAKKA-BRAKKA-
BRAKKA-BRAK-BRAKKA
VIP
V-VIP
VIP
SHE'S GOT SOME SORT OF REPULSOR TECH!
WHAT AM I PAYING YOU FOR, MR. RAVEN?
UP THE ANTE, IF YOU WOULD, PLEASE.
MA'AM.
BRAKKA-BRAKKA-BRAKKA
V-VIP VIP
VIP-VIP
OH--
#$%@ MUST PAY!
VRRRROOOOOSSH
SHAME.
GIRL'S GOT MOXIE.

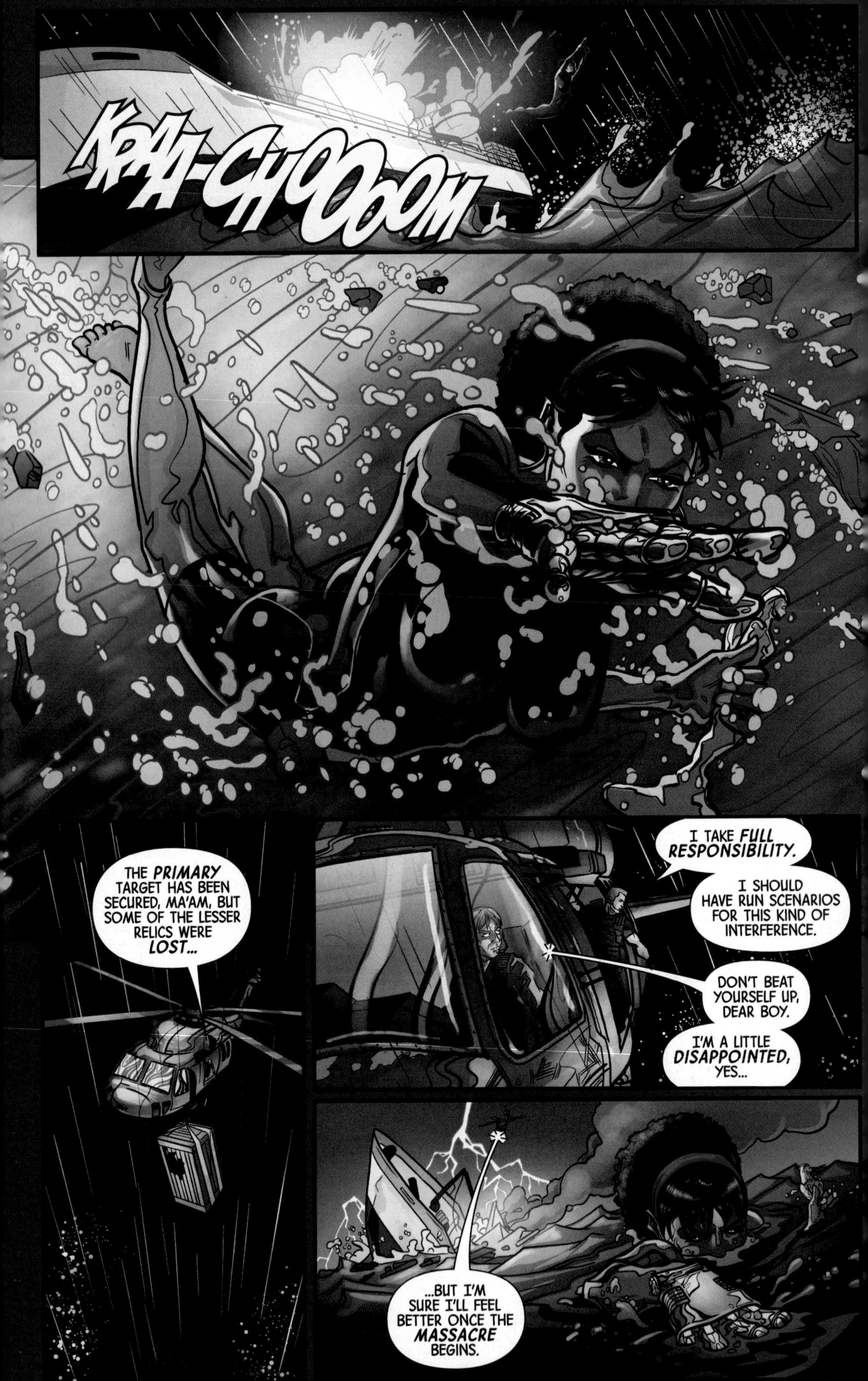
KRAA-CHOOOOOM
THE PRIMARY TARGET HAS BEEN SECURED, MA'AM, BUT SOME OF THE LESSER RELICS WERE LOST...
I TAKE FULL RESPONSIBILITY.
I SHOULD HAVE RUN SCENARIOS FOR THIS KIND OF INTERFERENCE.
DON'T BEAT YOURSELF UP, DEAR BOY.
I'M A LITTLE DISAPPOINTED, YES...
...BUT I'M SURE I'LL FEEL BETTER ONCE THE MASSACRE BEGINS.

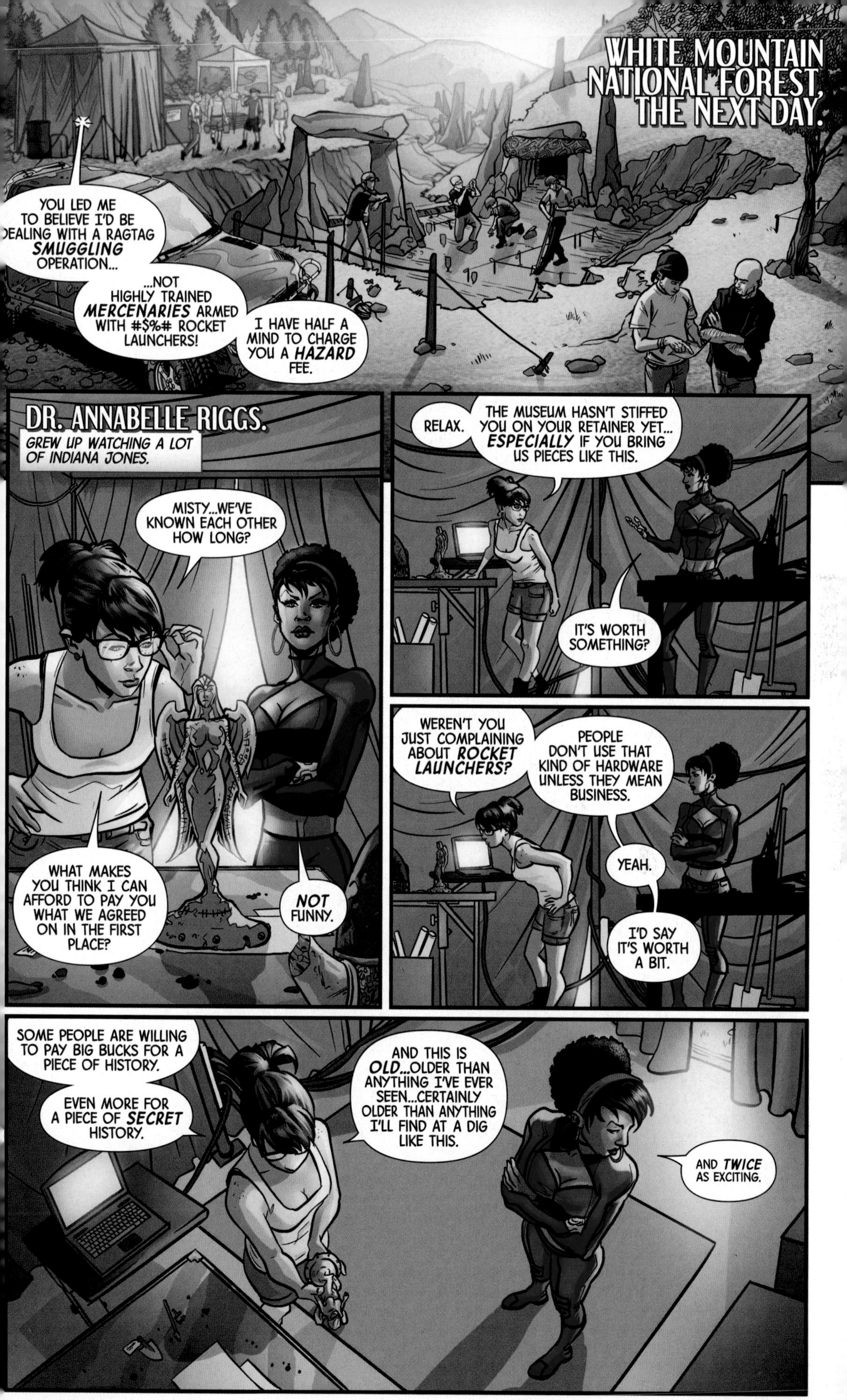
WHITE MOUNTAIN NATIONAL FOREST, THE NEXT DAY.
YOU LED ME TO BELIEVE I'D BE DEALING WITH A RAGTAG SMUGGLING OPERATION...
...NOT HIGHLY TRAINED MERCENARIES ARMED WITH #$%# ROCKET LAUNCHERS!
I HAVE HALF A MIND TO CHARGE YOU A HAZARD FEE.
DR. ANNABELLE RIGGS.
GREW UP WATCHING A LOT OF INDIANA JONES.
MISTY...WE'VE KNOWN EACH OTHER HOW LONG?
WHAT MAKES YOU THINK I CAN AFFORD TO PAY YOU WHAT WE AGREED ON IN THE FIRST PLACE?
NOT FUNNY.
RELAX.
THE MUSEUM HASN'T STIFFED YOU ON YOUR RETAINER YET... ESPECIALLY IF YOU BRING US PIECES LIKE THIS.
IT'S WORTH SOMETHING?
WEREN'T YOU JUST COMPLAINING ABOUT ROCKET LAUNCHERS?
PEOPLE DON'T USE THAT KIND OF HARDWARE UNLESS THEY MEAN BUSINESS.
YEAH.
I'D SAY IT'S WORTH A BIT.
SOME PEOPLE ARE WILLING TO PAY BIG BUCKS FOR A PIECE OF HISTORY.
EVEN MORE FOR A PIECE OF SECRET HISTORY.
AND THIS IS OLD...OLDER THAN ANYTHING I'VE EVER SEEN...CERTAINLY OLDER THAN ANYTHING I'LL FIND AT A DIG LIKE THIS.
AND TWICE AS EXCITING.

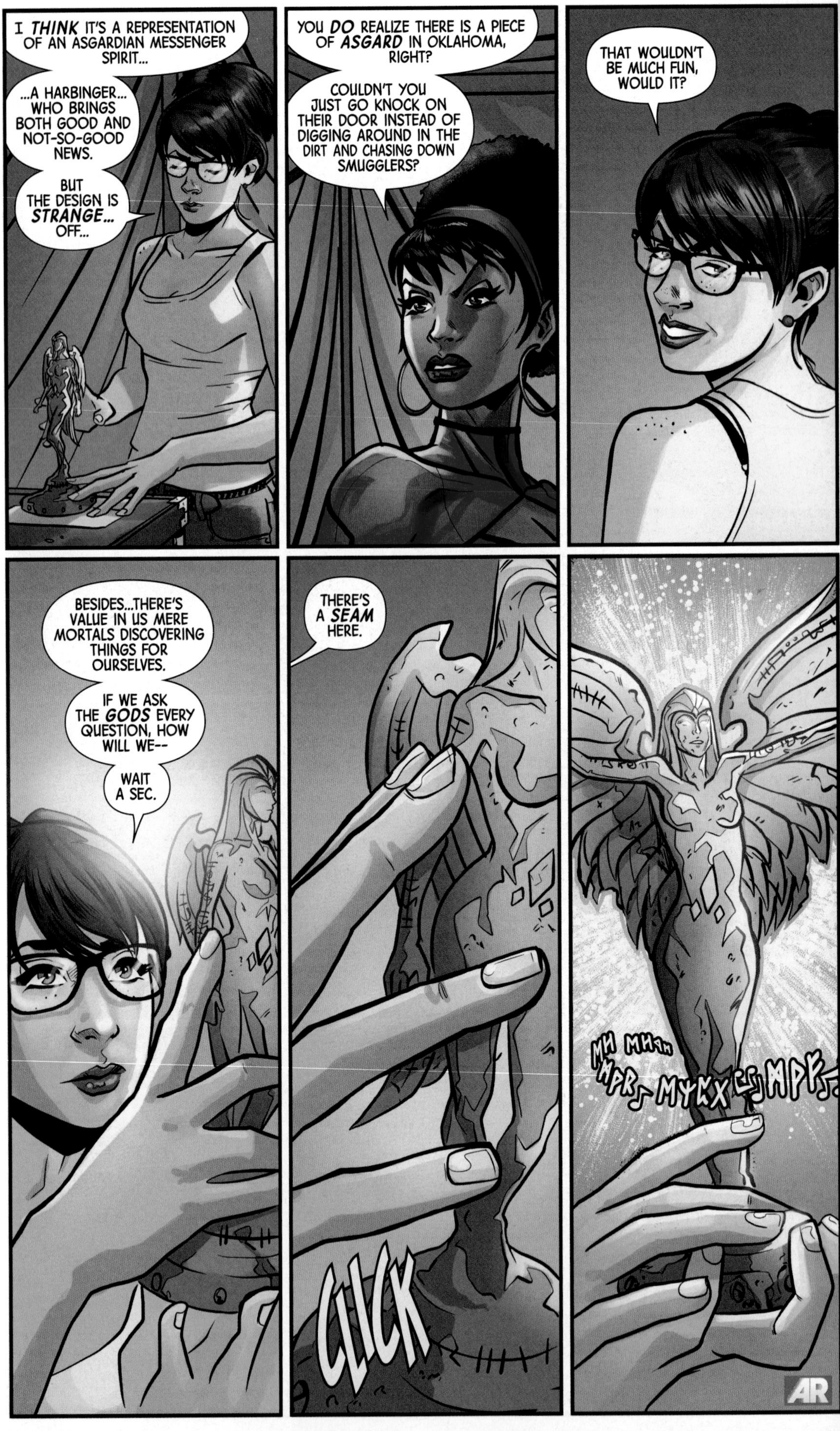
I THINK IT'S A REPRESENTATION OF AN ASGARDIAN MESSENGER SPIRIT...
...A HARBINGER... WHO BRINGS BOTH GOOD AND NOT-SO-GOOD NEWS.
BUT THE DESIGN IS STRANGE... OFF...
YOU DO REALIZE THERE IS A PIECE OF ASGARD IN OKLAHOMA, RIGHT?
COULDN'T YOU JUST GO KNOCK ON THEIR DOOR INSTEAD OF DIGGING AROUND IN THE DIRT AND CHASING DOWN SMUGGLERS?
THAT WOULDN'T BE MUCH FUN, WOULD IT?
BESIDES...THERE'S VALUE IN US MERE MORTALS DISCOVERING THINGS FOR OURSELVES.
IF WE ASK THE GODS EVERY QUESTION, HOW WILL WE--
WAIT A SEC.
THERE'S A SEAM HERE.
CLICK
AR

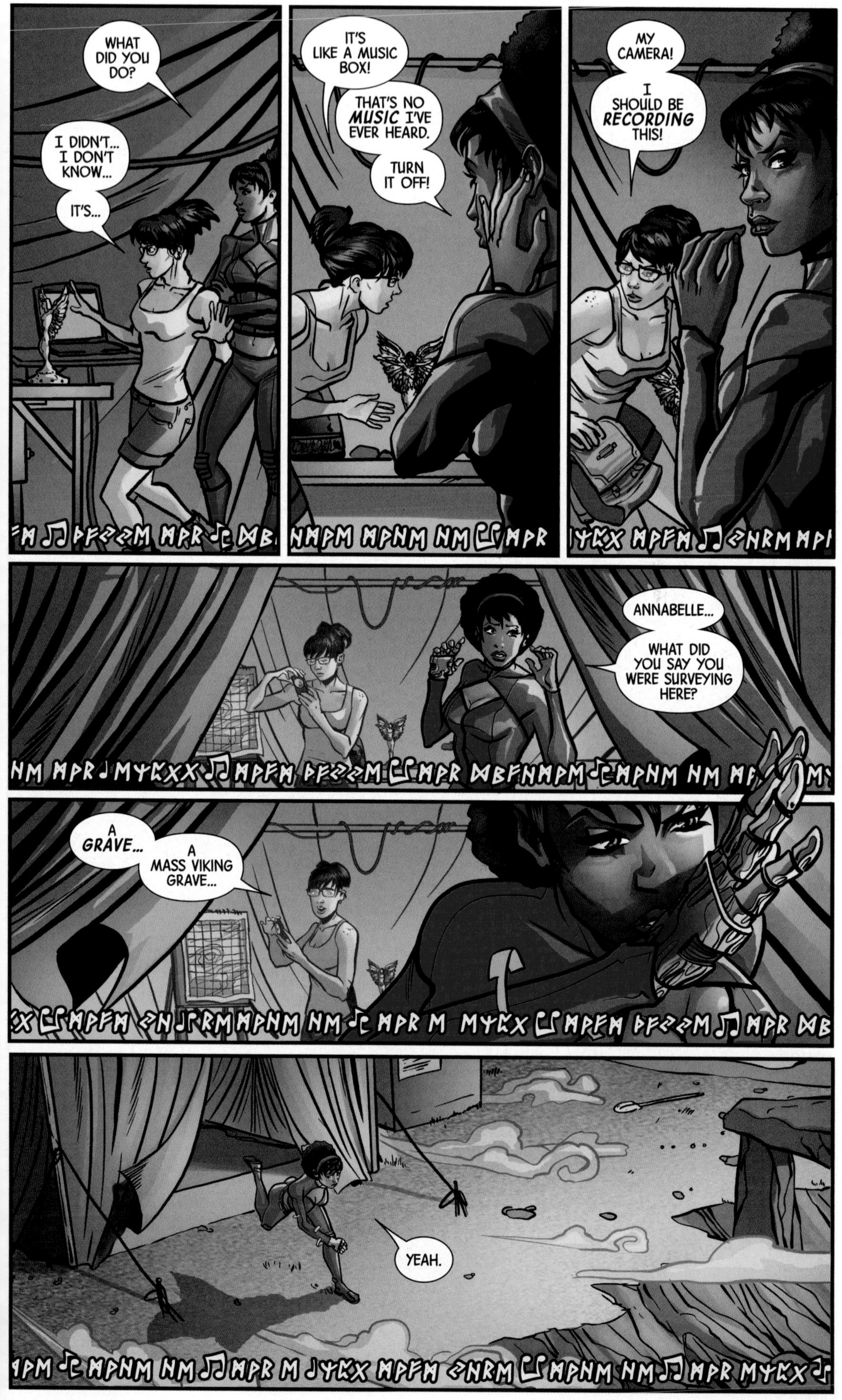
WHAT DID YOU DO?
I DIDN'T... I DON'T KNOW...
IT'S...
IT'S LIKE A MUSIC BOX!
THAT'S NO MUSIC I'VE EVER HEARD.
TURN IT OFF!
MY CAMERA!
I SHOULD BE RECORDING THIS!
ANNABELLE...
WHAT DID YOU SAY YOU WERE SURVEYING HERE?
A GRAVE...
A MASS VIKING GRAVE...
YEAH.

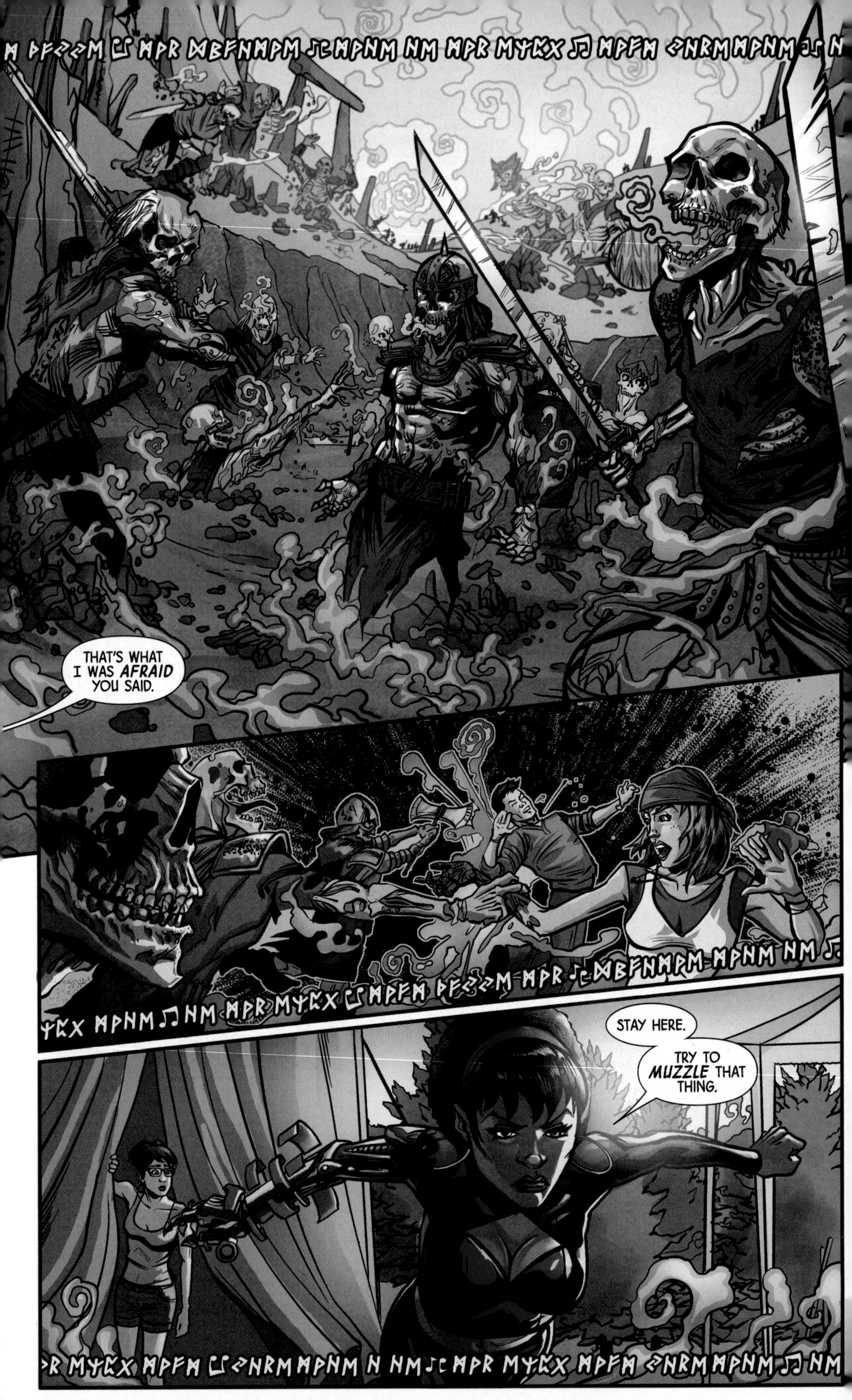
THAT'S WHAT I WAS AFRAID YOU SAID.
STAY HERE.
TRY TO MUZZLE THAT THING.

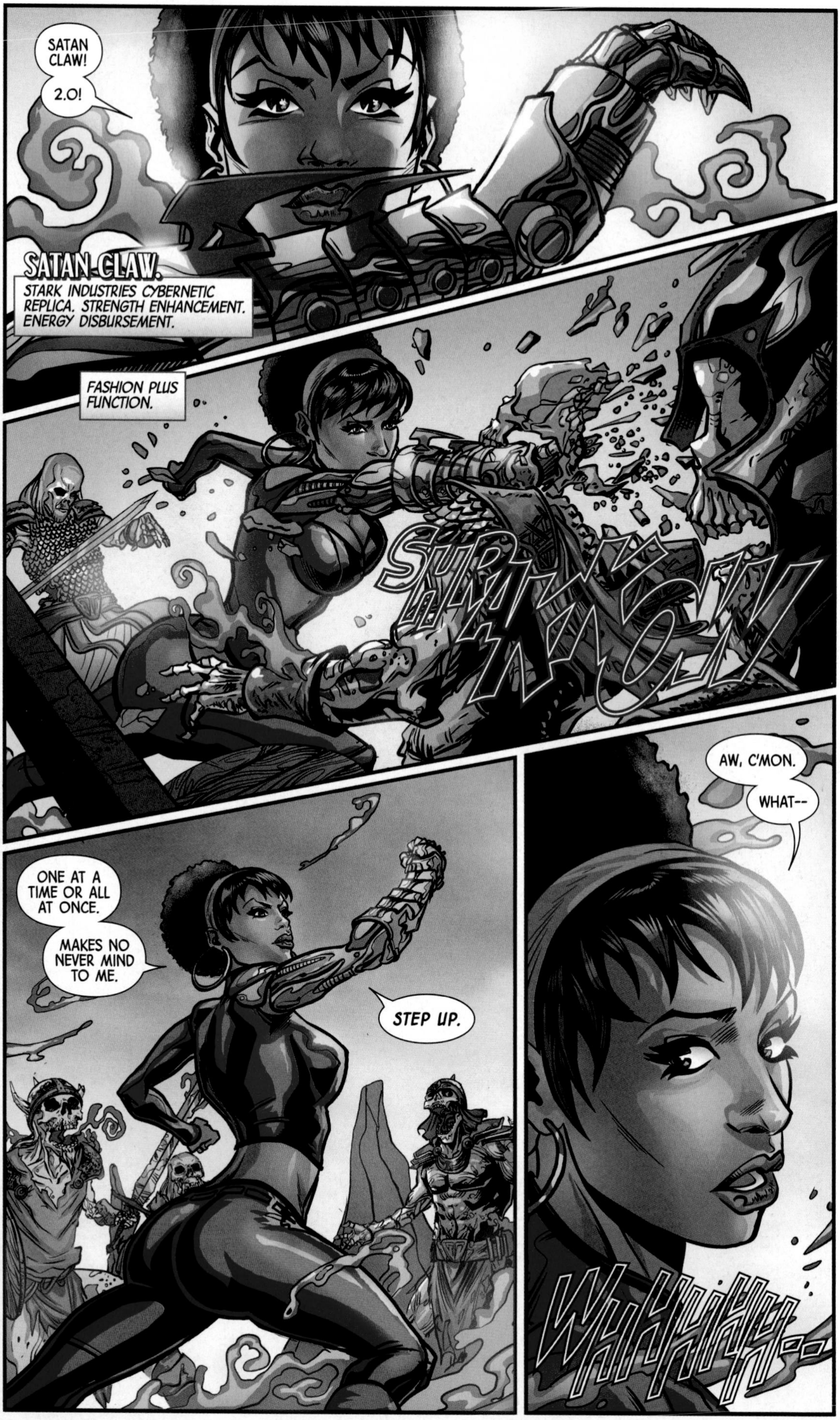
SATAN CLAW!
2.0!
SATAN CLAW.
STARK INDUSTRIES CYBERNETIC REPLICA. STRENGTH ENHANCEMENT. ENERGY DISBURSEMENT.
FASHION PLUS FUNCTION.
AW, C'MON.
WHAT--
ONE AT A TIME OR ALL AT ONCE.
MAKES NO NEVER MIND TO ME.
STEP UP.

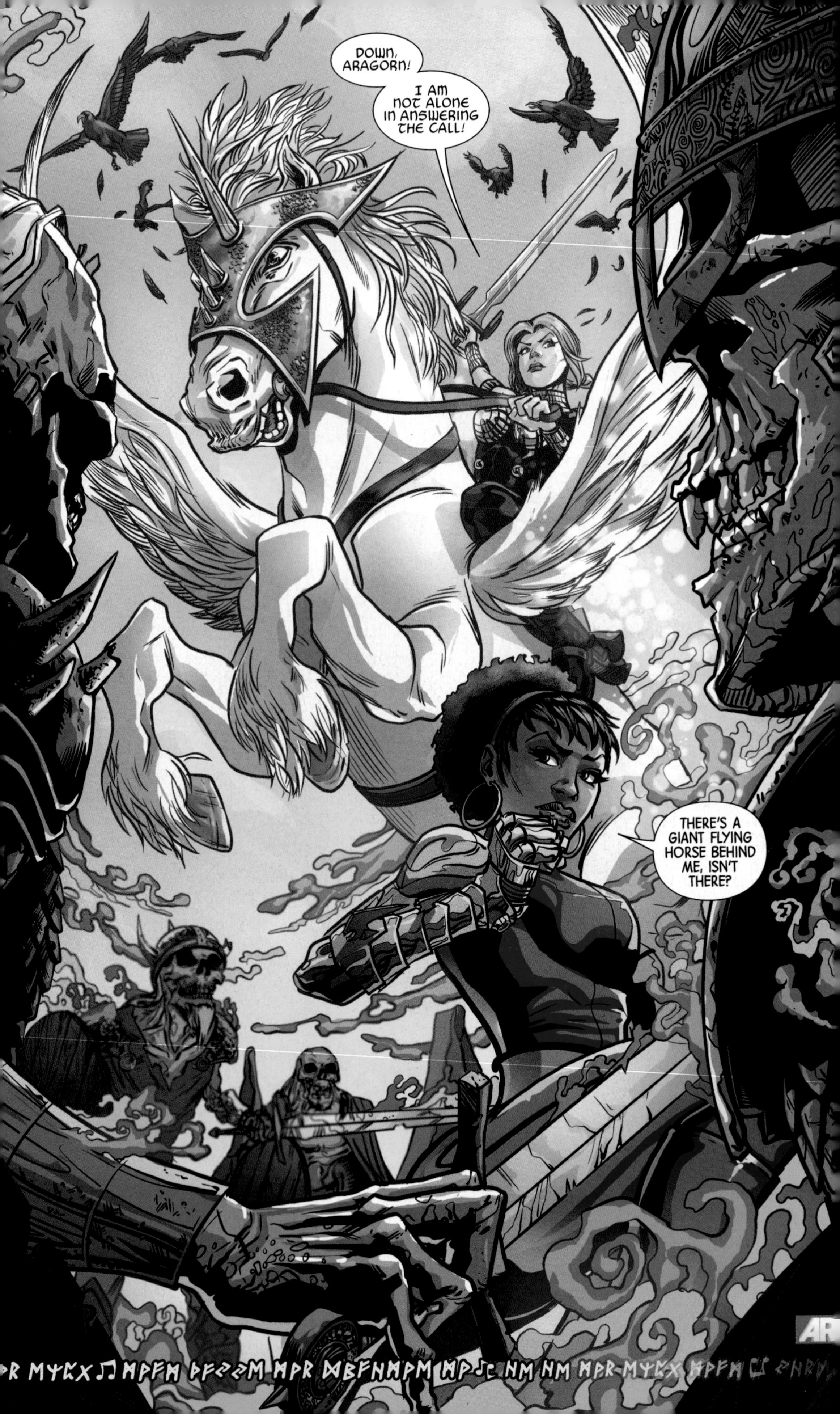
DOWN, ARAGORN!
I AM NOT ALONE IN ANSWERING THE CALL!
THERE'S A GIANT FLYING HORSE BEHIND ME, ISN'T THERE?

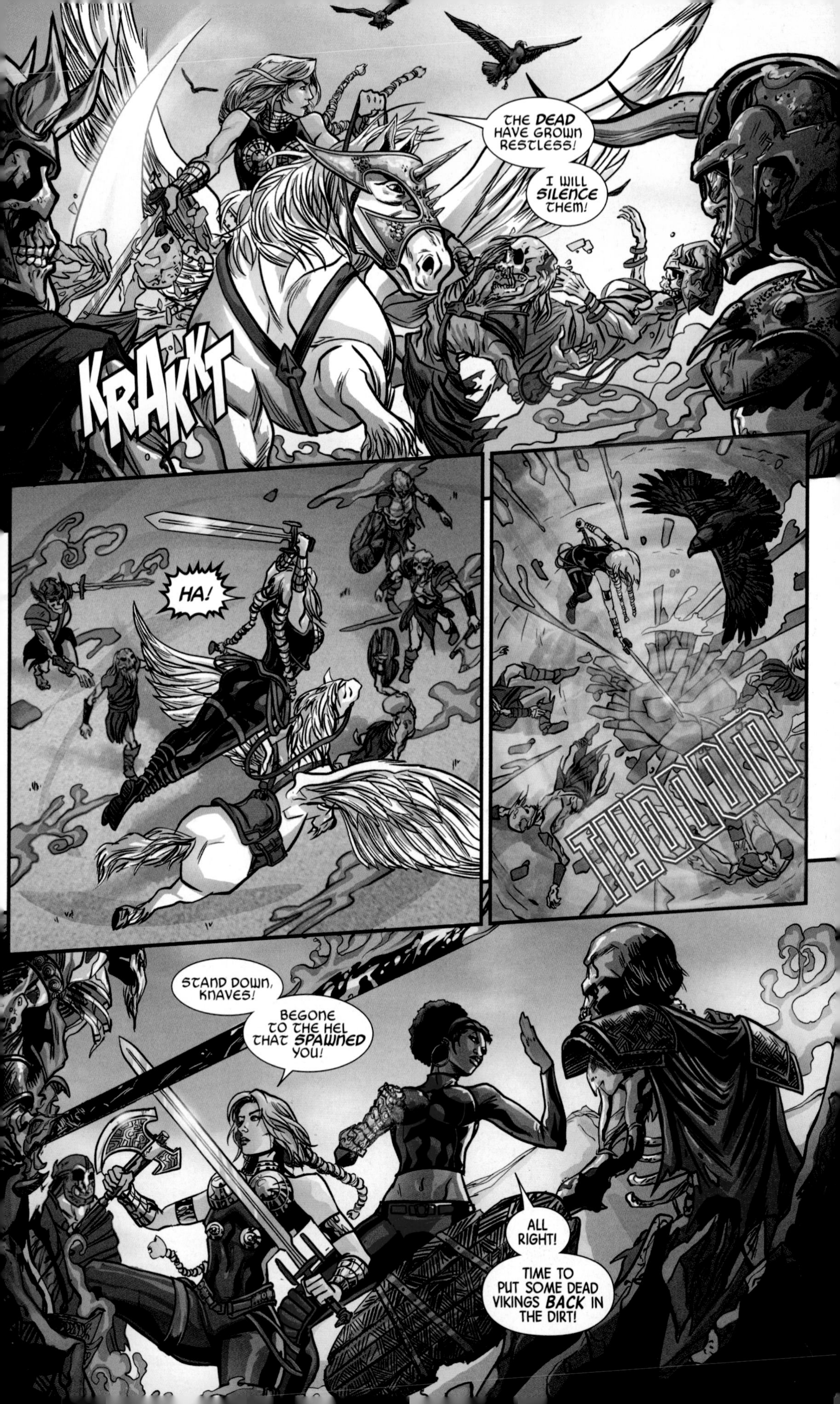
THE DEAD HAVE GROWN RESTLESS!
I WILL SILENCE THEM!
KRAKKT
HA!
THOOOM
STAND DOWN, KNAVES!
BEGONE TO THE HEL THAT SPAWNED YOU!
ALL RIGHT!
TIME TO PUT SOME DEAD VIKINGS BACK IN THE DIRT!

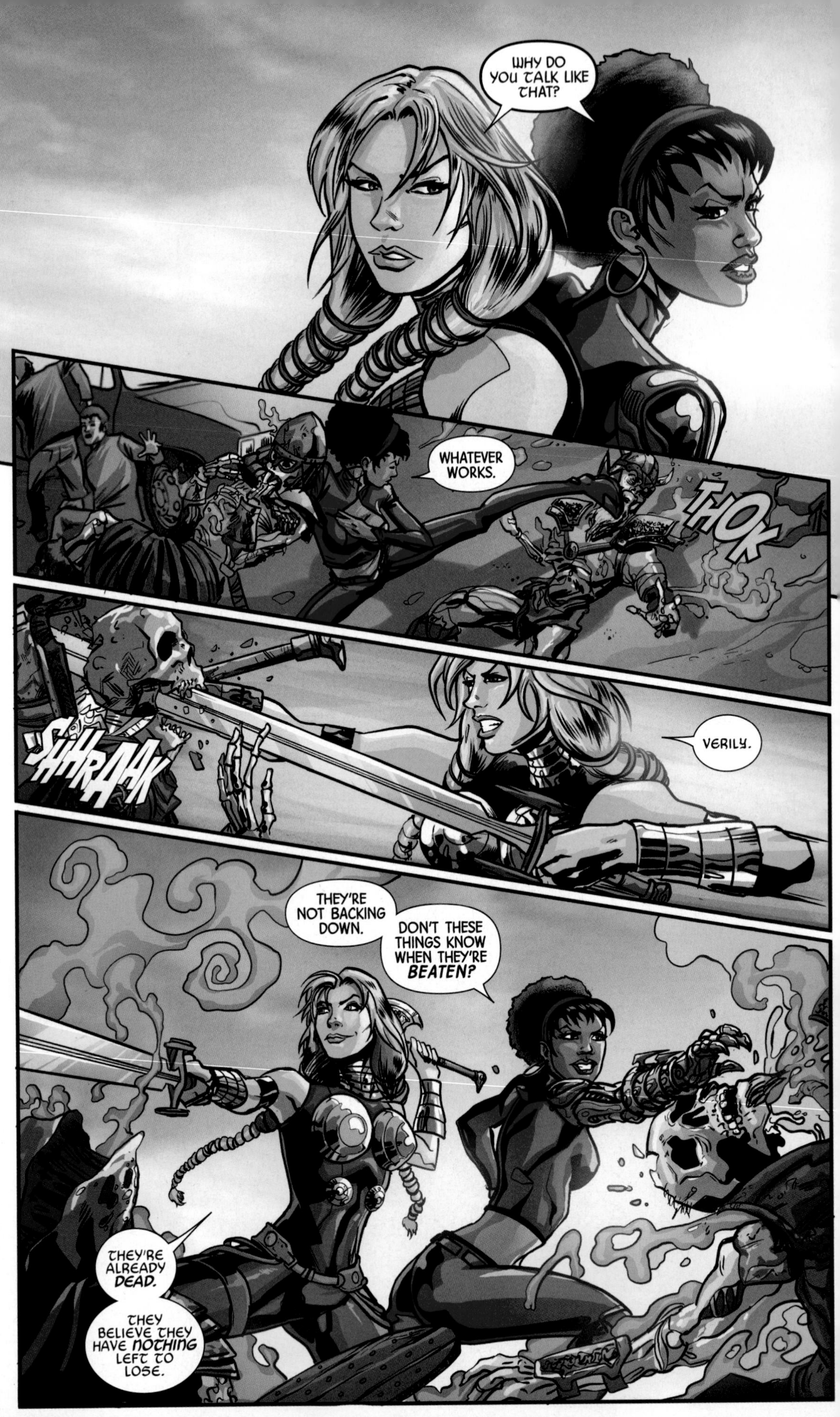
WHY DO YOU TALK LIKE THAT?
WHATEVER WORKS.
THOK
SHHRAAK
VERILY.
THEY'RE NOT BACKING DOWN.
DON'T THESE THINGS KNOW WHEN THEY'RE *BEATEN?*
THEY'RE ALREADY *DEAD.*
THEY BELIEVE THEY HAVE *NOTHING* LEFT TO LOSE.

STILL... THEY ARE BUT SHADOWS...

...STIRRED LIKE ASH FROM A FIRE...DISTURBED BY...

I DON'T KNOW WHAT THIS THING'S TRYING TO TELL US, BUT IT DOESN'T HAVE AN--

ᚾ�R M ᛘᛔR MᚤᛐX ᛋ ᛘᛔ! ᛍ ᛒᚠᛜᛜM ᛘᛔR ♪ ᛞᛒᚠᚾᛘᛘ ᛘᛔᚾM ᚾM ᛘᛔR ᛋ MᚤᛐX

--OFF SWITCH.

ᚾRM ᛋ ᛘᛔᚾM ᚾM ᛘᛔR MᚤᛐX ♪ ᛘᛔᚠM ᛒᚠᛜᛜM ᛘᛔR ᛞᛒᚠᚾᛘᛘ ᛋ ᛘᛔᚾM ᚾM

THAT SONG!

SHRAK

ᛘᛔR M ᛘᚤᛐX ᛘᛔᚠM ᛜᚾRM ᛋ ᛘᛔᚾM ᚾM

WHHSS-THRAKKOW

OH!

ᛘᛔR MᚤᛐX ♪ ᛘᛔᚠM ᛒᚠᛜᛜM ᛘᛔR ᛋᛞᛒᚠ

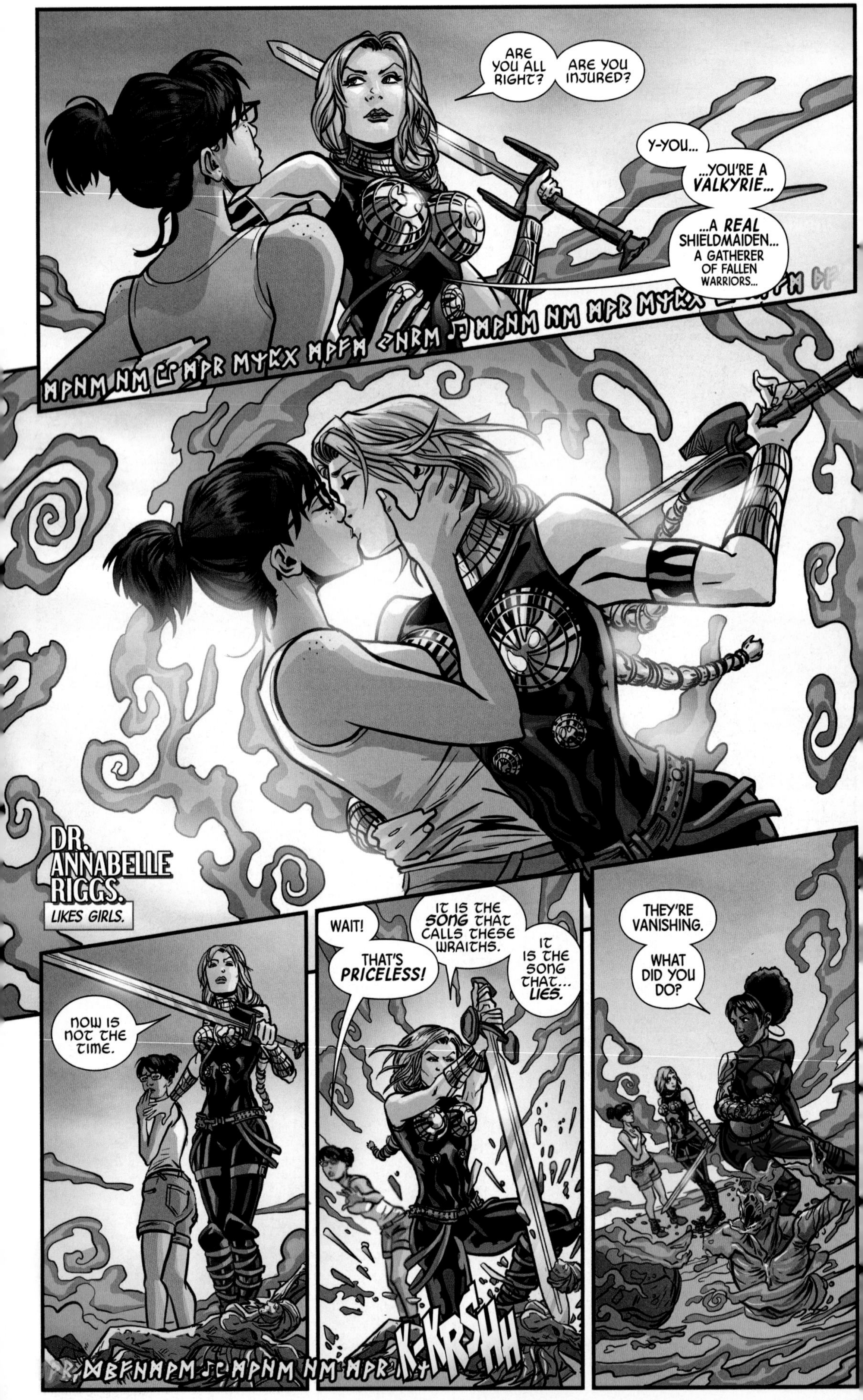
ARE YOU ALL RIGHT?
ARE YOU INJURED?
Y-YOU...
...YOU'RE A VALKYRIE...
...A REAL SHIELDMAIDEN... A GATHERER OF FALLEN WARRIORS...
DR. ANNABELLE RIGGS.
LIKES GIRLS.
NOW IS NOT THE TIME.
WAIT!
THAT'S PRICELESS!
IT IS THE SONG THAT CALLS THESE WRAITHS.
IT IS THE SONG THAT... LIES.
K-KRSHH
THEY'RE VANISHING.
WHAT DID YOU DO?

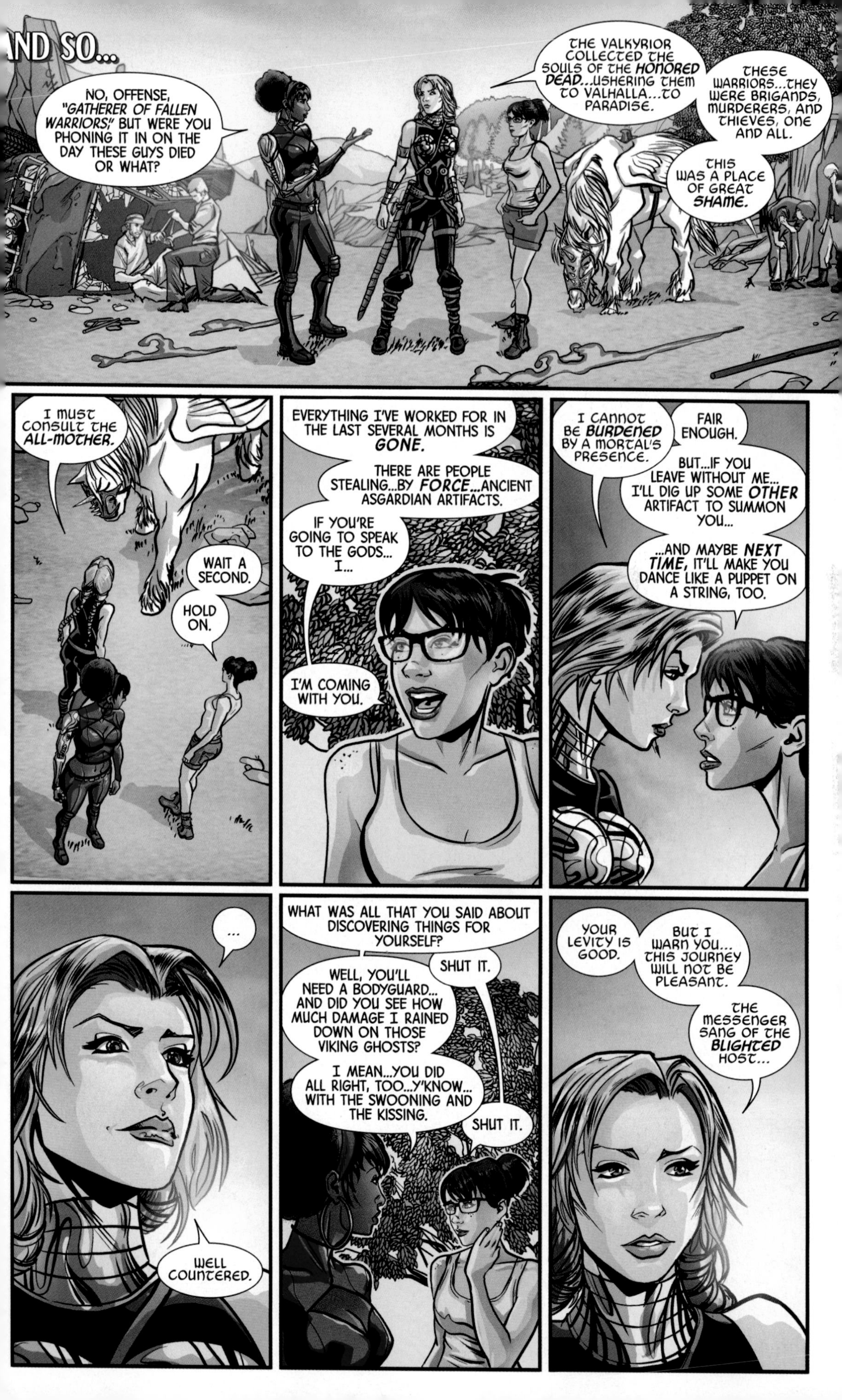
AND SO...
NO, OFFENSE, "GATHERER OF FALLEN WARRIORS," BUT WERE YOU PHONING IT IN ON THE DAY THESE GUYS DIED OR WHAT?
THE VALKYRIOR COLLECTED THE SOULS OF THE HONORED DEAD...USHERING THEM TO VALHALLA...TO PARADISE.
THESE WARRIORS...THEY WERE BRIGANDS, MURDERERS, AND THIEVES, ONE AND ALL.
THIS WAS A PLACE OF GREAT SHAME.
I MUST CONSULT THE ALL-MOTHER.
WAIT A SECOND.
HOLD ON.
EVERYTHING I'VE WORKED FOR IN THE LAST SEVERAL MONTHS IS GONE.
THERE ARE PEOPLE STEALING...BY FORCE...ANCIENT ASGARDIAN ARTIFACTS.
IF YOU'RE GOING TO SPEAK TO THE GODS... I...
I'M COMING WITH YOU.
I CANNOT BE BURDENED BY A MORTAL'S PRESENCE.
FAIR ENOUGH.
BUT...IF YOU LEAVE WITHOUT ME... I'LL DIG UP SOME OTHER ARTIFACT TO SUMMON YOU...
...AND MAYBE NEXT TIME, IT'LL MAKE YOU DANCE LIKE A PUPPET ON A STRING, TOO.
...
WELL COUNTERED.
WHAT WAS ALL THAT YOU SAID ABOUT DISCOVERING THINGS FOR YOURSELF?
SHUT IT.
WELL, YOU'LL NEED A BODYGUARD... AND DID YOU SEE HOW MUCH DAMAGE I RAINED DOWN ON THOSE VIKING GHOSTS?
I MEAN...YOU DID ALL RIGHT, TOO...Y'KNOW... WITH THE SWOONING AND THE KISSING.
SHUT IT.
YOUR LEVITY IS GOOD.
BUT I WARN YOU... THIS JOURNEY WILL NOT BE PLEASANT.
THE MESSENGER SANG OF THE BLIGHTED HOST...

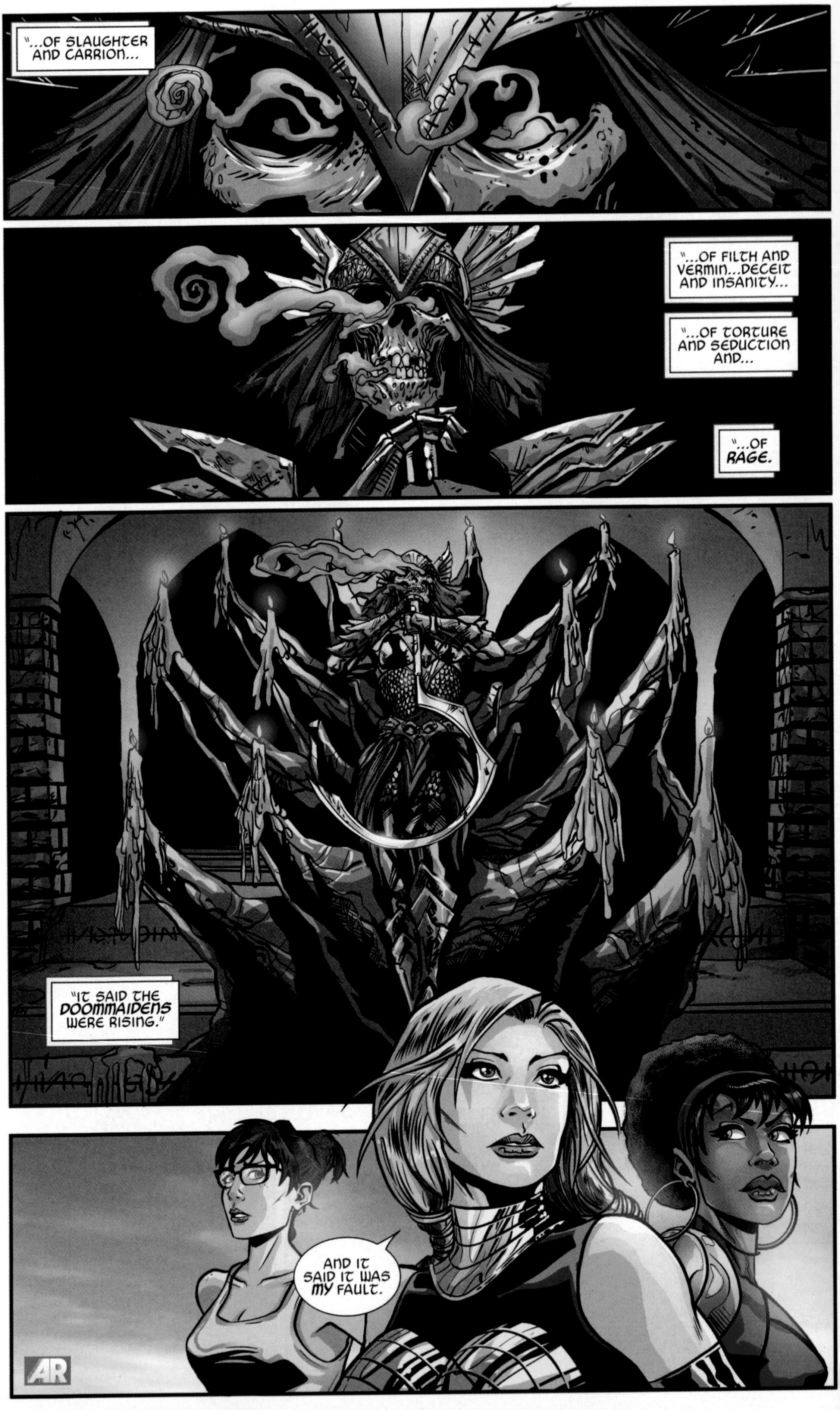
"...OF SLAUGHTER AND CARRION...
"...OF FILTH AND VERMIN...DECEIT AND INSANITY...
"...OF TORTURE AND SEDUCTION AND...
"...OF RAGE.
"IT SAID THE DOOMMAIDENS WERE RISING."
AND IT SAID IT WAS MY FAULT.

32675/78459 Asst.
THE FEARLESS
DEFENDERS
Misty Knight, Valkyrie, and others sold separately
DANI MOONSTAR
Includes bow, quiver and crown!
WARNING:
CHOKING HAZARD-Small parts. Not for children under 3 years.
BROOKS

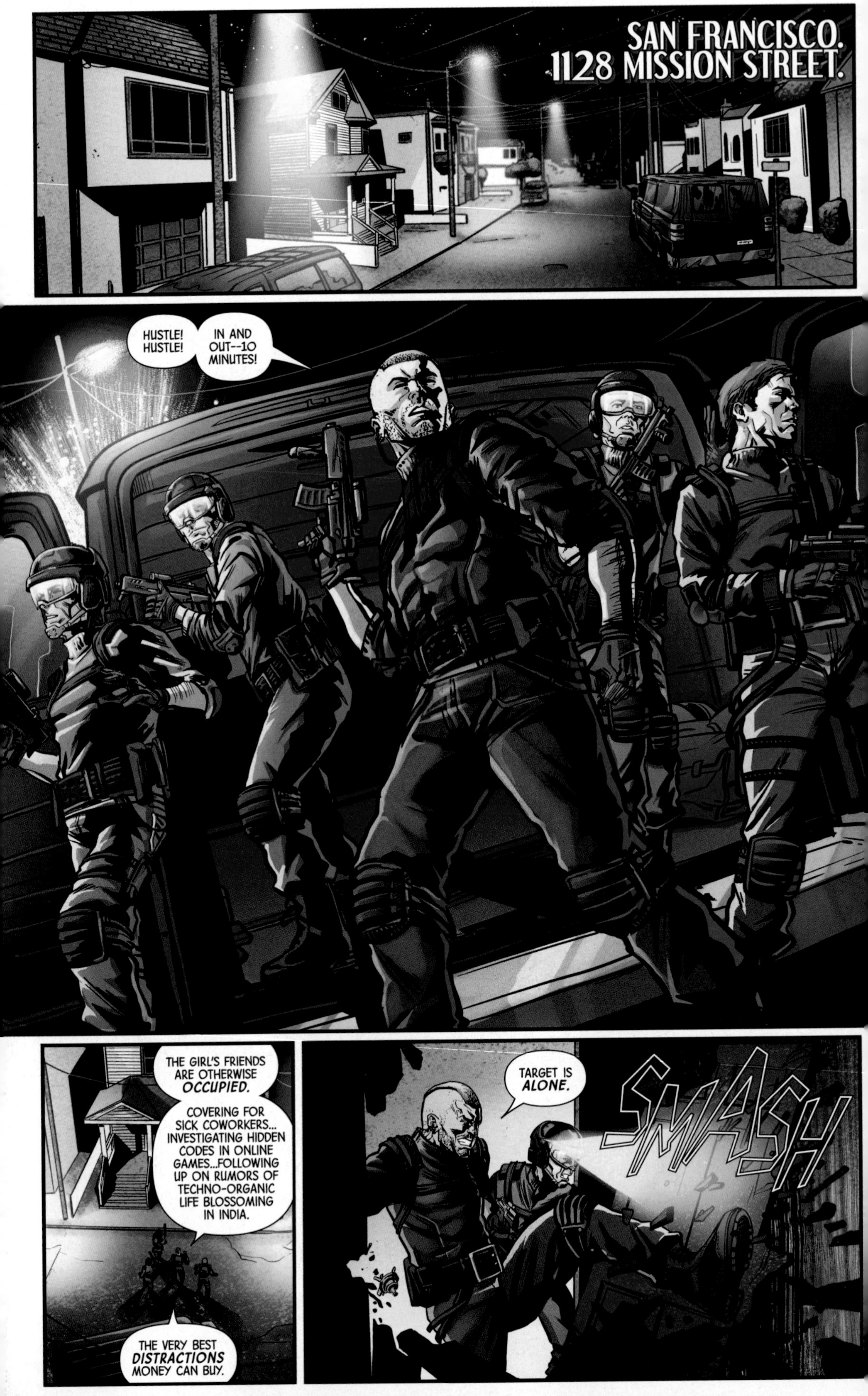
SAN FRANCISCO.
1128 MISSION STREET.
HUSTLE! HUSTLE!
IN AND OUT--10 MINUTES!
THE GIRL'S FRIENDS ARE OTHERWISE *OCCUPIED.*
COVERING FOR SICK COWORKERS... INVESTIGATING HIDDEN CODES IN ONLINE GAMES...FOLLOWING UP ON RUMORS OF TECHNO-ORGANIC LIFE BLOSSOMING IN INDIA.
THE VERY BEST *DISTRACTIONS* MONEY CAN BUY.
TARGET IS *ALONE.*
SMASH

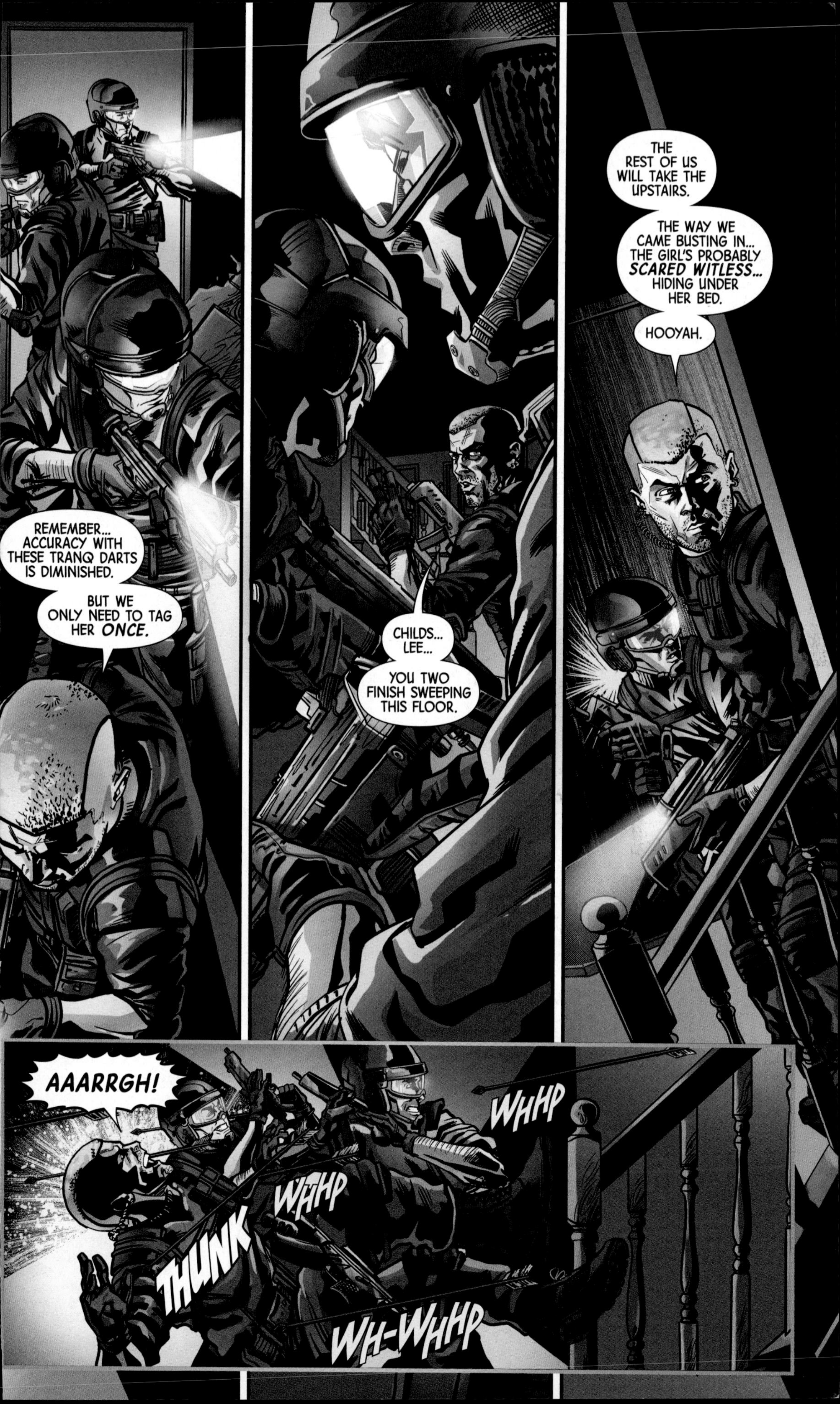
REMEMBER... ACCURACY WITH THESE TRANQ DARTS IS DIMINISHED.
BUT WE ONLY NEED TO TAG HER *ONCE.*
CHILDS... LEE...
YOU TWO FINISH SWEEPING THIS FLOOR.
THE REST OF US WILL TAKE THE UPSTAIRS.
THE WAY WE CAME BUSTING IN... THE GIRL'S PROBABLY *SCARED WITLESS...* HIDING UNDER HER BED.
HOOYAH.
AAARRGH!
WHHP
WHHP
THUNK
WH-WHHP

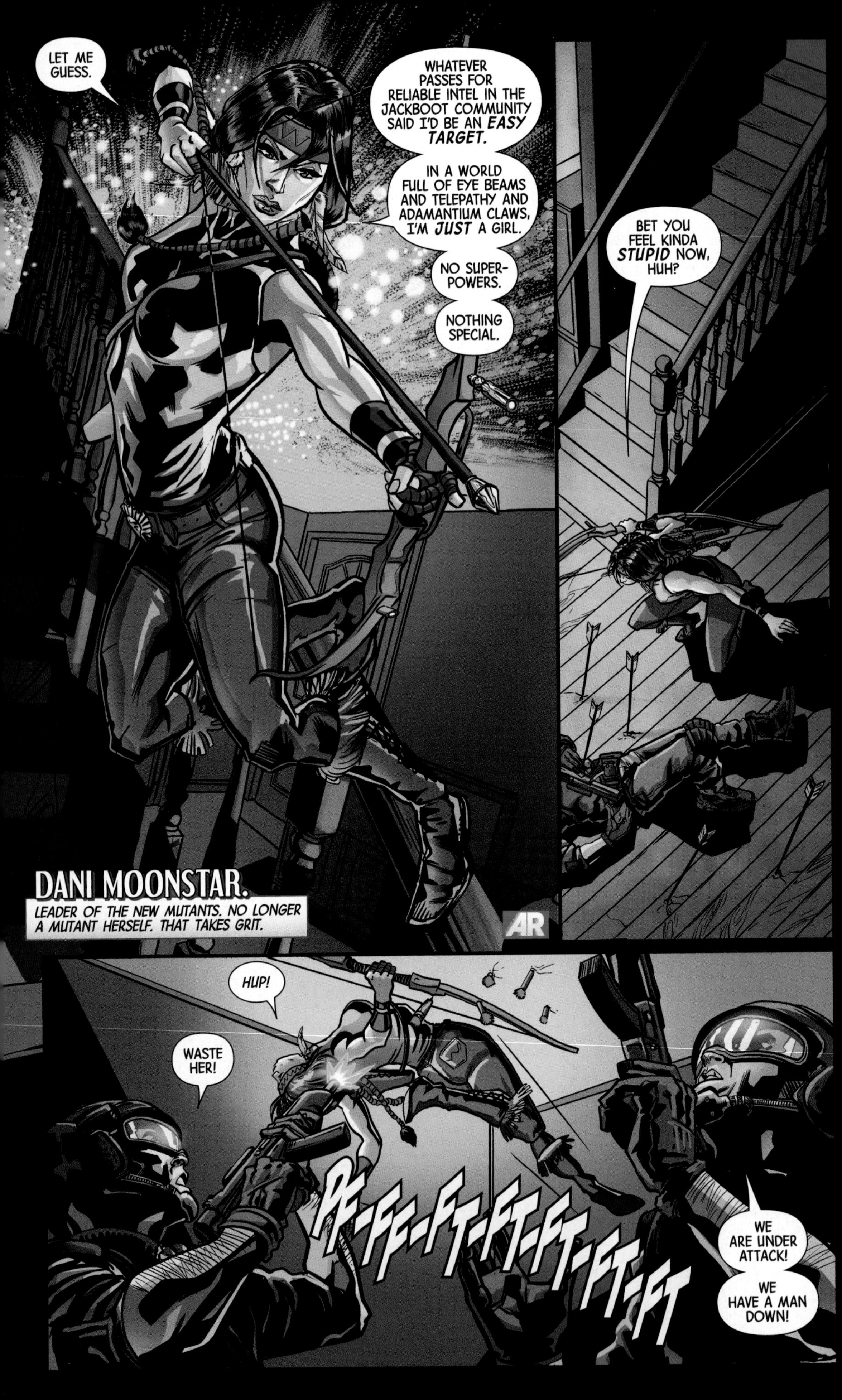

LET ME GUESS.
WHATEVER PASSES FOR RELIABLE INTEL IN THE JACKBOOT COMMUNITY SAID I'D BE AN *EASY TARGET.*
IN A WORLD FULL OF EYE BEAMS AND TELEPATHY AND ADAMANTIUM CLAWS, I'M *JUST* A GIRL.
NO SUPER-POWERS.
NOTHING SPECIAL.
BET YOU FEEL KINDA *STUPID* NOW, HUH?
DANI MOONSTAR.
LEADER OF THE NEW MUTANTS. NO LONGER A MUTANT HERSELF. THAT TAKES GRIT.
HUP!
WASTE HER!
PF-F-F-FT-FT-FT-FT-FT-FT
WE ARE UNDER ATTACK!
WE HAVE A MAN DOWN!

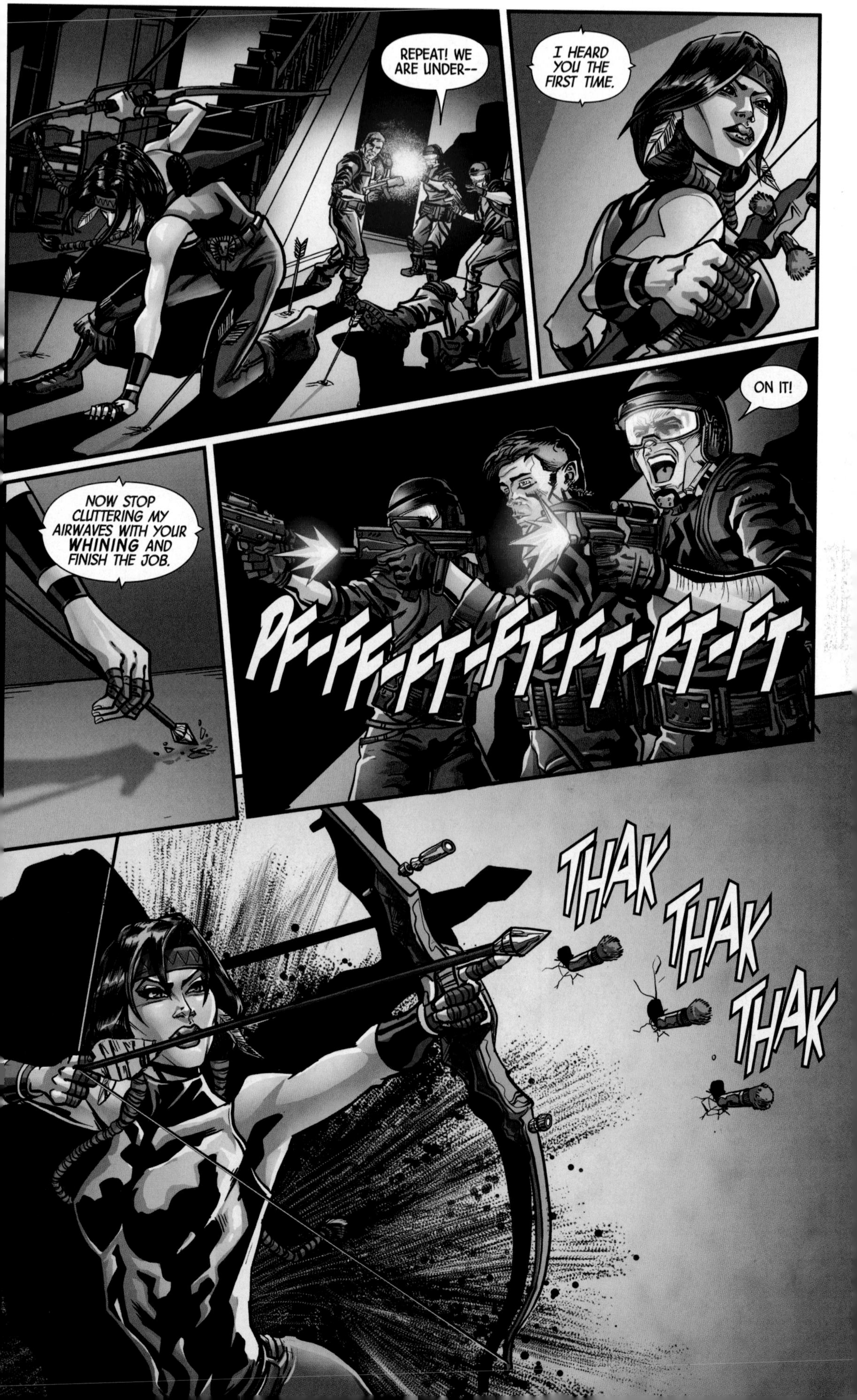
REPEAT! WE ARE UNDER--
I HEARD YOU THE FIRST TIME.
ON IT!
NOW STOP CLUTTERING MY AIRWAVES WITH YOUR **WHINING** AND FINISH THE JOB.
PF-FF-FT-FT-FT-FT-FT
THAK
THAK
THAK

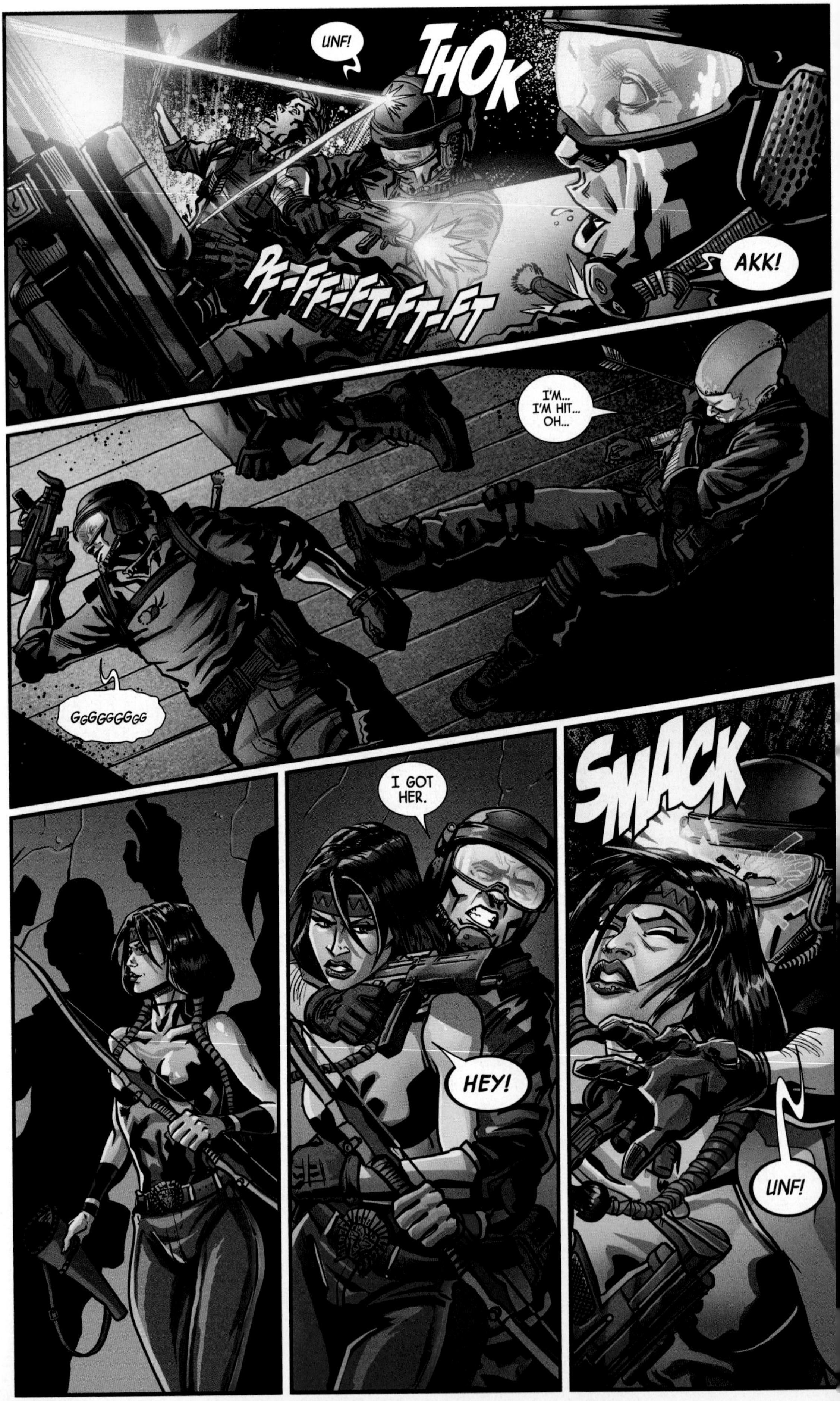
UNF!
THOK
PF-FF-FT-FT-FT
AKK!
I'M... I'M HIT... OH...
GGGGGGGGG
I GOT HER.
HEY!
SMACK
UNF!

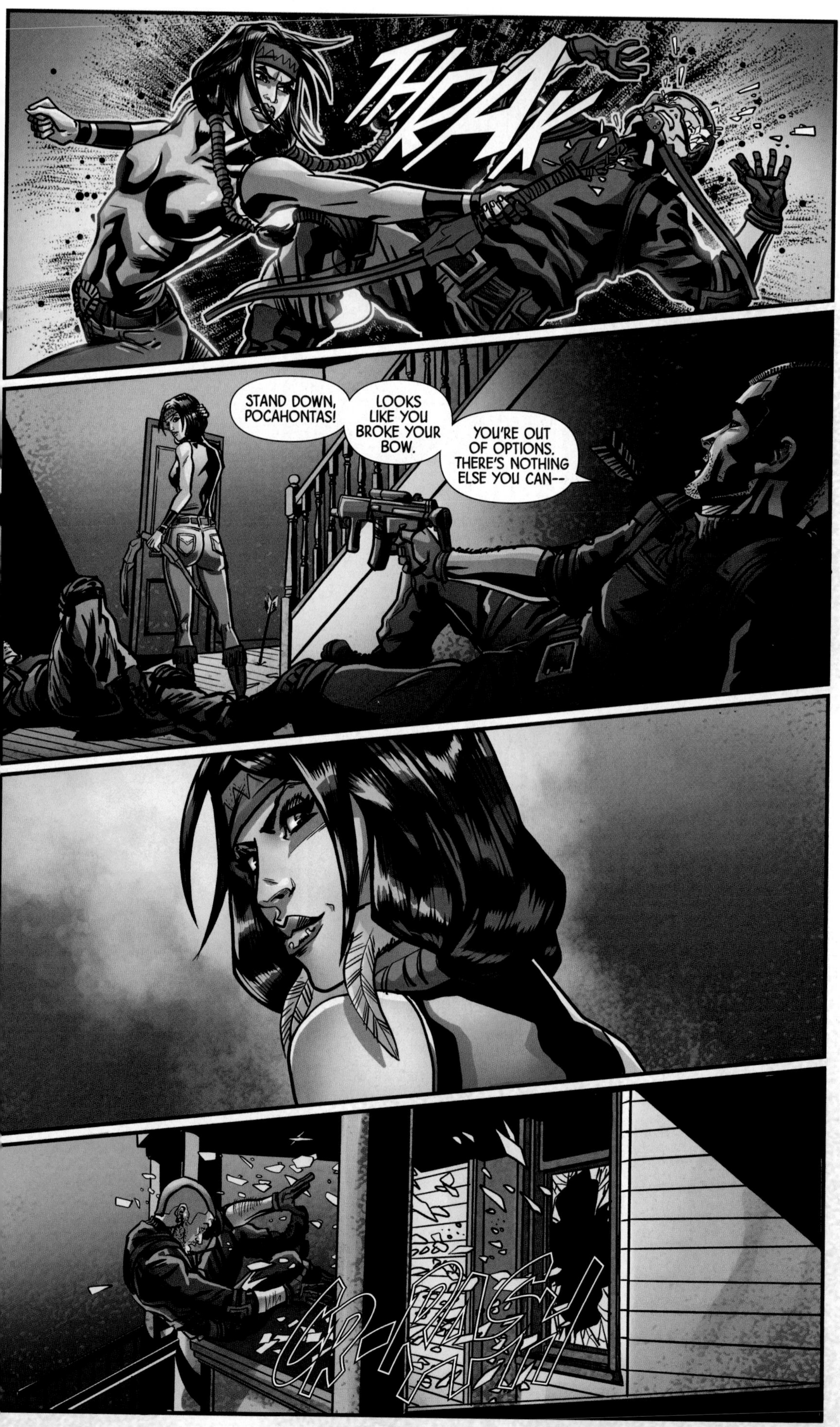
THRAK
STAND DOWN, POCAHONTAS!
LOOKS LIKE YOU BROKE YOUR BOW.
YOU'RE OUT OF OPTIONS. THERE'S NOTHING ELSE YOU CAN--
CRASH

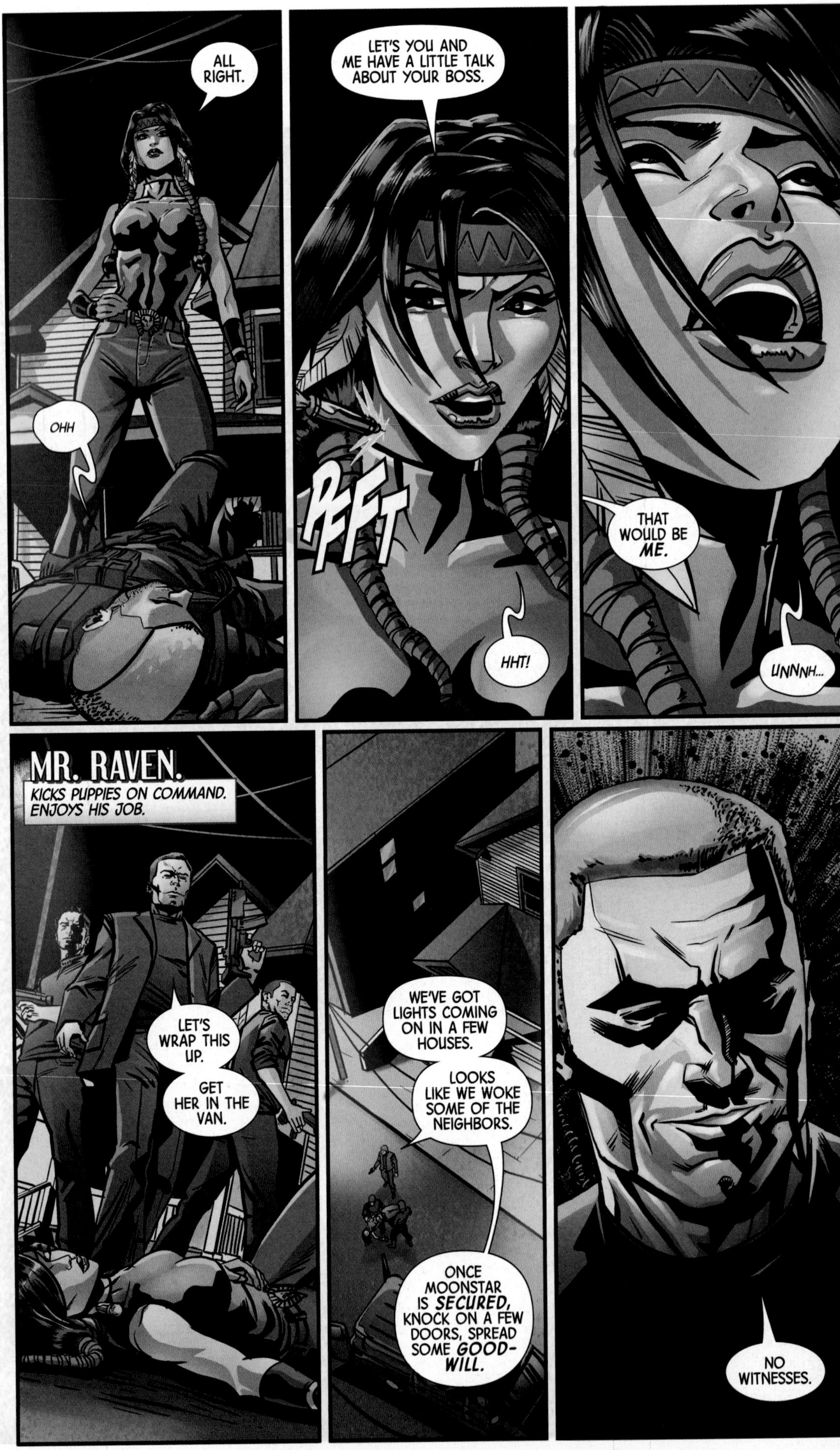
ALL RIGHT.
OHH
LET'S YOU AND ME HAVE A LITTLE TALK ABOUT YOUR BOSS.
PFFT
HHT!
THAT WOULD BE *ME*.
UNNNH...
MR. RAVEN.
KICKS PUPPIES ON COMMAND. ENJOYS HIS JOB.
LET'S WRAP THIS UP.
GET HER IN THE VAN.
WE'VE GOT LIGHTS COMING ON IN A FEW HOUSES.
LOOKS LIKE WE WOKE SOME OF THE NEIGHBORS.
ONCE MOONSTAR IS *SECURED*, KNOCK ON A FEW DOORS, SPREAD SOME *GOOD-WILL.*
NO WITNESSES.

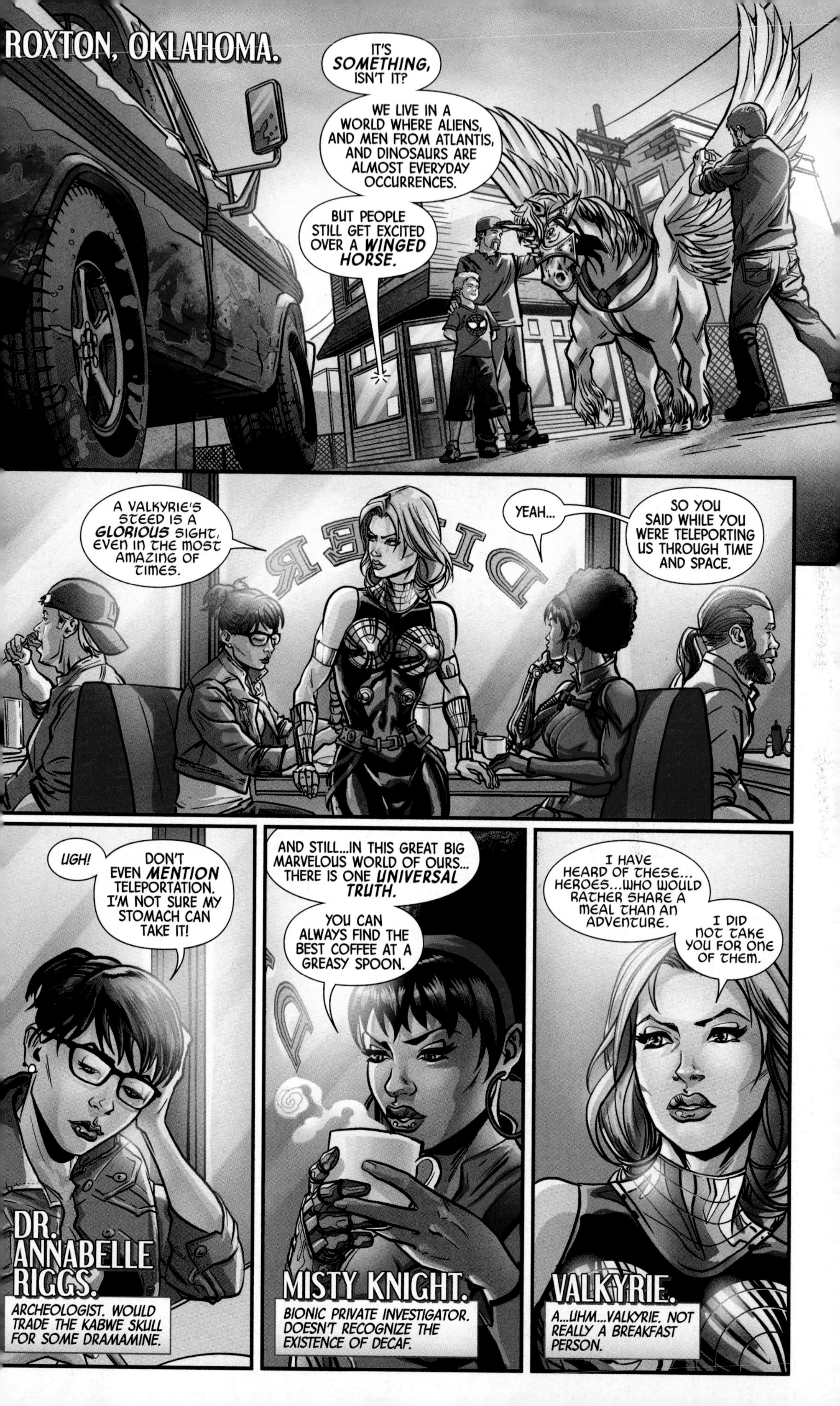

ROXTON, OKLAHOMA.
IT'S SOMETHING, ISN'T IT?
WE LIVE IN A WORLD WHERE ALIENS, AND MEN FROM ATLANTIS, AND DINOSAURS ARE ALMOST EVERYDAY OCCURRENCES.
BUT PEOPLE STILL GET EXCITED OVER A WINGED HORSE.
A VALKYRIE'S STEED IS A GLORIOUS SIGHT, EVEN IN THE MOST AMAZING OF TIMES.
YEAH...
SO YOU SAID WHILE YOU WERE TELEPORTING US THROUGH TIME AND SPACE.
UGH!
DON'T EVEN MENTION TELEPORTATION. I'M NOT SURE MY STOMACH CAN TAKE IT!
DR. ANNABELLE RIGGS.
ARCHEOLOGIST. WOULD TRADE THE KABWE SKULL FOR SOME DRAMAMINE.
AND STILL...IN THIS GREAT BIG MARVELOUS WORLD OF OURS... THERE IS ONE UNIVERSAL TRUTH.
YOU CAN ALWAYS FIND THE BEST COFFEE AT A GREASY SPOON.
MISTY KNIGHT.
BIONIC PRIVATE INVESTIGATOR. DOESN'T RECOGNIZE THE EXISTENCE OF DECAF.
I HAVE HEARD OF THESE... HEROES...WHO WOULD RATHER SHARE A MEAL THAN AN ADVENTURE.
I DID NOT TAKE YOU FOR ONE OF THEM.
VALKYRIE.
A...UHM...VALKYRIE. NOT REALLY A BREAKFAST PERSON.

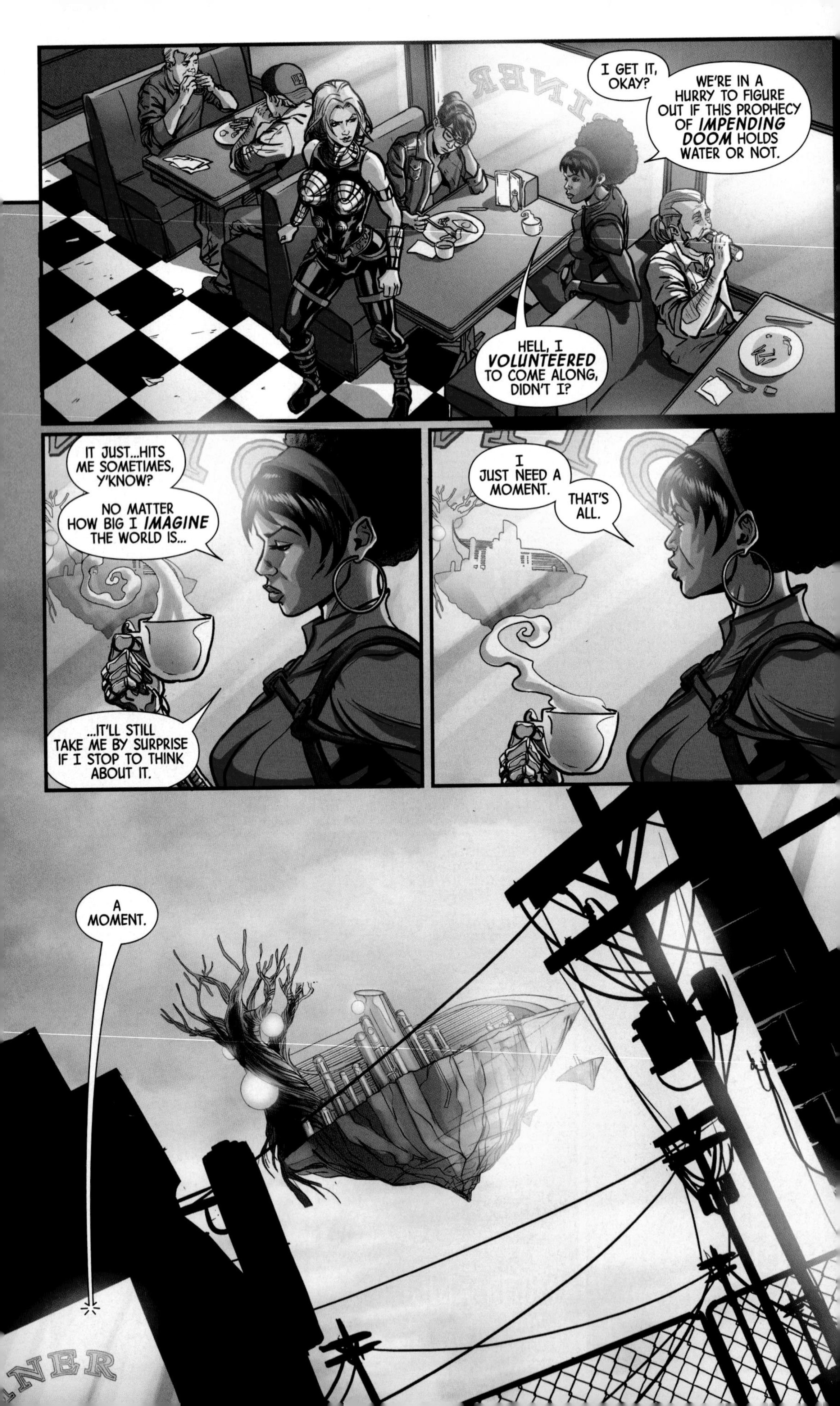

I GET IT, OKAY?
WE'RE IN A HURRY TO FIGURE OUT IF THIS PROPHECY OF *IMPENDING DOOM* HOLDS WATER OR NOT.
HELL, I *VOLUNTEERED* TO COME ALONG, DIDN'T I?
IT JUST...HITS ME SOMETIMES, Y'KNOW?
NO MATTER HOW BIG I *IMAGINE* THE WORLD IS...
...IT'LL STILL TAKE ME BY SURPRISE IF I STOP TO THINK ABOUT IT.
I JUST NEED A MOMENT.
THAT'S ALL.
A MOMENT.

OPEN YOUR EYES, MISS MOONSTAR.

I ASSURE YOU, FEIGNING UNCONSCIOUSNESS WILL NOT AFFORD YOU ANY TIME TO PLOT AN *ESCAPE.*

I CAN *APPRECIATE* THE EFFORT, BUT--TRUST ME-- IT'S *WASTED.*

YOU'RE NOT GOING ANYWHERE.

WHERE AM I?

WHO THE HELL ARE YOU?

SEE? ISN'T THIS MUCH NICER?

ONCE WE DISMISS WITH THE CHARADES AND SCHEMING, WE CAN HAVE A PLEASANT DISCUSSION LIKE TWO SENSIBLE WOMEN WHO *RESPECT* ONE ANOTHER.

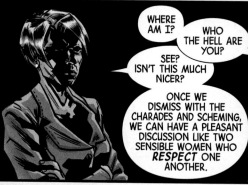

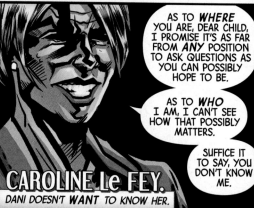

AS TO *WHERE* YOU ARE, DEAR CHILD, I PROMISE IT'S AS FAR FROM *ANY* POSITION TO ASK QUESTIONS AS YOU CAN POSSIBLY HOPE TO BE.

AS TO *WHO* I AM, I CAN'T SEE HOW THAT POSSIBLY MATTERS.

SUFFICE IT TO SAY, YOU DON'T KNOW ME.

CAROLINE Le FEY.
DANI DOESN'T *WANT* TO KNOW HER.

AND YOUR REMAINING TIME ON THIS EARTH ISN'T SUFFICIENT FOR THE TWO OF US TO BECOME--

--WHAT DO YOU GIRLS SAY--

--B.F.FS.

LADY...I MIGHT NOT KNOW WHO YOU ARE, BUT IF YOU THINK YOU CAN *JUST* KIDNAP ME, YOU'VE GOT ANOTHER THING COMING.

I'VE GOT *FRIENDS* WHO--

TSK TSK TSK.

DON'T, SWEETIE. JUST *DON'T.*

IT'S *INSULTING* TO BOTH OF US.

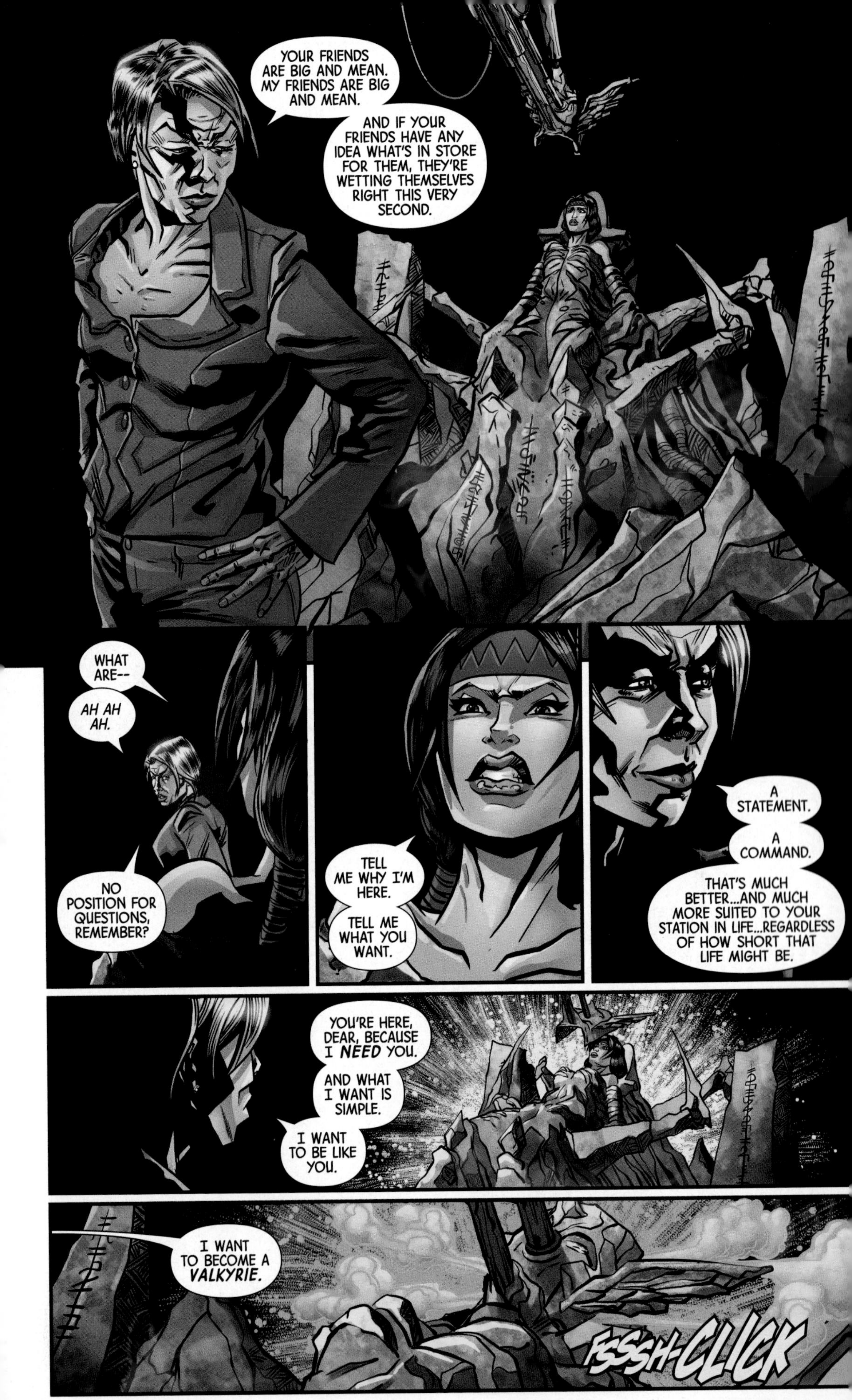
YOUR FRIENDS ARE BIG AND MEAN. MY FRIENDS ARE BIG AND MEAN.
AND IF YOUR FRIENDS HAVE ANY IDEA WHAT'S IN STORE FOR THEM, THEY'RE WETTING THEMSELVES RIGHT THIS VERY SECOND.
WHAT ARE--
AH AH AH.
NO POSITION FOR QUESTIONS, REMEMBER?
TELL ME WHY I'M HERE.
TELL ME WHAT YOU WANT.
A STATEMENT.
A COMMAND.
THAT'S MUCH BETTER...AND MUCH MORE SUITED TO YOUR STATION IN LIFE...REGARDLESS OF HOW SHORT THAT LIFE MIGHT BE.
YOU'RE HERE, DEAR, BECAUSE I NEED YOU.
AND WHAT I WANT IS SIMPLE.
I WANT TO BE LIKE YOU.
I WANT TO BECOME A VALKYRIE.
FSSSH-CLICK

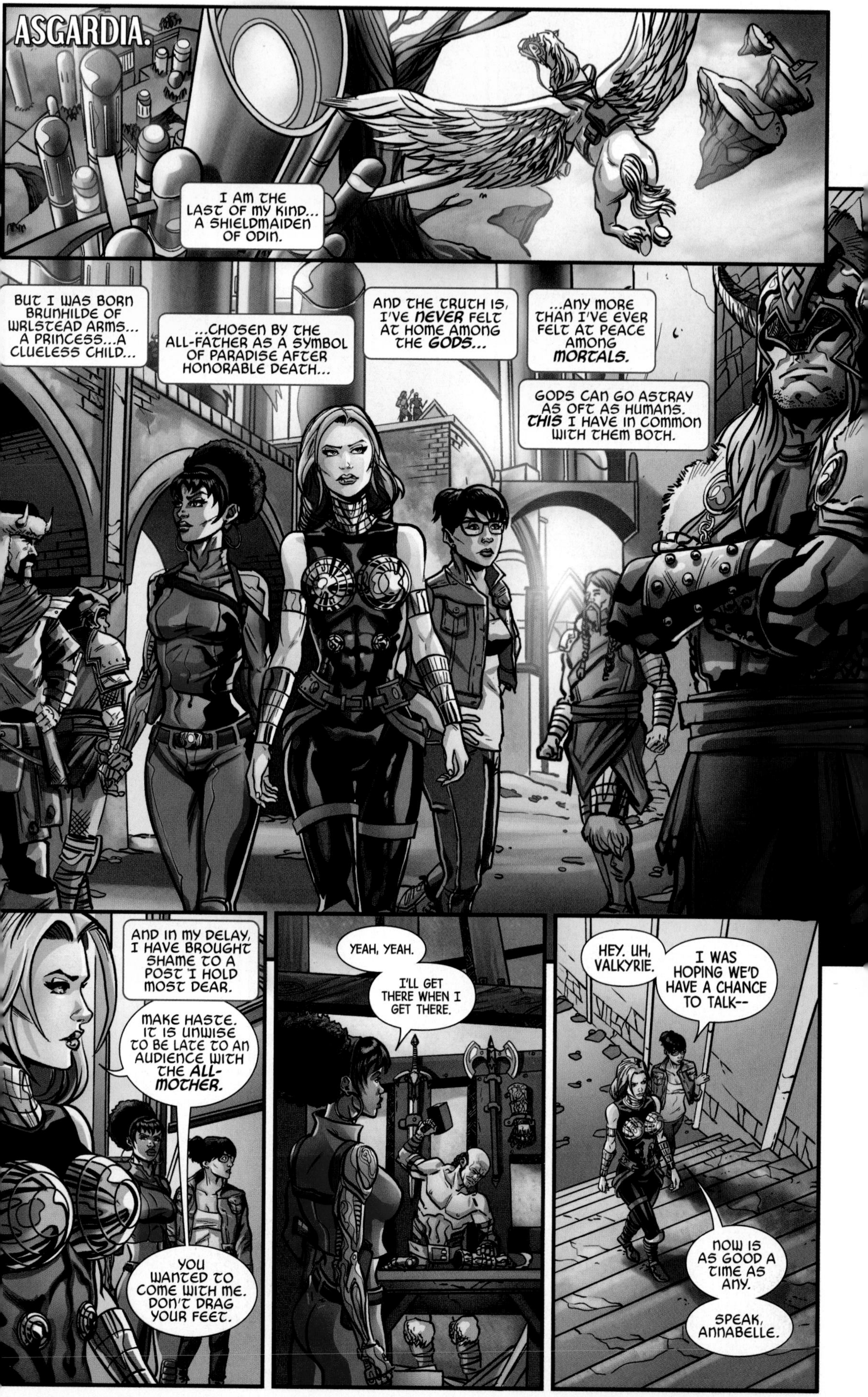

ASGARDIA.
I AM THE LAST OF MY KIND... A SHIELDMAIDEN OF ODIN.
BUT I WAS BORN BRUNHILDE OF WRLSTEAD ARMS... A PRINCESS...A CLUELESS CHILD...
...CHOSEN BY THE ALL-FATHER AS A SYMBOL OF PARADISE AFTER HONORABLE DEATH...
AND THE TRUTH IS, I'VE NEVER FELT AT HOME AMONG THE GODS...
...ANY MORE THAN I'VE EVER FELT AT PEACE AMONG MORTALS.
GODS CAN GO ASTRAY AS OFT AS HUMANS. THIS I HAVE IN COMMON WITH THEM BOTH.
AND IN MY DELAY, I HAVE BROUGHT SHAME TO A POST I HOLD MOST DEAR.
MAKE HASTE. IT IS UNWISE TO BE LATE TO AN AUDIENCE WITH THE ALL-MOTHER.
YOU WANTED TO COME WITH ME. DON'T DRAG YOUR FEET.
YEAH, YEAH.
I'LL GET THERE WHEN I GET THERE.
HEY. UH, VALKYRIE.
I WAS HOPING WE'D HAVE A CHANCE TO TALK--
NOW IS AS GOOD A TIME AS ANY.
SPEAK, ANNABELLE.

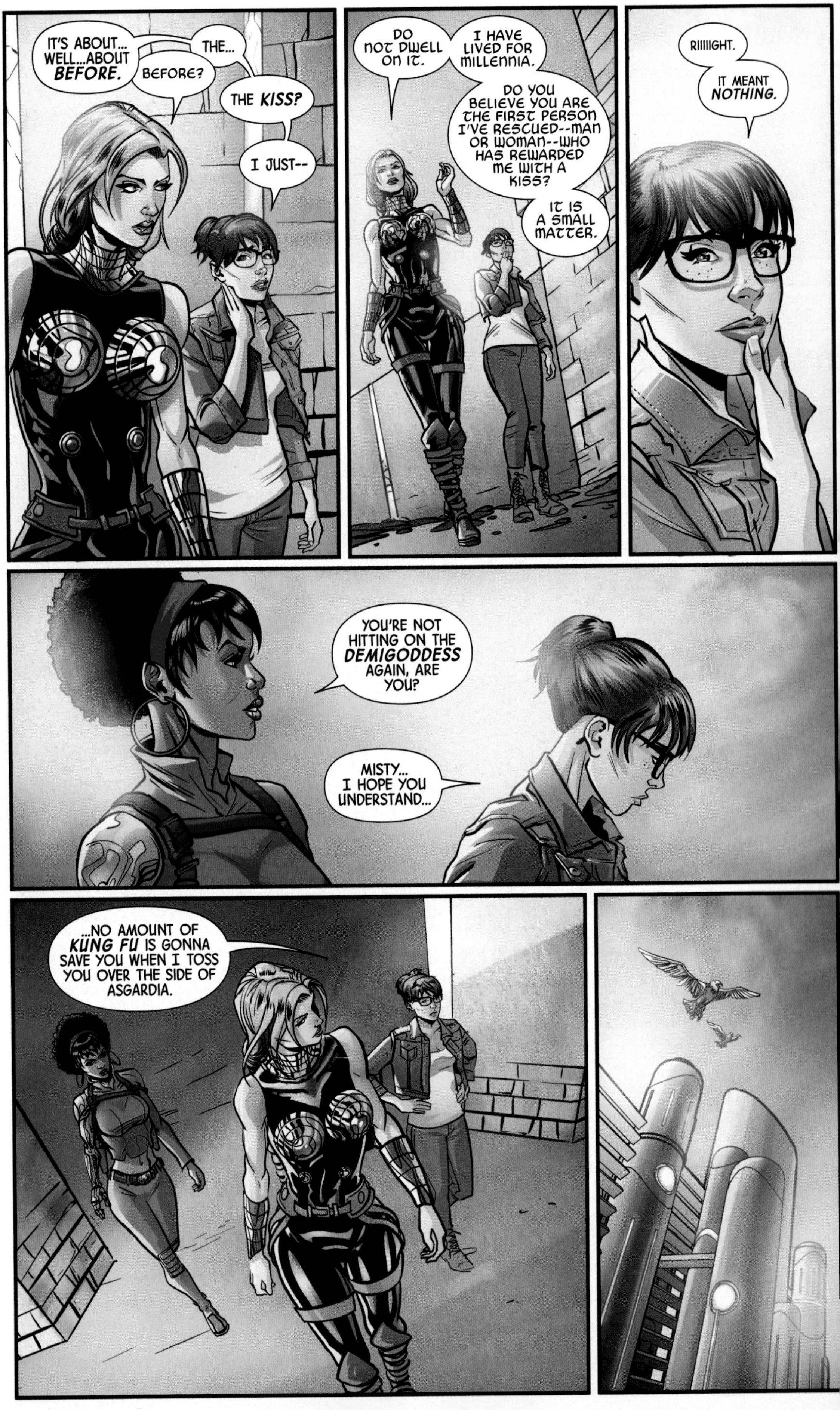
IT'S ABOUT... WELL...ABOUT BEFORE.
THE...
BEFORE?
THE KISS?
I JUST--
DO NOT DWELL ON IT.
I HAVE LIVED FOR MILLENNIA.
DO YOU BELIEVE YOU ARE THE FIRST PERSON I'VE RESCUED--MAN OR WOMAN--WHO HAS REWARDED ME WITH A KISS?
IT IS A SMALL MATTER.
RIIIIIGHT.
IT MEANT NOTHING.
YOU'RE NOT HITTING ON THE DEMIGODDESS AGAIN, ARE YOU?
MISTY... I HOPE YOU UNDERSTAND...
...NO AMOUNT OF KÜNG FU IS GONNA SAVE YOU WHEN I TOSS YOU OVER THE SIDE OF ASGARDIA.

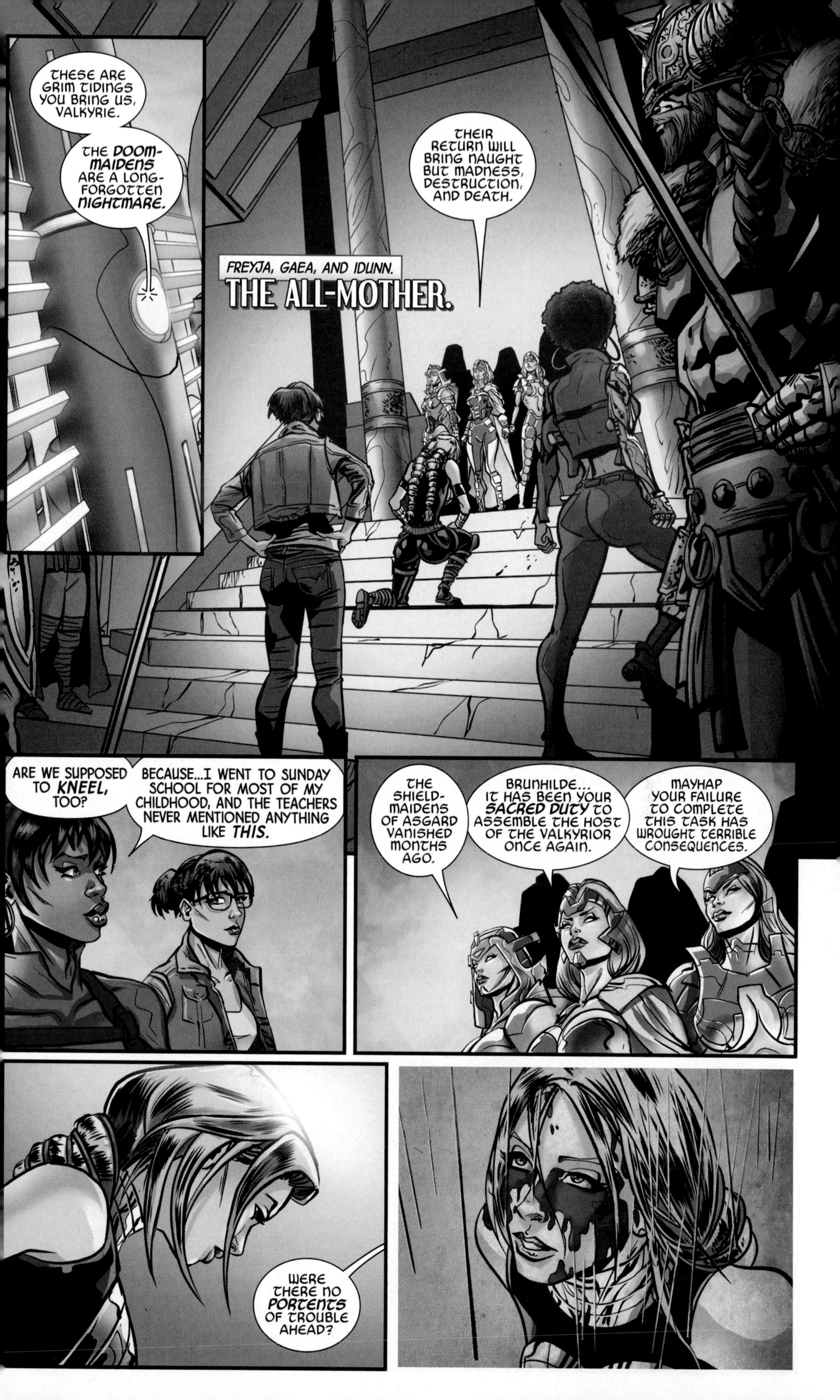

THESE ARE GRIM TIDINGS YOU BRING US, VALKYRIE.
THE DOOM-MAIDENS ARE A LONG-FORGOTTEN NIGHTMARE.
THEIR RETURN WILL BRING NAUGHT BUT MADNESS, DESTRUCTION, AND DEATH.
FREYJA, GAEA, AND IDUNN.
THE ALL-MOTHER.
ARE WE SUPPOSED TO KNEEL, TOO?
BECAUSE...I WENT TO SUNDAY SCHOOL FOR MOST OF MY CHILDHOOD, AND THE TEACHERS NEVER MENTIONED ANYTHING LIKE THIS.
THE SHIELD-MAIDENS OF ASGARD VANISHED MONTHS AGO.
BRUNHILDE... IT HAS BEEN YOUR SACRED DUTY TO ASSEMBLE THE HOST OF THE VALKYRIOR ONCE AGAIN.
MAYHAP YOUR FAILURE TO COMPLETE THIS TASK HAS WROUGHT TERRIBLE CONSEQUENCES.
WERE THERE NO PORTENTS OF TROUBLE AHEAD?

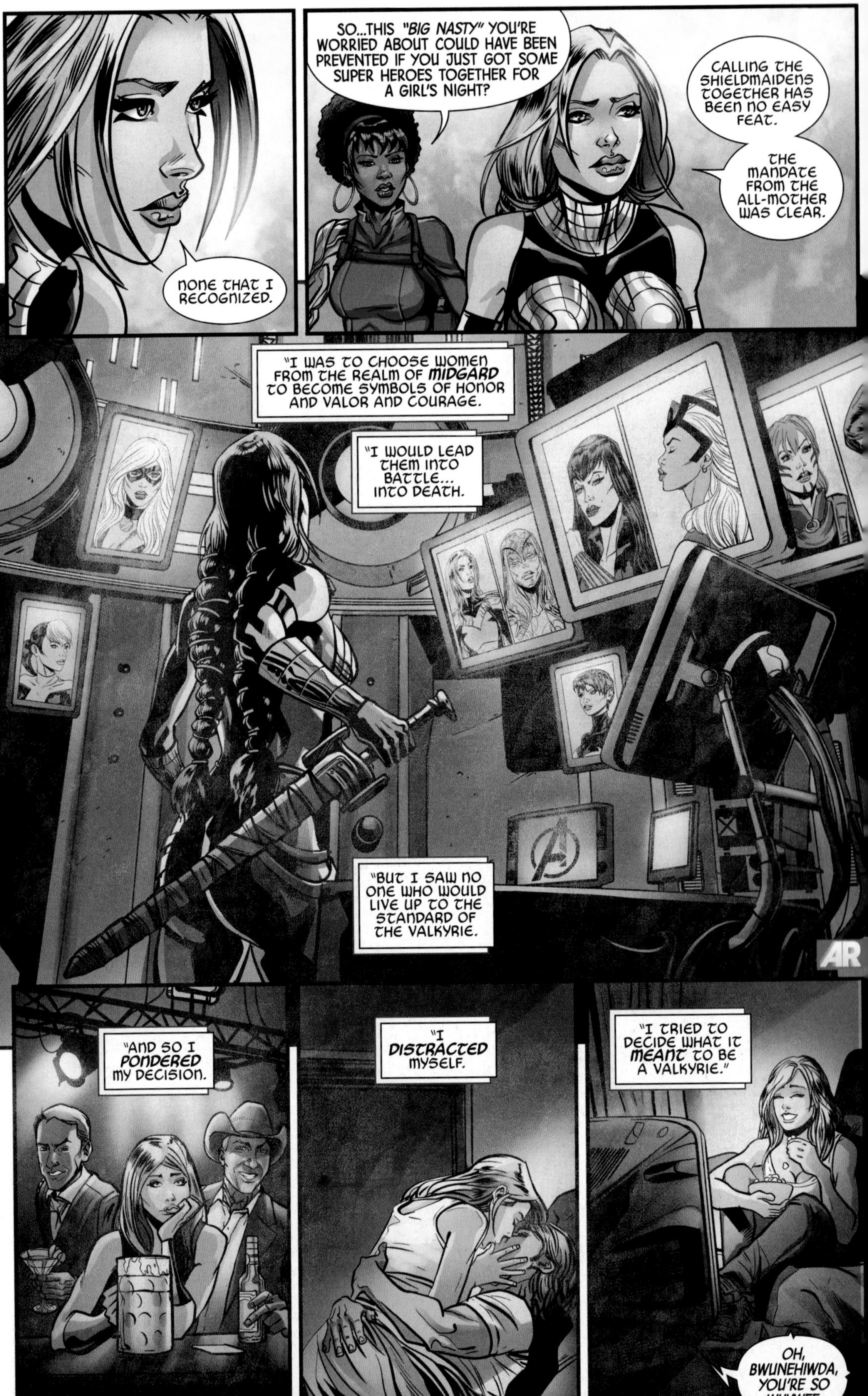
NONE THAT I RECOGNIZED.
SO...THIS "BIG NASTY" YOU'RE WORRIED ABOUT COULD HAVE BEEN PREVENTED IF YOU JUST GOT SOME SUPER HEROES TOGETHER FOR A GIRL'S NIGHT?
CALLING THE SHIELDMAIDENS TOGETHER HAS BEEN NO EASY FEAT.
THE MANDATE FROM THE ALL-MOTHER WAS CLEAR.
"I WAS TO CHOOSE WOMEN FROM THE REALM OF MIDGARD TO BECOME SYMBOLS OF HONOR AND VALOR AND COURAGE.
"I WOULD LEAD THEM INTO BATTLE... INTO DEATH.
"BUT I SAW NO ONE WHO WOULD LIVE UP TO THE STANDARD OF THE VALKYRIE.
"AND SO I PONDERED MY DECISION.
"I DISTRACTED MYSELF.
"I TRIED TO DECIDE WHAT IT MEANT TO BE A VALKYRIE."
OH, BWUNEHIWDA, YOU'RE SO WUVWEE.

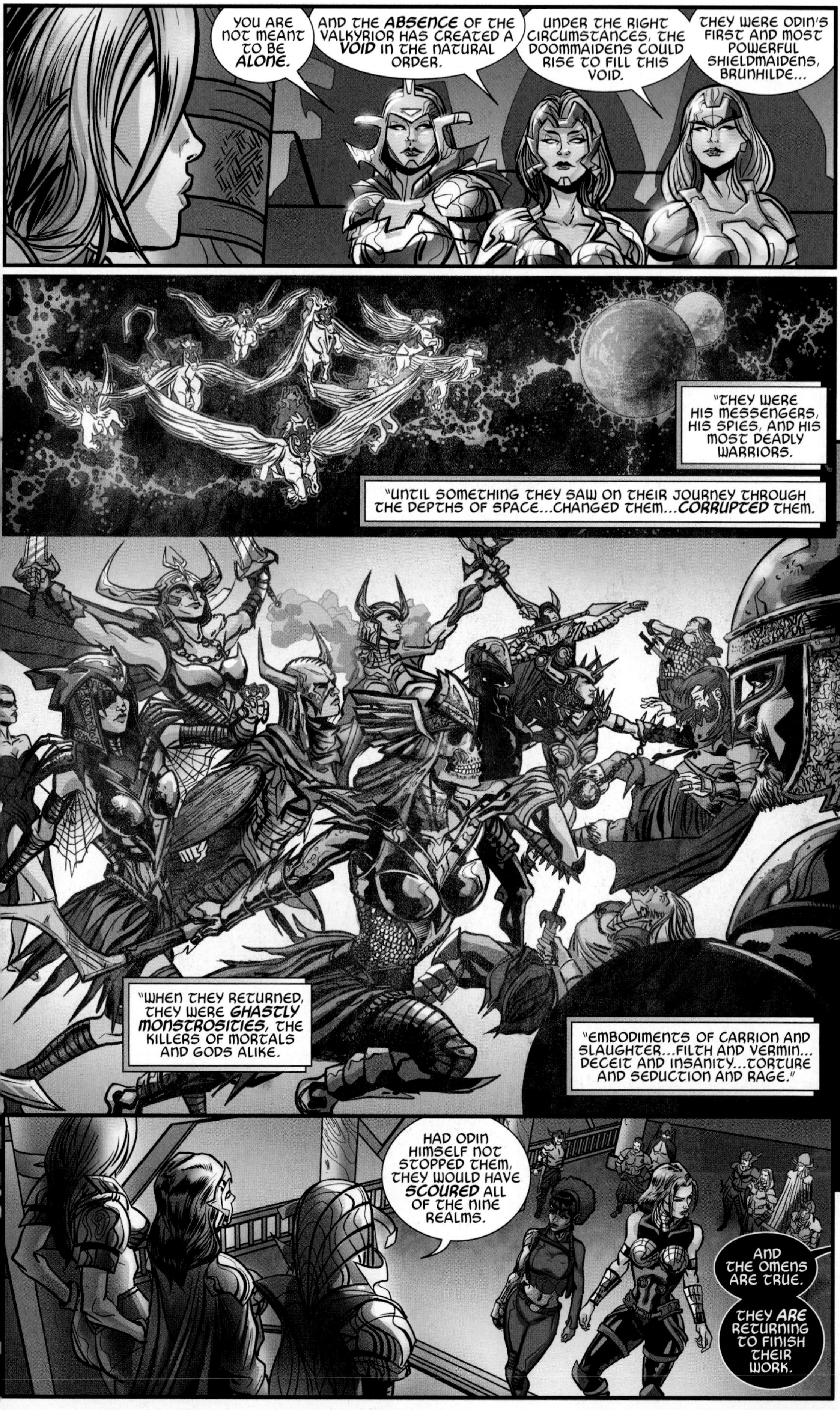

YOU ARE NOT MEANT TO BE ALONE.
AND THE ABSENCE OF THE VALKYRIOR HAS CREATED A VOID IN THE NATURAL ORDER.
UNDER THE RIGHT CIRCUMSTANCES, THE DOOMMAIDENS COULD RISE TO FILL THIS VOID.
THEY WERE ODIN'S FIRST AND MOST POWERFUL SHIELDMAIDENS, BRUNHILDE...
"THEY WERE HIS MESSENGERS, HIS SPIES, AND HIS MOST DEADLY WARRIORS.
"UNTIL SOMETHING THEY SAW ON THEIR JOURNEY THROUGH THE DEPTHS OF SPACE...CHANGED THEM...CORRUPTED THEM.
"WHEN THEY RETURNED, THEY WERE GHASTLY MONSTROSITIES, THE KILLERS OF MORTALS AND GODS ALIKE.
"EMBODIMENTS OF CARRION AND SLAUGHTER...FILTH AND VERMIN... DECEIT AND INSANITY...TORTURE AND SEDUCTION AND RAGE."
HAD ODIN HIMSELF NOT STOPPED THEM, THEY WOULD HAVE SCOURED ALL OF THE NINE REALMS.
AND THE OMENS ARE TRUE.
THEY ARE RETURNING TO FINISH THEIR WORK.

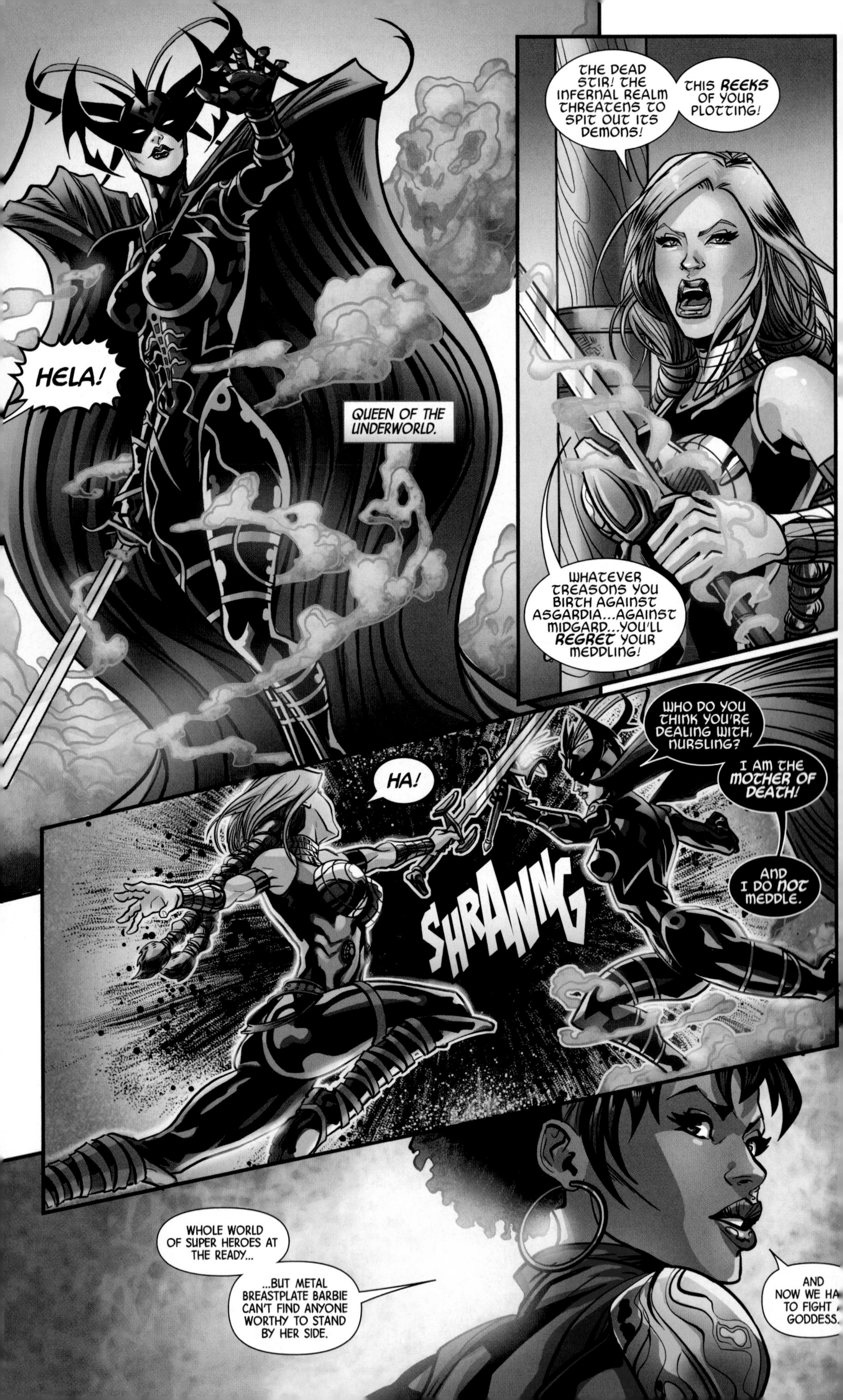
THE DEAD STIR! THE INFERNAL REALM THREATENS TO SPIT OUT ITS DEMONS!
THIS REEKS OF YOUR PLOTTING!
HELA!
QUEEN OF THE UNDERWORLD.
WHATEVER TREASONS YOU BIRTH AGAINST ASGARDIA...AGAINST MIDGARD...YOU'LL REGRET YOUR MEDDLING!
WHO DO YOU THINK YOU'RE DEALING WITH, NURSLING?
I AM THE MOTHER OF DEATH!
HA!
AND I DO NOT MEDDLE.
SHRANNG
WHOLE WORLD OF SUPER HEROES AT THE READY...
...BUT METAL BREASTPLATE BARBIE CAN'T FIND ANYONE WORTHY TO STAND BY HER SIDE.

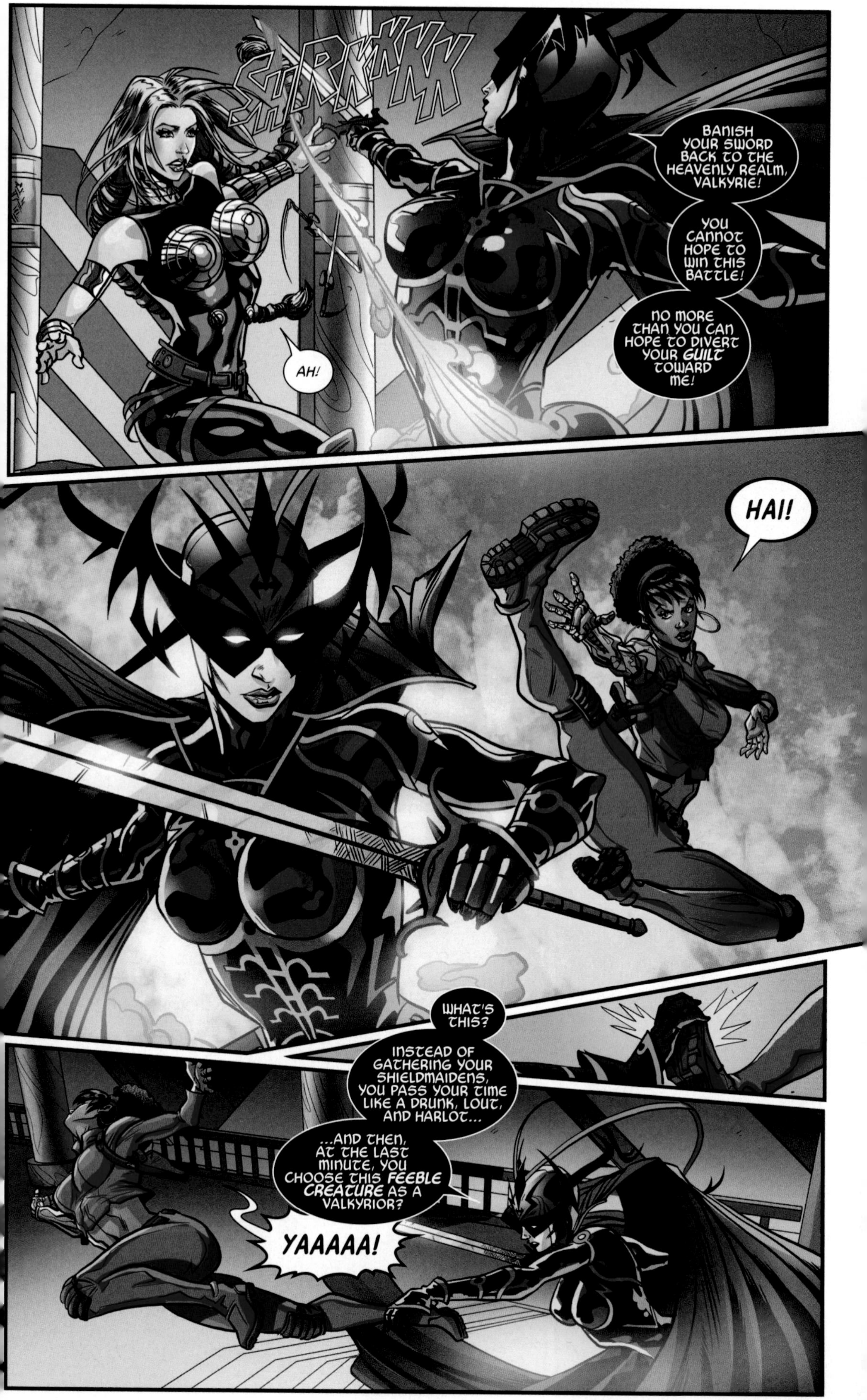
SHRKKK
BANISH YOUR SWORD BACK TO THE HEAVENLY REALM, VALKYRIE!
YOU CANNOT HOPE TO WIN THIS BATTLE!
NO MORE THAN YOU CAN HOPE TO DIVERT YOUR GUILT TOWARD ME!
AH!
HAI!
WHAT'S THIS?
INSTEAD OF GATHERING YOUR SHIELDMAIDENS, YOU PASS YOUR TIME LIKE A DRUNK, LOUT, AND HARLOT...
...AND THEN, AT THE LAST MINUTE, YOU CHOOSE THIS FEEBLE CREATURE AS A VALKYRIOR?
YAAAAA!

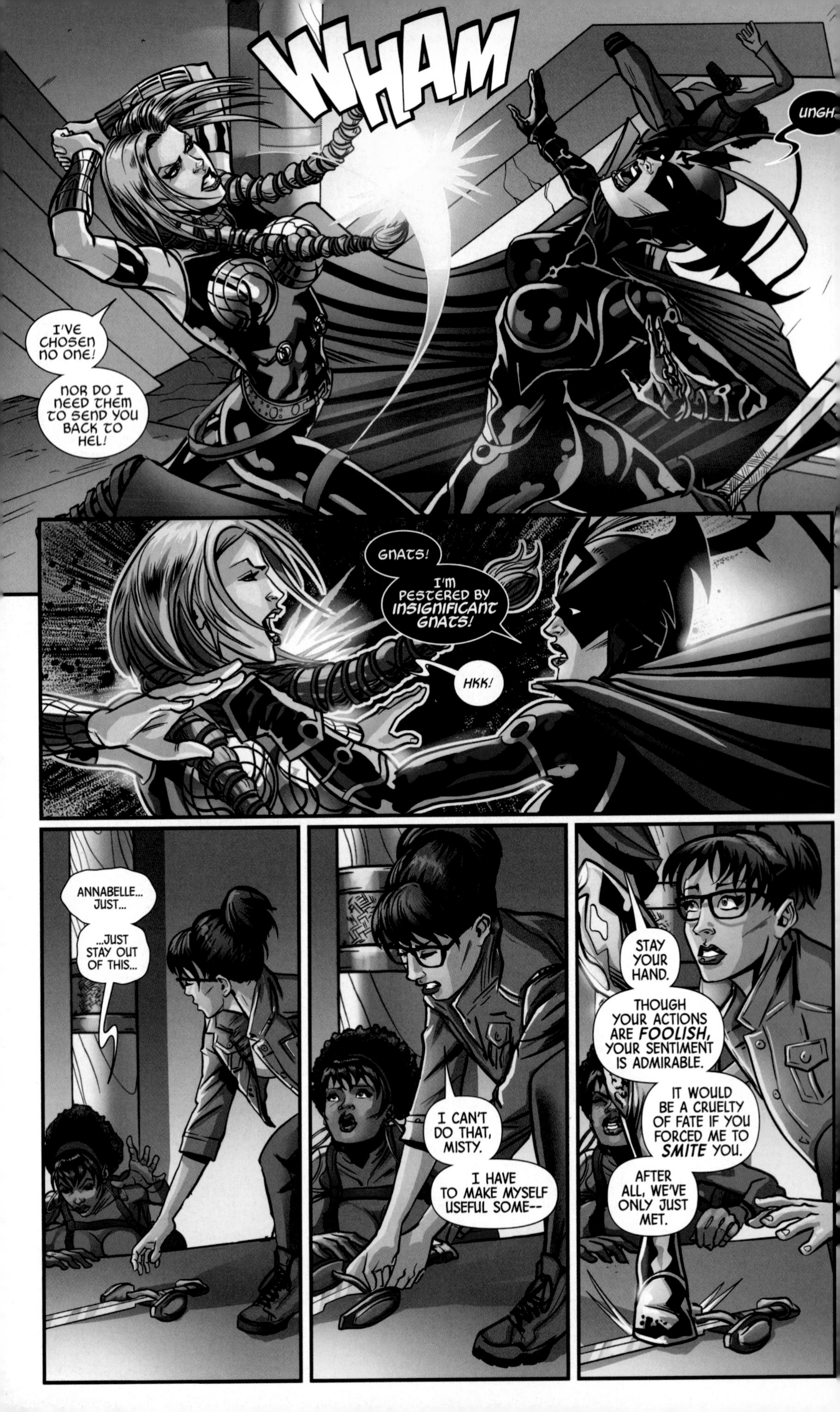
WHAM
UNGH
I'VE CHOSEN NO ONE!
NOR DO I NEED THEM TO SEND YOU BACK TO HEL!
GNATS!
I'M PESTERED BY INSIGNIFICANT GNATS!
HKK!
ANNABELLE... JUST...
...JUST STAY OUT OF THIS...
I CAN'T DO THAT, MISTY.
I HAVE TO MAKE MYSELF USEFUL SOME--
STAY YOUR HAND.
THOUGH YOUR ACTIONS ARE FOOLISH, YOUR SENTIMENT IS ADMIRABLE.
IT WOULD BE A CRUELTY OF FATE IF YOU FORCED ME TO SMITE YOU.
AFTER ALL, WE'VE ONLY JUST MET.

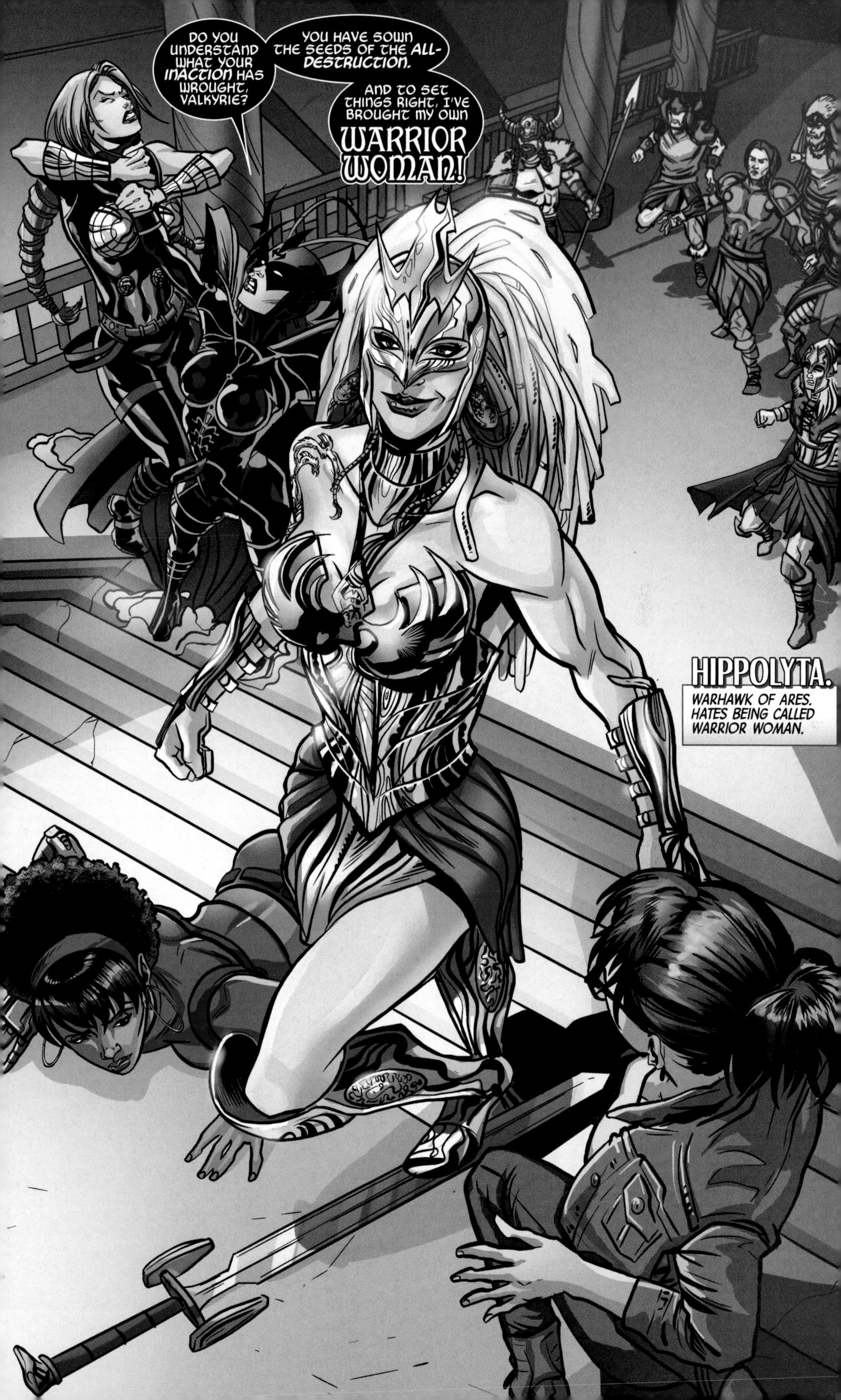
DO YOU UNDERSTAND WHAT YOUR INACTION HAS WROUGHT, VALKYRIE?
YOU HAVE SOWN THE SEEDS OF THE ALL-DESTRUCTION.
AND TO SET THINGS RIGHT, I'VE BROUGHT MY OWN
WARRIOR WOMAN!
HIPPOLYTA.
WARHAWK OF ARES. HATES BEING CALLED WARRIOR WOMAN.

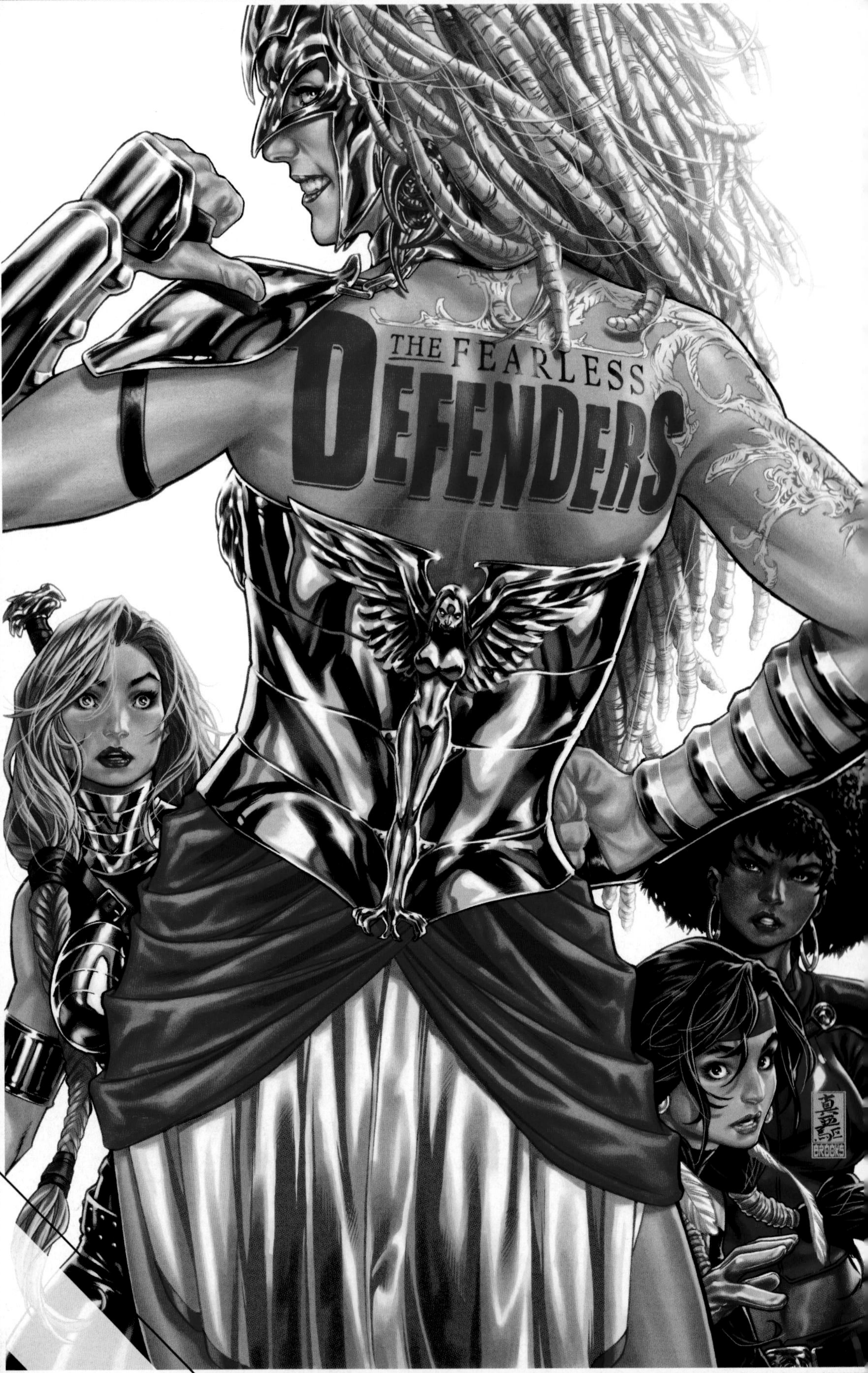
THE FEARLESS
DEFENDERS
BROOKS

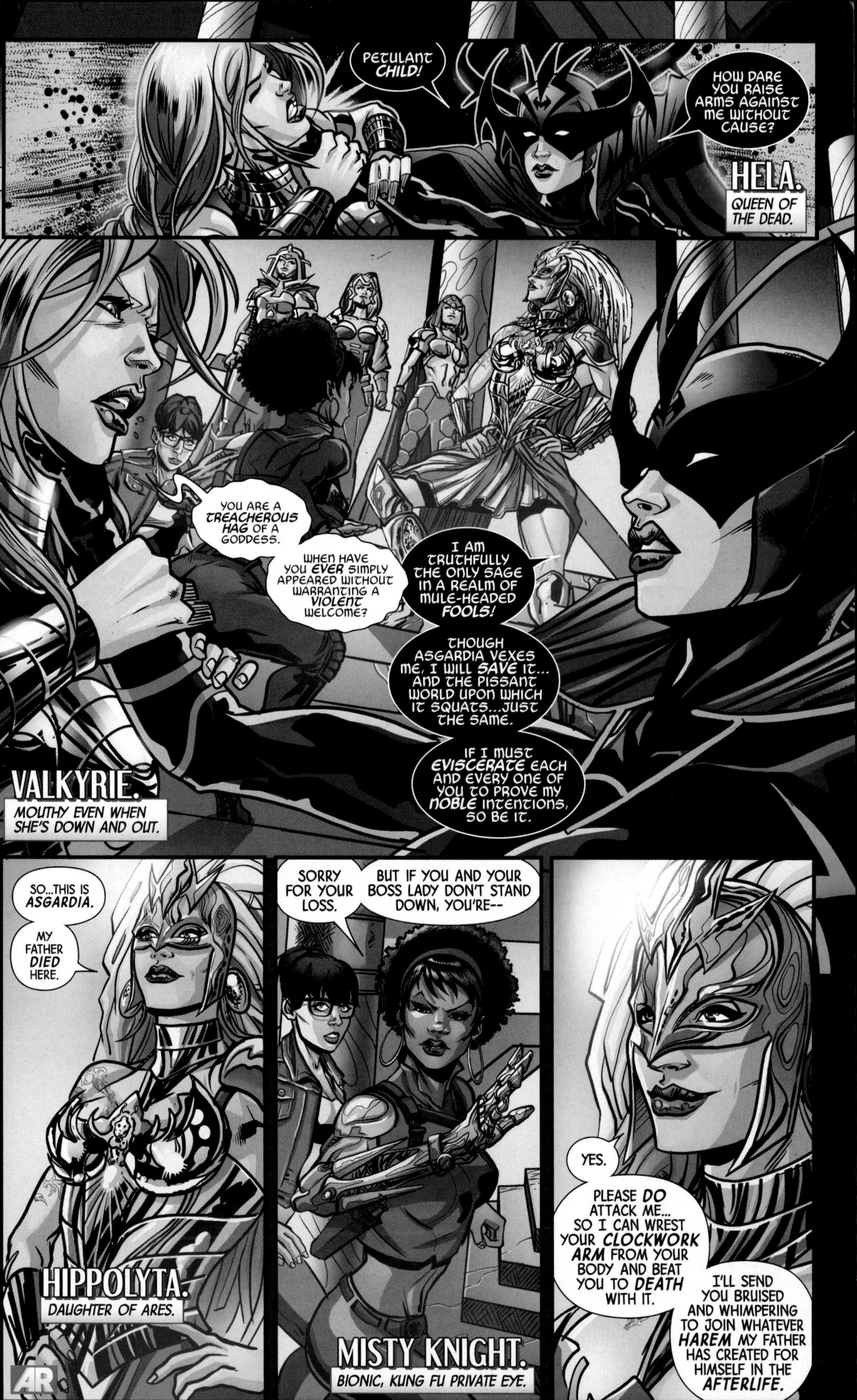

PETULANT CHILD!
HOW DARE YOU RAISE ARMS AGAINST ME WITHOUT CAUSE?
HELA.
QUEEN OF THE DEAD.
YOU ARE A TREACHEROUS HAG OF A GODDESS.
WHEN HAVE YOU EVER SIMPLY APPEARED WITHOUT WARRANTING A VIOLENT WELCOME?
I AM TRUTHFULLY THE ONLY SAGE IN A REALM OF MULE-HEADED FOOLS!
THOUGH ASGARDIA VEXES ME, I WILL SAVE IT... AND THE PISSANT WORLD UPON WHICH IT SQUATS...JUST THE SAME.
IF I MUST EVISCERATE EACH AND EVERY ONE OF YOU TO PROVE MY NOBLE INTENTIONS, SO BE IT.
VALKYRIE.
MOUTHY EVEN WHEN SHE'S DOWN AND OUT.
SO...THIS IS ASGARDIA.
MY FATHER DIED HERE.
HIPPOLYTA.
DAUGHTER OF ARES.
SORRY FOR YOUR LOSS.
BUT IF YOU AND YOUR BOSS LADY DON'T STAND DOWN, YOU'RE--
MISTY KNIGHT.
BIONIC, KUNG FU PRIVATE EYE.
YES.
PLEASE DO ATTACK ME... SO I CAN WREST YOUR CLOCKWORK ARM FROM YOUR BODY AND BEAT YOU TO DEATH WITH IT.
I'LL SEND YOU BRUISED AND WHIMPERING TO JOIN WHATEVER HAREM MY FATHER HAS CREATED FOR HIMSELF IN THE AFTERLIFE.

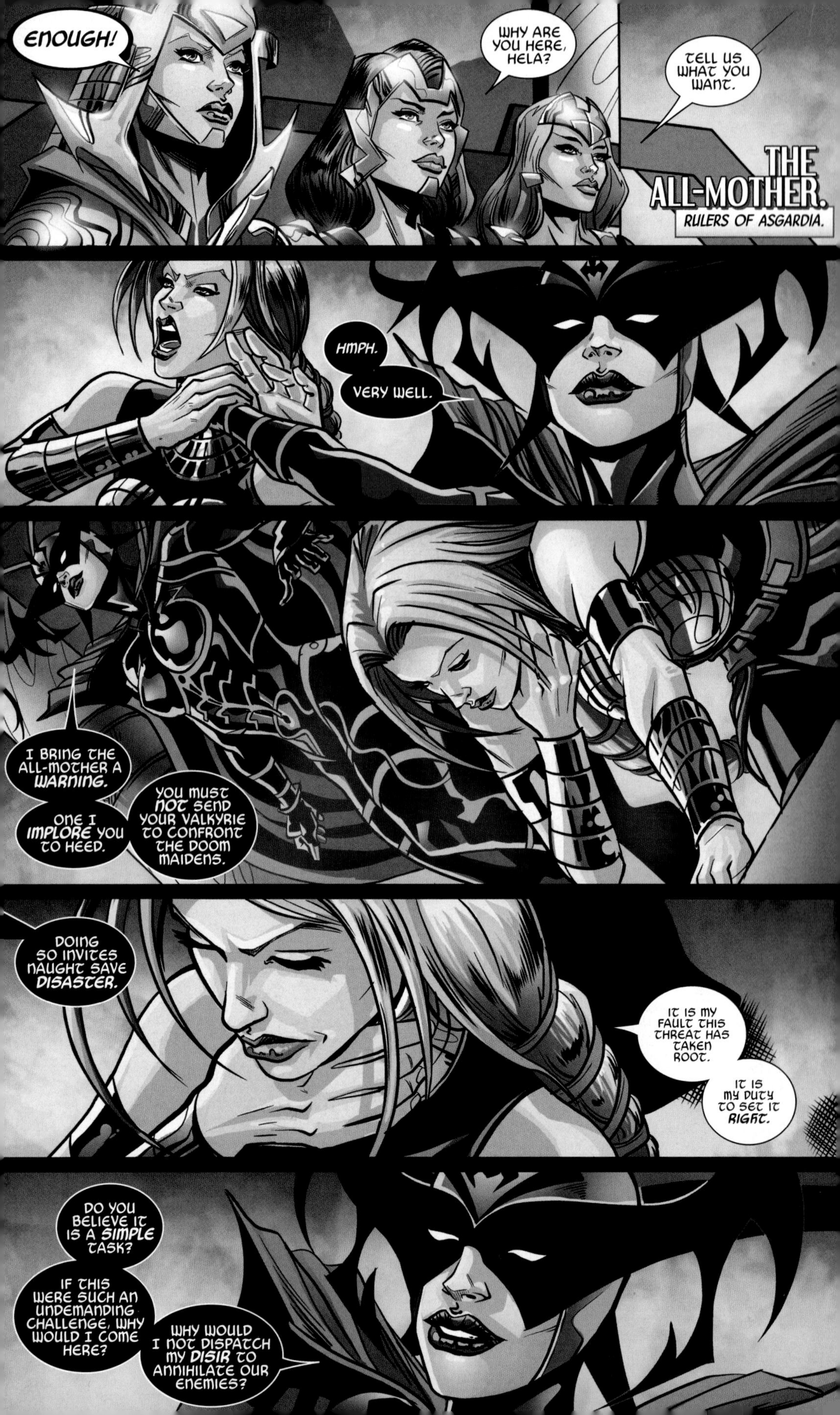
ENOUGH!
WHY ARE YOU HERE, HELA?
TELL US WHAT YOU WANT.
THE ALL-MOTHER.
RULERS OF ASGARDIA.
HMPH.
VERY WELL.
I BRING THE ALL-MOTHER A WARNING.
ONE I IMPLORE YOU TO HEED.
YOU MUST NOT SEND YOUR VALKYRIE TO CONFRONT THE DOOM MAIDENS.
DOING SO INVITES NAUGHT SAVE DISASTER.
IT IS MY FAULT THIS THREAT HAS TAKEN ROOT.
IT IS MY DUTY TO SET IT RIGHT.
DO YOU BELIEVE IT IS A SIMPLE TASK?
IF THIS WERE SUCH AN UNDEMANDING CHALLENGE, WHY WOULD I COME HERE?
WHY WOULD I NOT DISPATCH MY DISIR TO ANNIHILATE OUR ENEMIES?

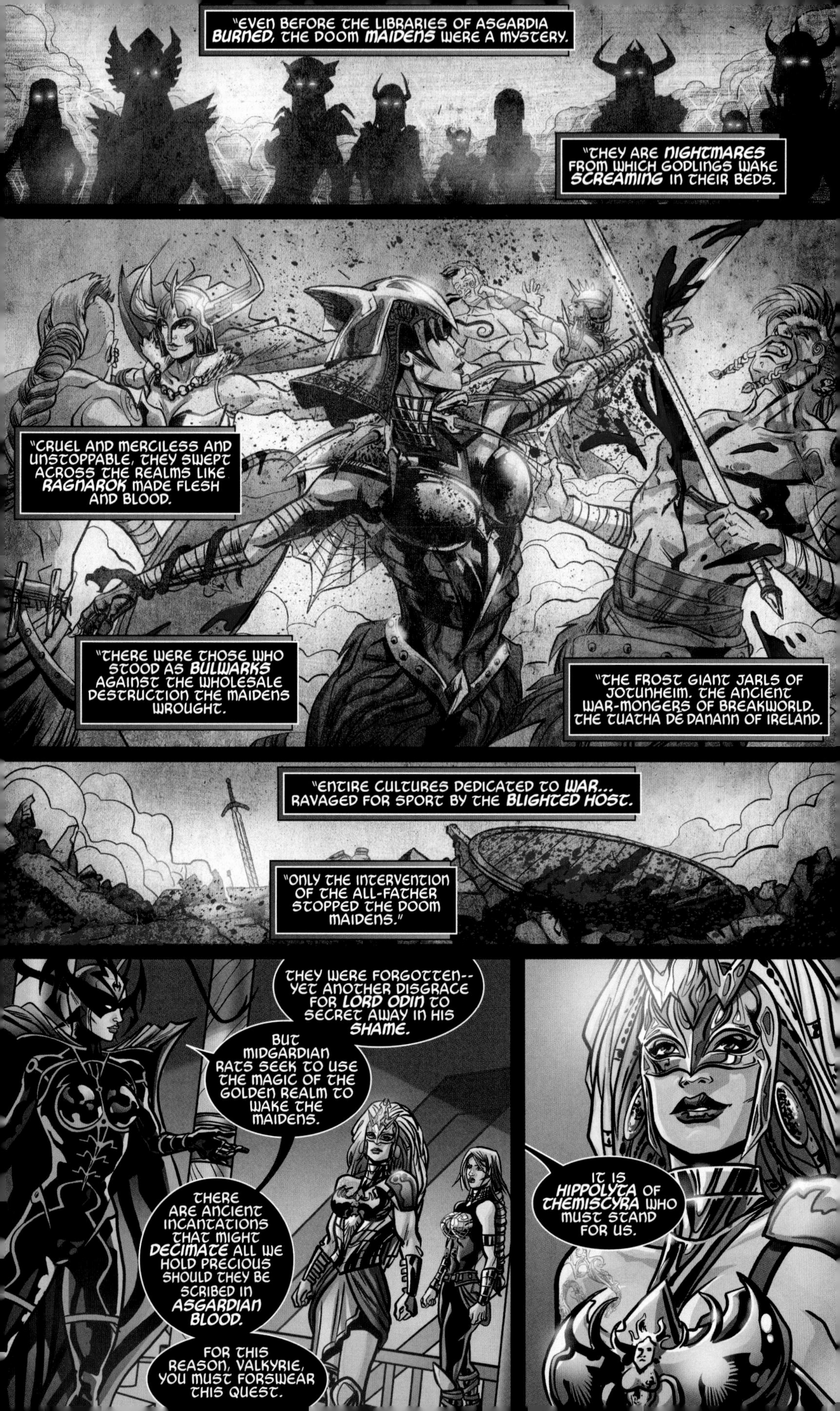

"EVEN BEFORE THE LIBRARIES OF ASGARDIA BURNED, THE DOOM MAIDENS WERE A MYSTERY.
"THEY ARE NIGHTMARES FROM WHICH GODLINGS WAKE SCREAMING IN THEIR BEDS.
"CRUEL AND MERCILESS AND UNSTOPPABLE, THEY SWEPT ACROSS THE REALMS LIKE RAGNAROK MADE FLESH AND BLOOD.
"THERE WERE THOSE WHO STOOD AS BULWARKS AGAINST THE WHOLESALE DESTRUCTION THE MAIDENS WROUGHT.
"THE FROST GIANT JARLS OF JOTUNHEIM. THE ANCIENT WAR-MONGERS OF BREAKWORLD. THE TUATHA DE DANANN OF IRELAND.
"ENTIRE CULTURES DEDICATED TO WAR... RAVAGED FOR SPORT BY THE BLIGHTED HOST.
"ONLY THE INTERVENTION OF THE ALL-FATHER STOPPED THE DOOM MAIDENS."
THEY WERE FORGOTTEN-- YET ANOTHER DISGRACE FOR LORD ODIN TO SECRET AWAY IN HIS SHAME.
BUT MIDGARDIAN RATS SEEK TO USE THE MAGIC OF THE GOLDEN REALM TO WAKE THE MAIDENS.
THERE ARE ANCIENT INCANTATIONS THAT MIGHT DECIMATE ALL WE HOLD PRECIOUS SHOULD THEY BE SCRIBED IN ASGARDIAN BLOOD.
FOR THIS REASON, VALKYRIE, YOU MUST FORSWEAR THIS QUEST.
IT IS HIPPOLYTA OF THEMISCYRA WHO MUST STAND FOR US.

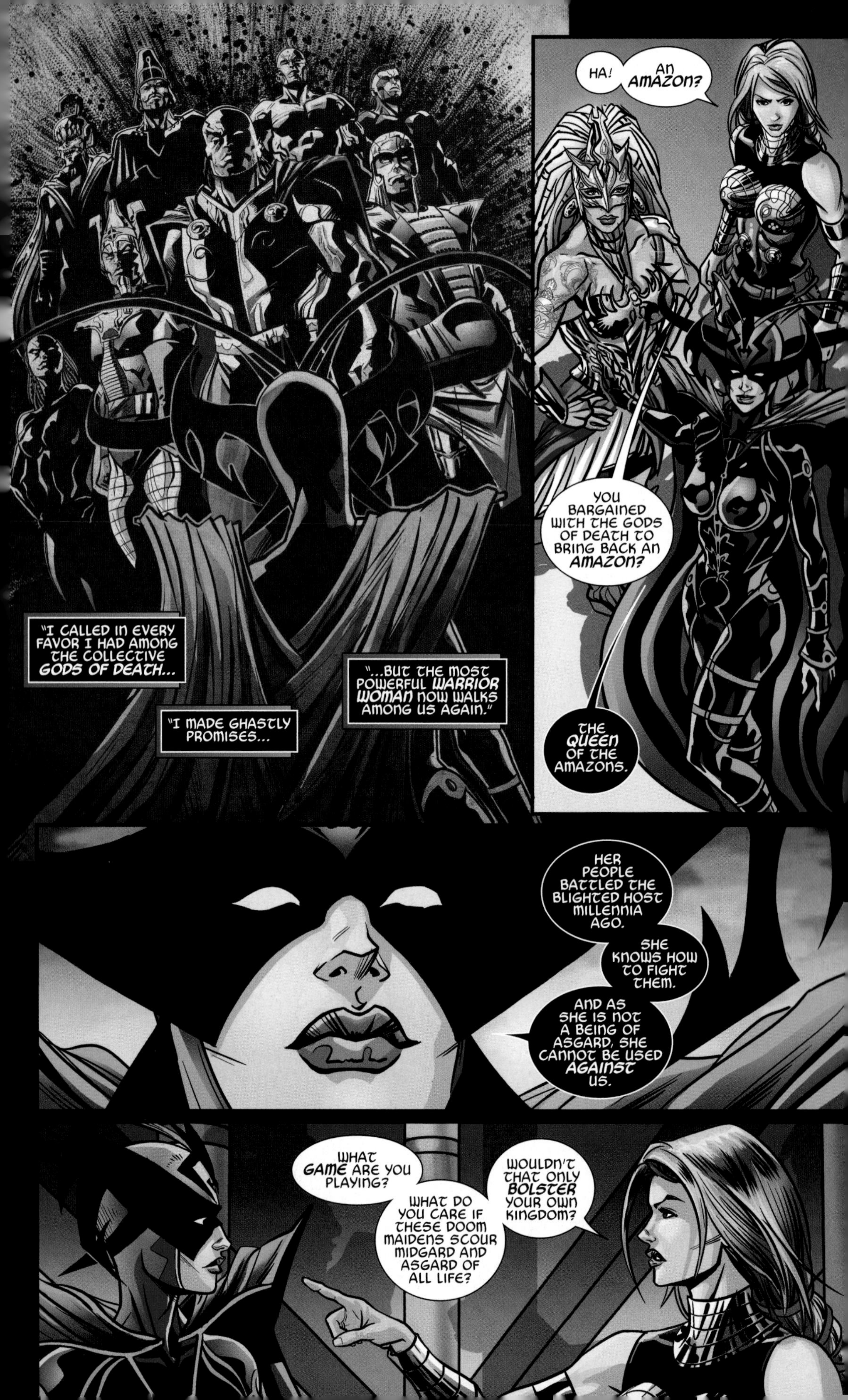
"I CALLED IN EVERY FAVOR I HAD AMONG THE COLLECTIVE GODS OF DEATH...
"I MADE GHASTLY PROMISES...
"...BUT THE MOST POWERFUL WARRIOR WOMAN NOW WALKS AMONG US AGAIN."
HA!
AN AMAZON?
YOU BARGAINED WITH THE GODS OF DEATH TO BRING BACK AN AMAZON?
THE QUEEN OF THE AMAZONS.
HER PEOPLE BATTLED THE BLIGHTED HOST MILLENNIA AGO.
SHE KNOWS HOW TO FIGHT THEM.
AND AS SHE IS NOT A BEING OF ASGARD, SHE CANNOT BE USED AGAINST US.
WHAT GAME ARE YOU PLAYING?
WHAT DO YOU CARE IF THESE DOOM MAIDENS SCOUR MIDGARD AND ASGARD OF ALL LIFE?
WOULDN'T THAT ONLY BOLSTER YOUR OWN KINGDOM?

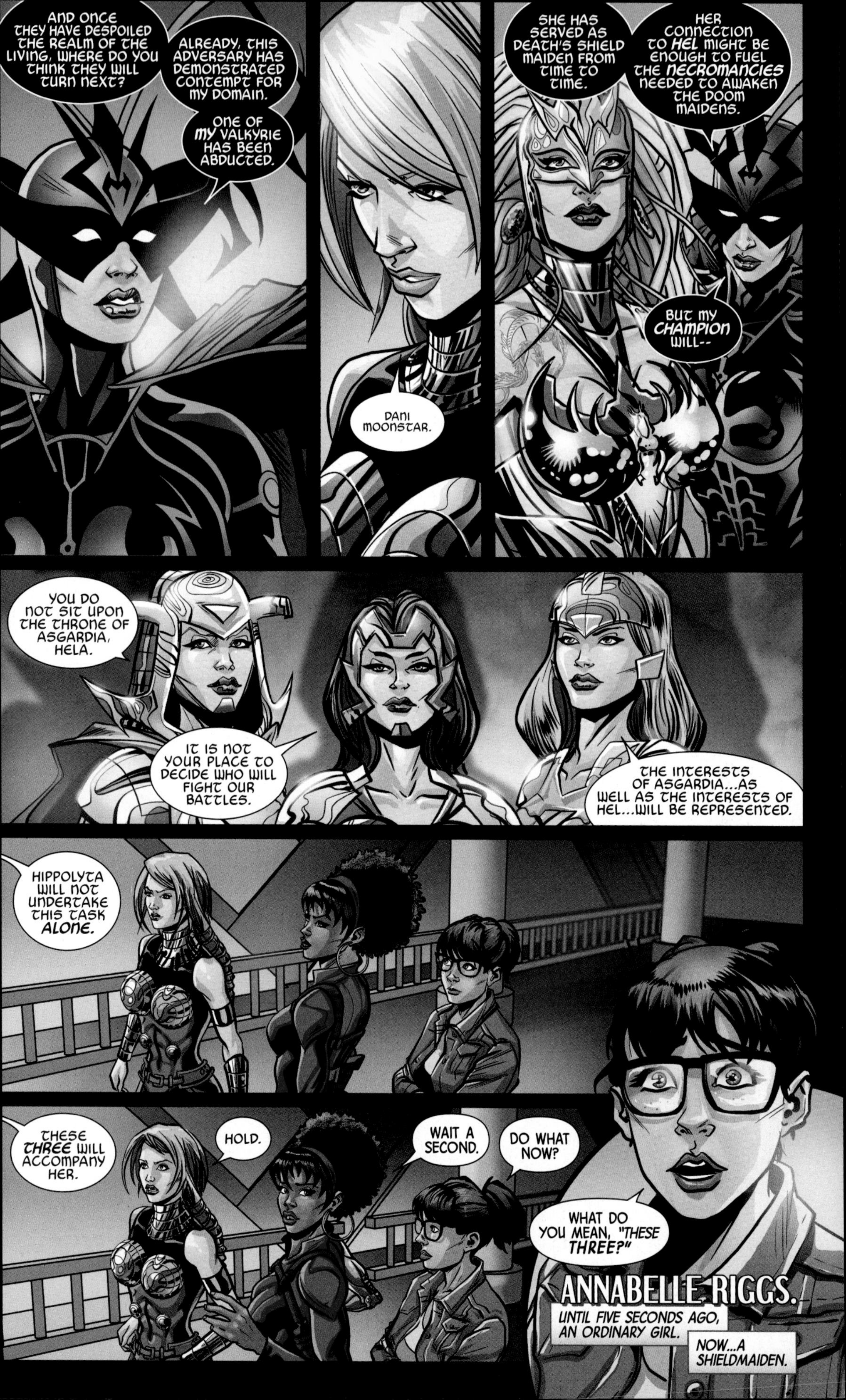
AND ONCE THEY HAVE DESPOILED THE REALM OF THE LIVING, WHERE DO YOU THINK THEY WILL TURN NEXT?
ALREADY, THIS ADVERSARY HAS DEMONSTRATED CONTEMPT FOR MY DOMAIN.
ONE OF *MY* VALKYRIE HAS BEEN ABDUCTED.
DANI MOONSTAR.
SHE HAS SERVED AS DEATH'S SHIELD MAIDEN FROM TIME TO TIME.
HER CONNECTION TO *HEL* MIGHT BE ENOUGH TO FUEL THE *NECROMANCIES* NEEDED TO AWAKEN THE DOOM MAIDENS.
BUT MY *CHAMPION* WILL--
YOU DO NOT SIT UPON THE THRONE OF ASGARDIA, HELA.
IT IS NOT YOUR PLACE TO DECIDE WHO WILL FIGHT OUR BATTLES.
THE INTERESTS OF ASGARDIA...AS WELL AS THE INTERESTS OF HEL...WILL BE REPRESENTED.
HIPPOLYTA WILL NOT UNDERTAKE THIS TASK *ALONE.*
THESE *THREE* WILL ACCOMPANY HER.
HOLD.
WAIT A SECOND.
DO WHAT NOW?
WHAT DO YOU MEAN, "THESE *THREE?*"
ANNABELLE RIGGS.
UNTIL FIVE SECONDS AGO, AN ORDINARY GIRL.
NOW...A SHIELDMAIDEN.

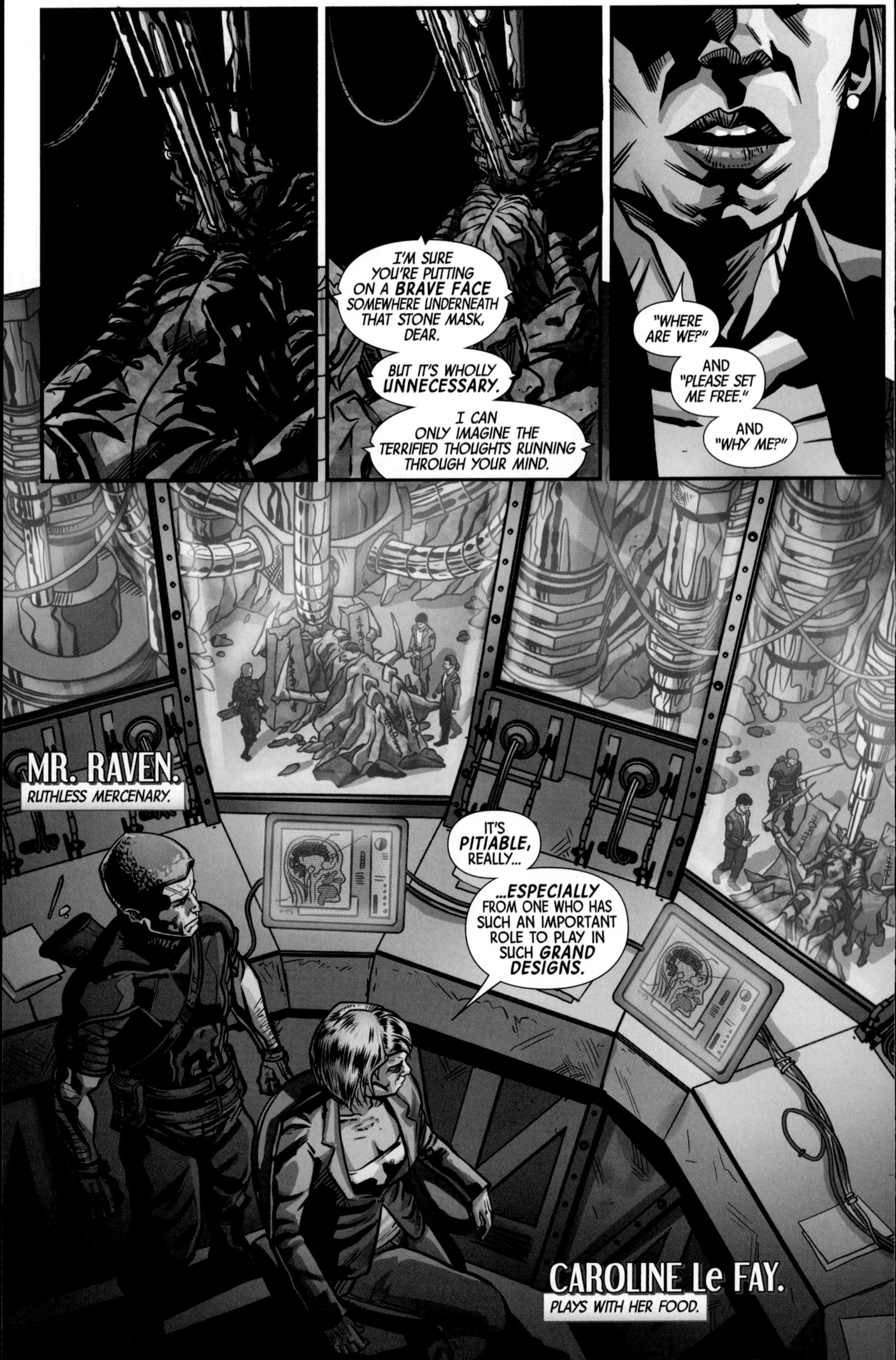
I'M SURE YOU'RE PUTTING ON A BRAVE FACE SOMEWHERE UNDERNEATH THAT STONE MASK, DEAR.
BUT IT'S WHOLLY UNNECESSARY.
I CAN ONLY IMAGINE THE TERRIFIED THOUGHTS RUNNING THROUGH YOUR MIND.
"WHERE ARE WE?"
AND "PLEASE SET ME FREE."
AND "WHY ME?"
MR. RAVEN.
RUTHLESS MERCENARY.
IT'S PITIABLE, REALLY...
...ESPECIALLY FROM ONE WHO HAS SUCH AN IMPORTANT ROLE TO PLAY IN SUCH GRAND DESIGNS.
CAROLINE Le FAY.
PLAYS WITH HER FOOD.

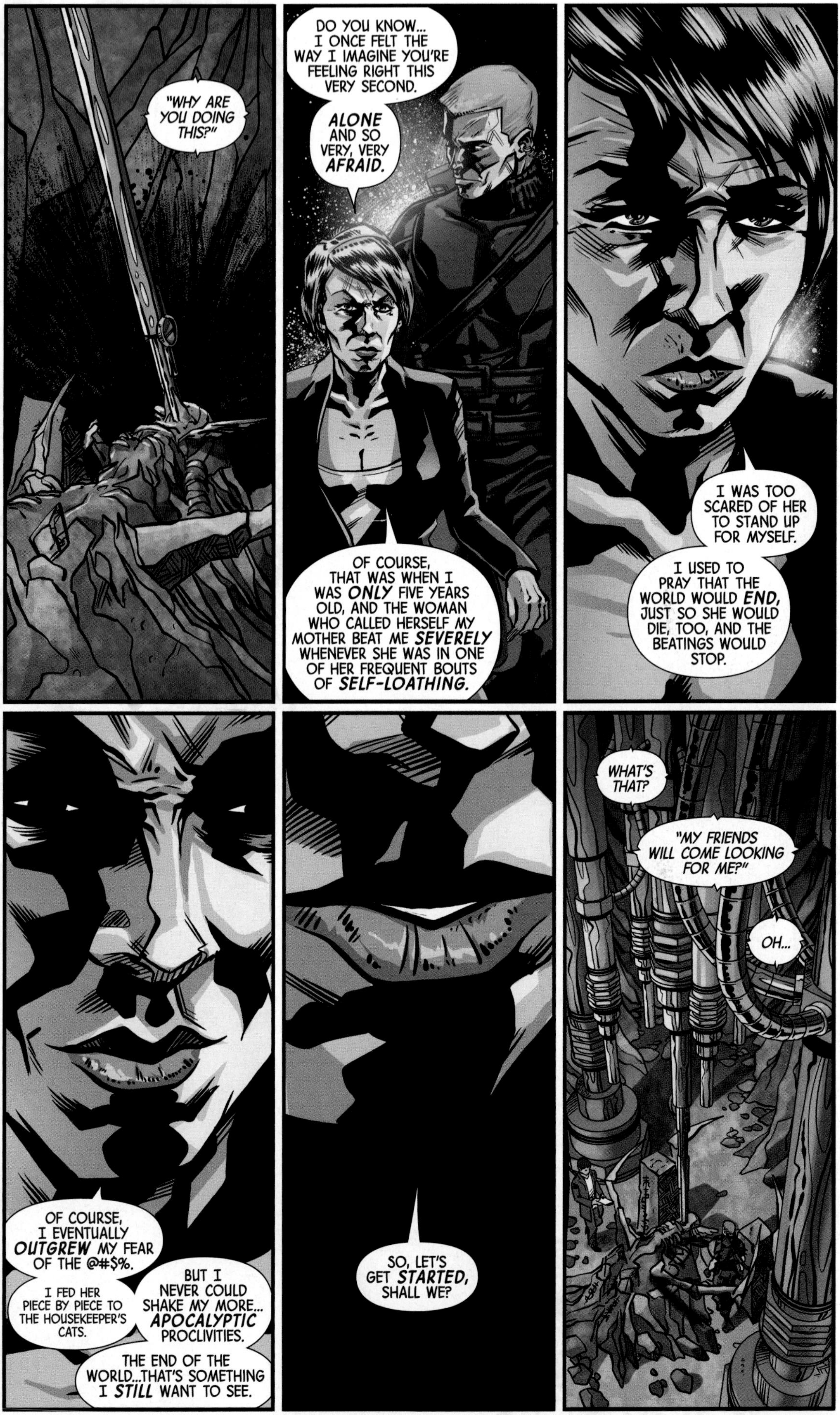
"WHY ARE YOU DOING THIS?"
DO YOU KNOW... I ONCE FELT THE WAY I IMAGINE YOU'RE FEELING RIGHT THIS VERY SECOND.
ALONE AND SO VERY, VERY AFRAID.
OF COURSE, THAT WAS WHEN I WAS ONLY FIVE YEARS OLD, AND THE WOMAN WHO CALLED HERSELF MY MOTHER BEAT ME SEVERELY WHENEVER SHE WAS IN ONE OF HER FREQUENT BOUTS OF SELF-LOATHING.
I WAS TOO SCARED OF HER TO STAND UP FOR MYSELF.
I USED TO PRAY THAT THE WORLD WOULD END, JUST SO SHE WOULD DIE, TOO, AND THE BEATINGS WOULD STOP.
OF COURSE, I EVENTUALLY OUTGREW MY FEAR OF THE @#$%.
I FED HER PIECE BY PIECE TO THE HOUSEKEEPER'S CATS.
BUT I NEVER COULD SHAKE MY MORE... APOCALYPTIC PROCLIVITIES.
THE END OF THE WORLD...THAT'S SOMETHING I STILL WANT TO SEE.
SO, LET'S GET STARTED, SHALL WE?
WHAT'S THAT?
"MY FRIENDS WILL COME LOOKING FOR ME?"
OH...

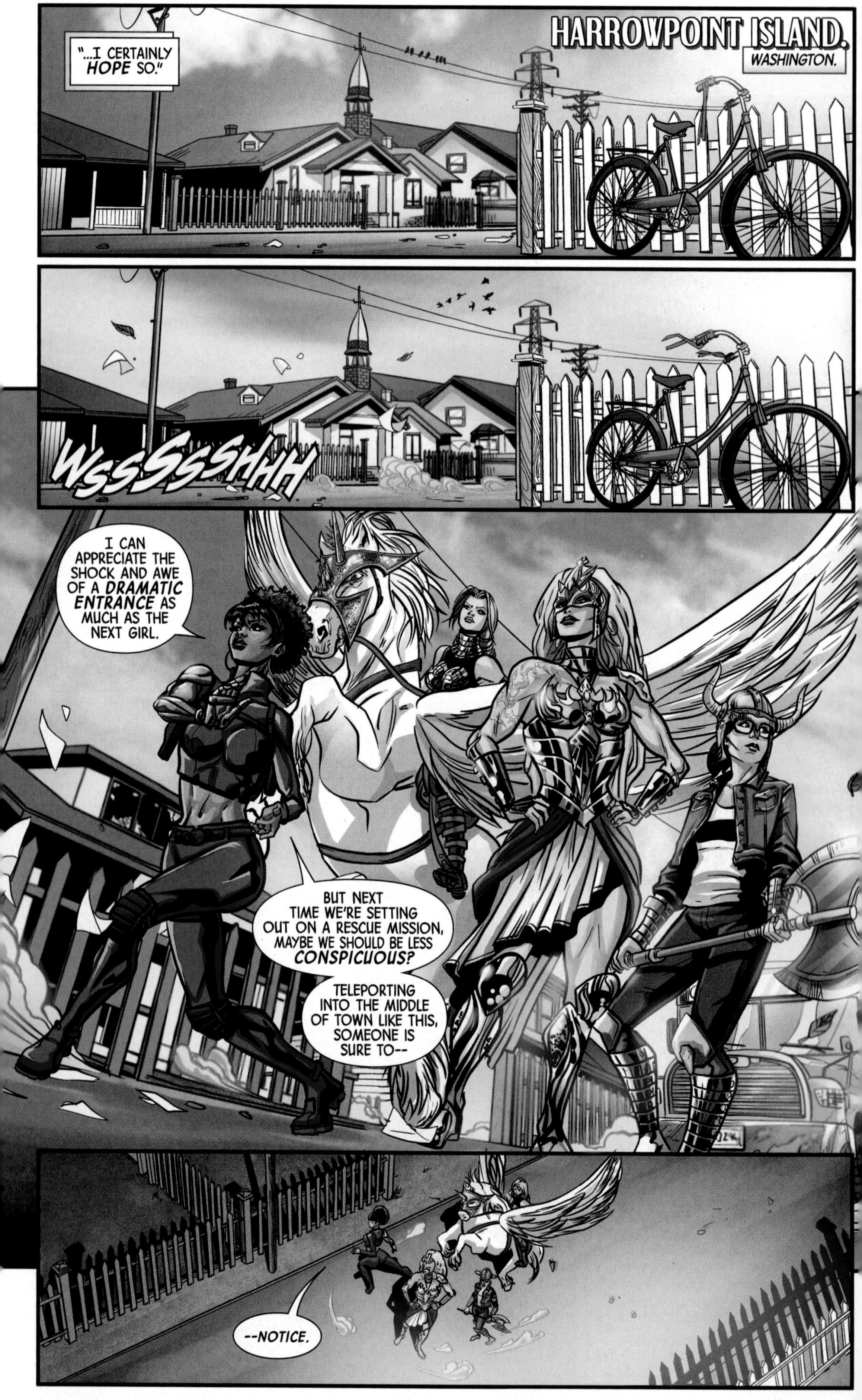

HARROWPOINT ISLAND.
WASHINGTON.
"...I CERTAINLY HOPE SO."
WSSSSSHHH
I CAN APPRECIATE THE SHOCK AND AWE OF A DRAMATIC ENTRANCE AS MUCH AS THE NEXT GIRL.
BUT NEXT TIME WE'RE SETTING OUT ON A RESCUE MISSION, MAYBE WE SHOULD BE LESS CONSPICUOUS?
TELEPORTING INTO THE MIDDLE OF TOWN LIKE THIS, SOMEONE IS SURE TO--
--NOTICE.

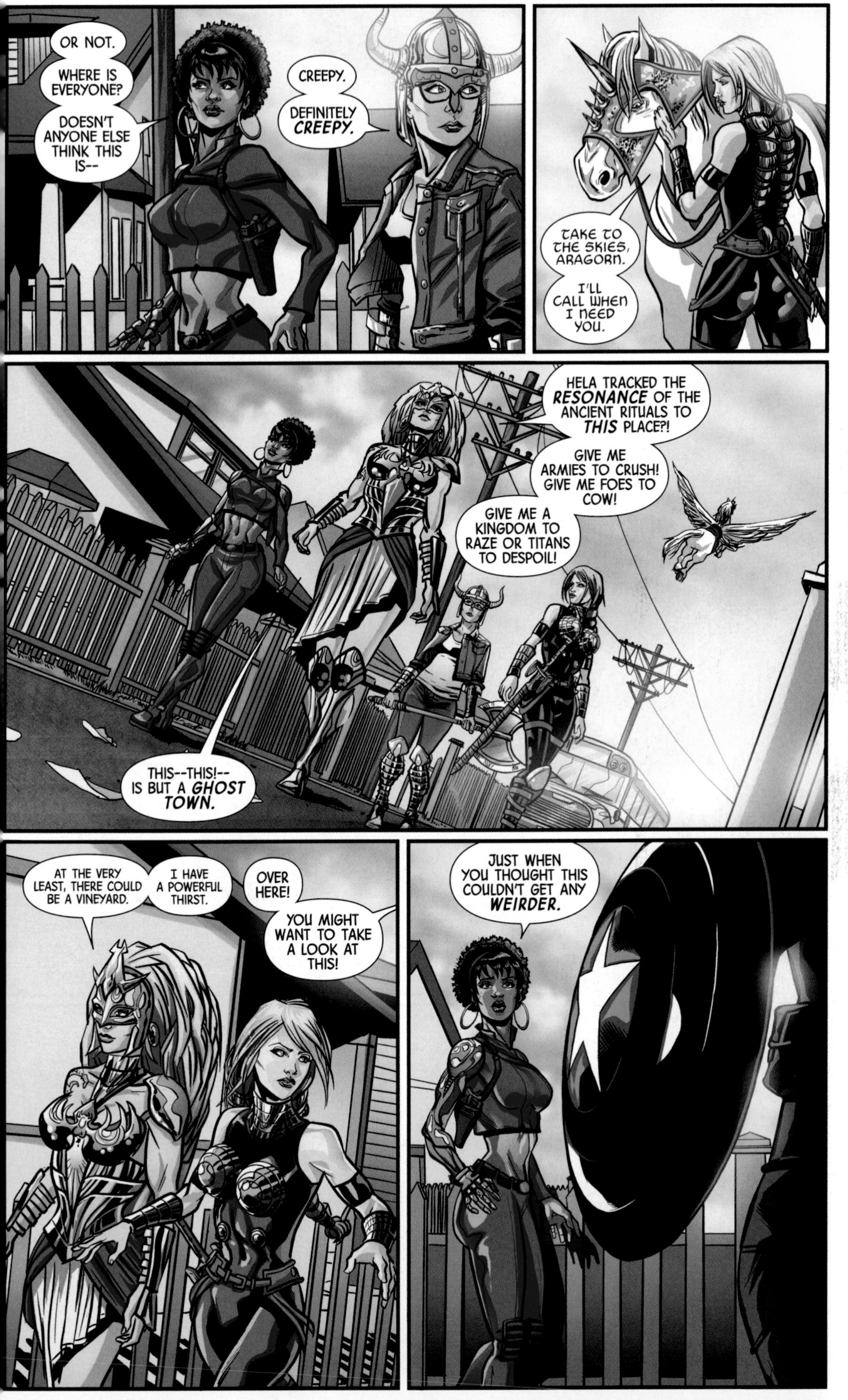
OR NOT.
WHERE IS EVERYONE?
DOESN'T ANYONE ELSE THINK THIS IS--
CREEPY.
DEFINITELY *CREEPY.*
TAKE TO THE SKIES, ARAGORN.
I'LL CALL WHEN I NEED YOU.
HELA TRACKED THE *RESONANCE* OF THE ANCIENT RITUALS TO *THIS* PLACE?!
GIVE ME ARMIES TO CRUSH! GIVE ME FOES TO COW!
GIVE ME A KINGDOM TO RAZE OR TITANS TO DESPOIL!
THIS--THIS!-- IS BUT A *GHOST TOWN.*
AT THE VERY LEAST, THERE COULD BE A VINEYARD.
I HAVE A POWERFUL THIRST.
OVER HERE!
YOU MIGHT WANT TO TAKE A LOOK AT THIS!
JUST WHEN YOU THOUGHT THIS COULDN'T GET ANY *WEIRDER.*

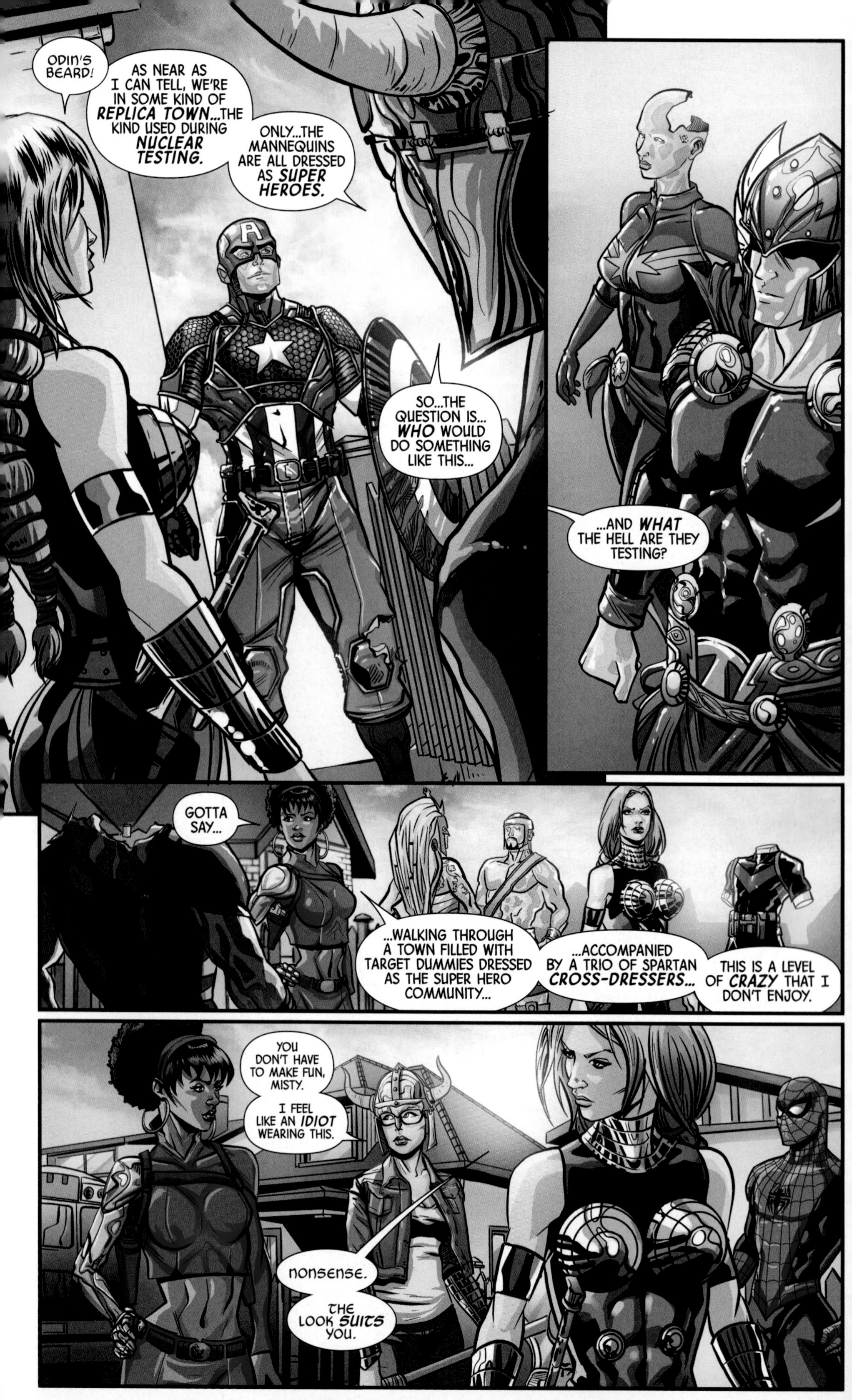
ODIN'S BEARD!
AS NEAR AS I CAN TELL, WE'RE IN SOME KIND OF REPLICA TOWN...THE KIND USED DURING NUCLEAR TESTING.
ONLY...THE MANNEQUINS ARE ALL DRESSED AS SUPER HEROES.
SO...THE QUESTION IS... WHO WOULD DO SOMETHING LIKE THIS...
...AND WHAT THE HELL ARE THEY TESTING?
GOTTA SAY...
...WALKING THROUGH A TOWN FILLED WITH TARGET DUMMIES DRESSED AS THE SUPER HERO COMMUNITY...
...ACCOMPANIED BY A TRIO OF SPARTAN CROSS-DRESSERS...
THIS IS A LEVEL OF CRAZY THAT I DON'T ENJOY.
YOU DON'T HAVE TO MAKE FUN, MISTY.
I FEEL LIKE AN IDIOT WEARING THIS.
NONSENSE.
THE LOOK SUITS YOU.

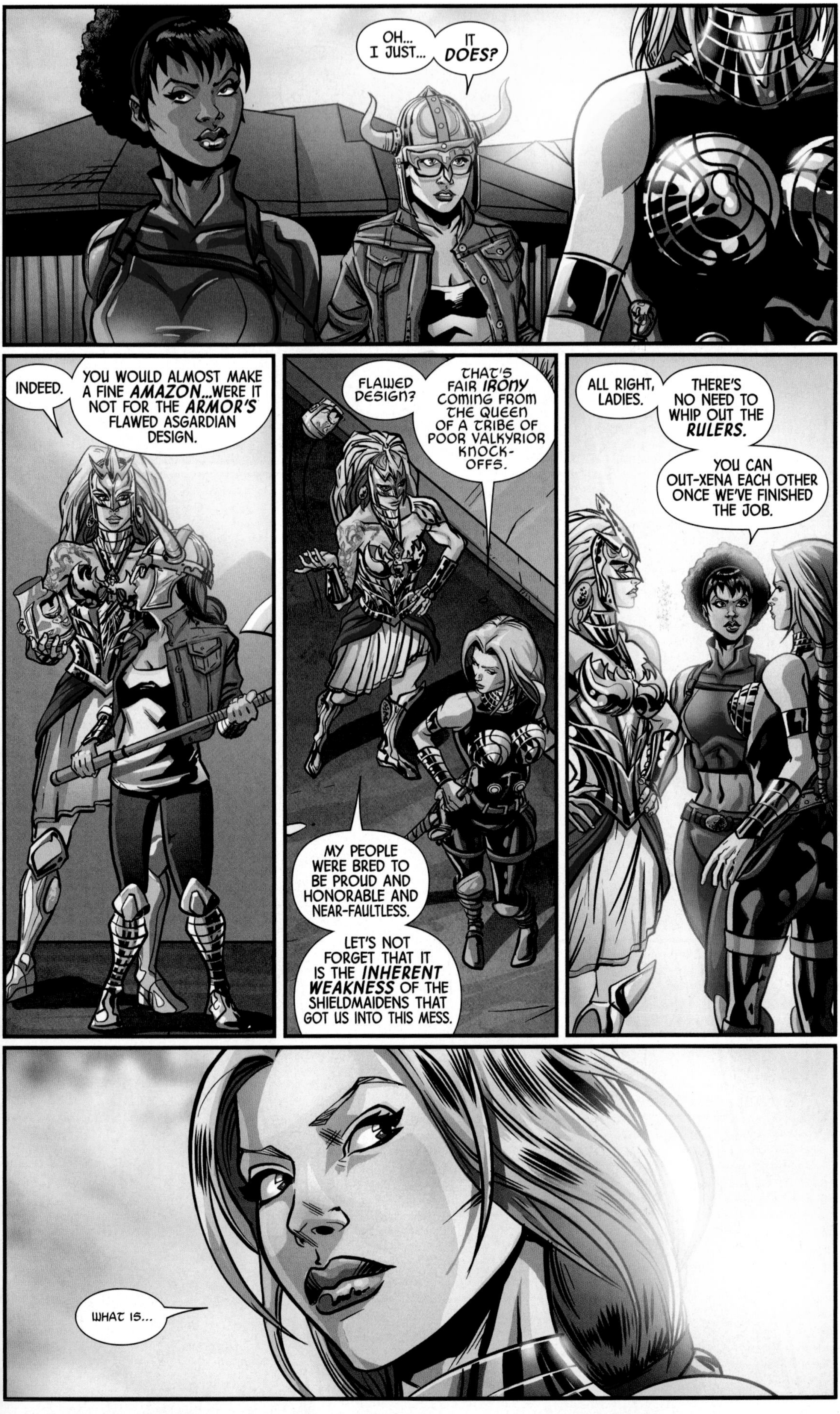
OH... I JUST...
IT DOES?
INDEED.
YOU WOULD ALMOST MAKE A FINE AMAZON...WERE IT NOT FOR THE ARMOR'S FLAWED ASGARDIAN DESIGN.
FLAWED DESIGN?
THAT'S FAIR IRONY COMING FROM THE QUEEN OF A TRIBE OF POOR VALKYRIOR KNOCK-OFFS.
MY PEOPLE WERE BRED TO BE PROUD AND HONORABLE AND NEAR-FAULTLESS.
LET'S NOT FORGET THAT IT IS THE INHERENT WEAKNESS OF THE SHIELDMAIDENS THAT GOT US INTO THIS MESS.
ALL RIGHT, LADIES.
THERE'S NO NEED TO WHIP OUT THE RULERS.
YOU CAN OUT-XENA EACH OTHER ONCE WE'VE FINISHED THE JOB.
WHAT IS...

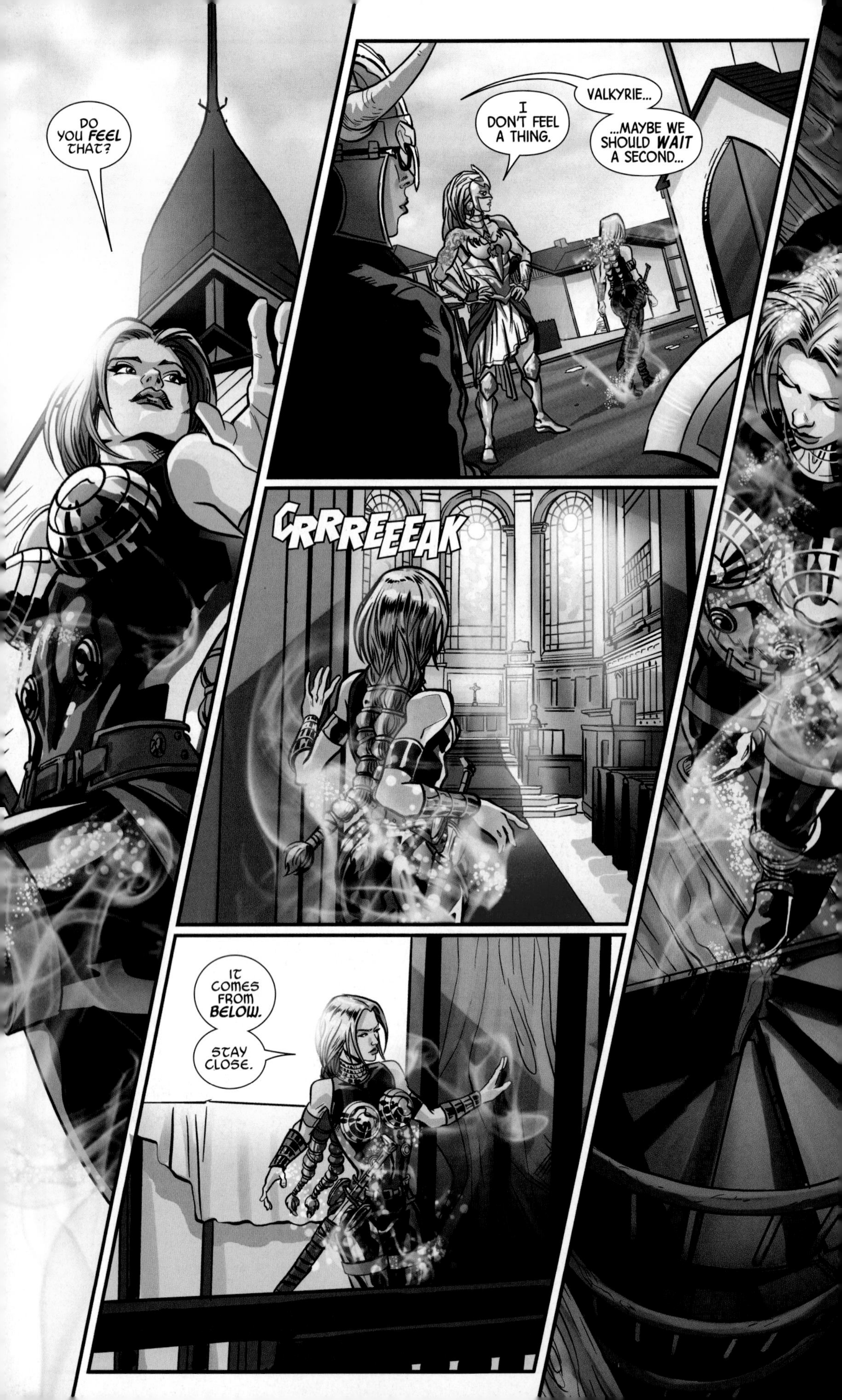
DO YOU FEEL THAT?
I DON'T FEEL A THING.
VALKYRIE...
...MAYBE WE SHOULD WAIT A SECOND...
CRRREEEAK
IT COMES FROM BELOW.
STAY CLOSE.

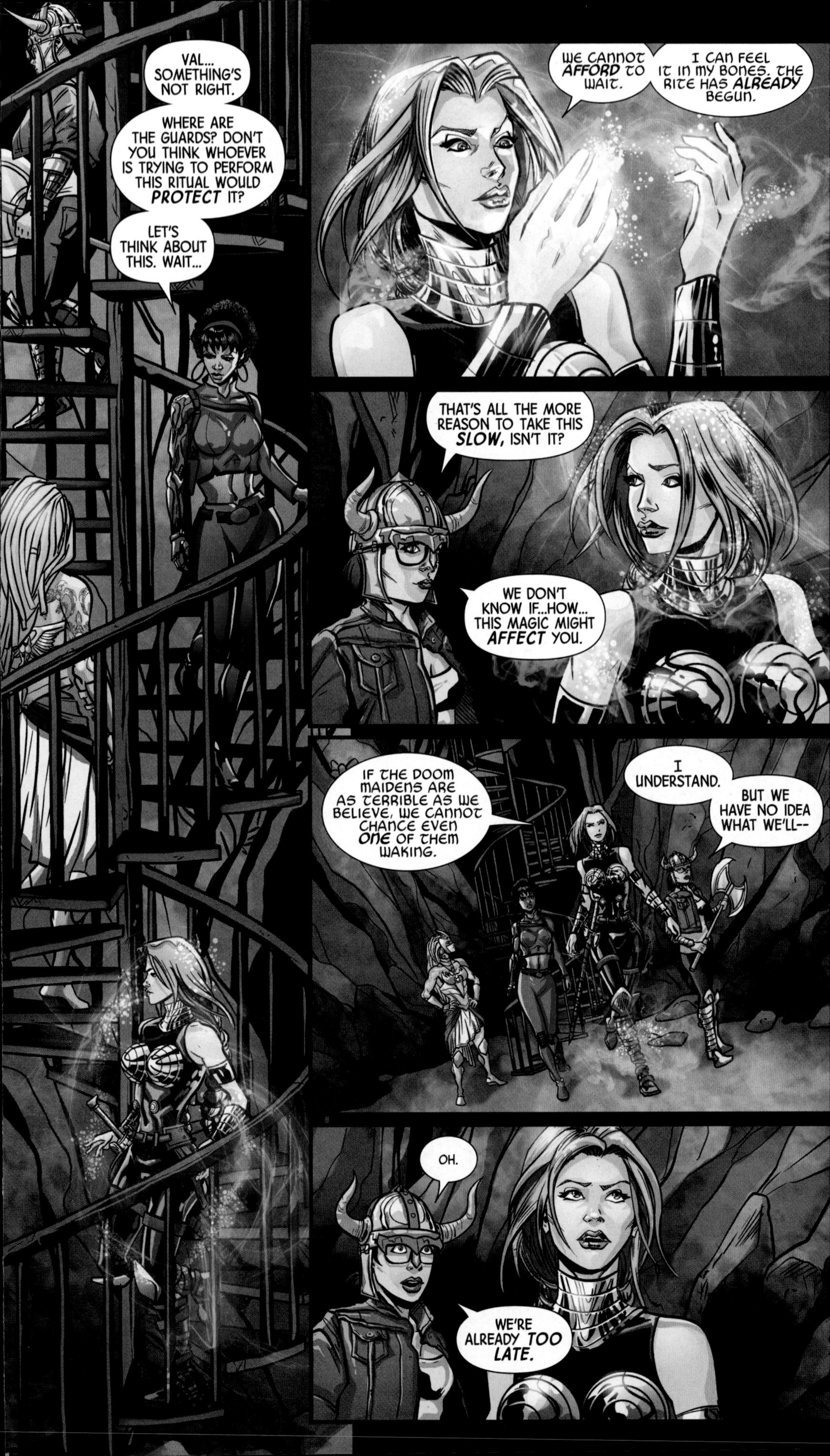

VAL... SOMETHING'S NOT RIGHT.
WHERE ARE THE GUARDS? DON'T YOU THINK WHOEVER IS TRYING TO PERFORM THIS RITUAL WOULD PROTECT IT?
LET'S THINK ABOUT THIS. WAIT...
WE CANNOT AFFORD TO WAIT.
I CAN FEEL IT IN MY BONES. THE RITE HAS ALREADY BEGUN.
THAT'S ALL THE MORE REASON TO TAKE THIS SLOW, ISN'T IT?
WE DON'T KNOW IF...HOW... THIS MAGIC MIGHT AFFECT YOU.
IF THE DOOM MAIDENS ARE AS TERRIBLE AS WE BELIEVE, WE CANNOT CHANCE EVEN ONE OF THEM WAKING.
I UNDERSTAND.
BUT WE HAVE NO IDEA WHAT WE'LL--
OH.
WE'RE ALREADY TOO LATE.

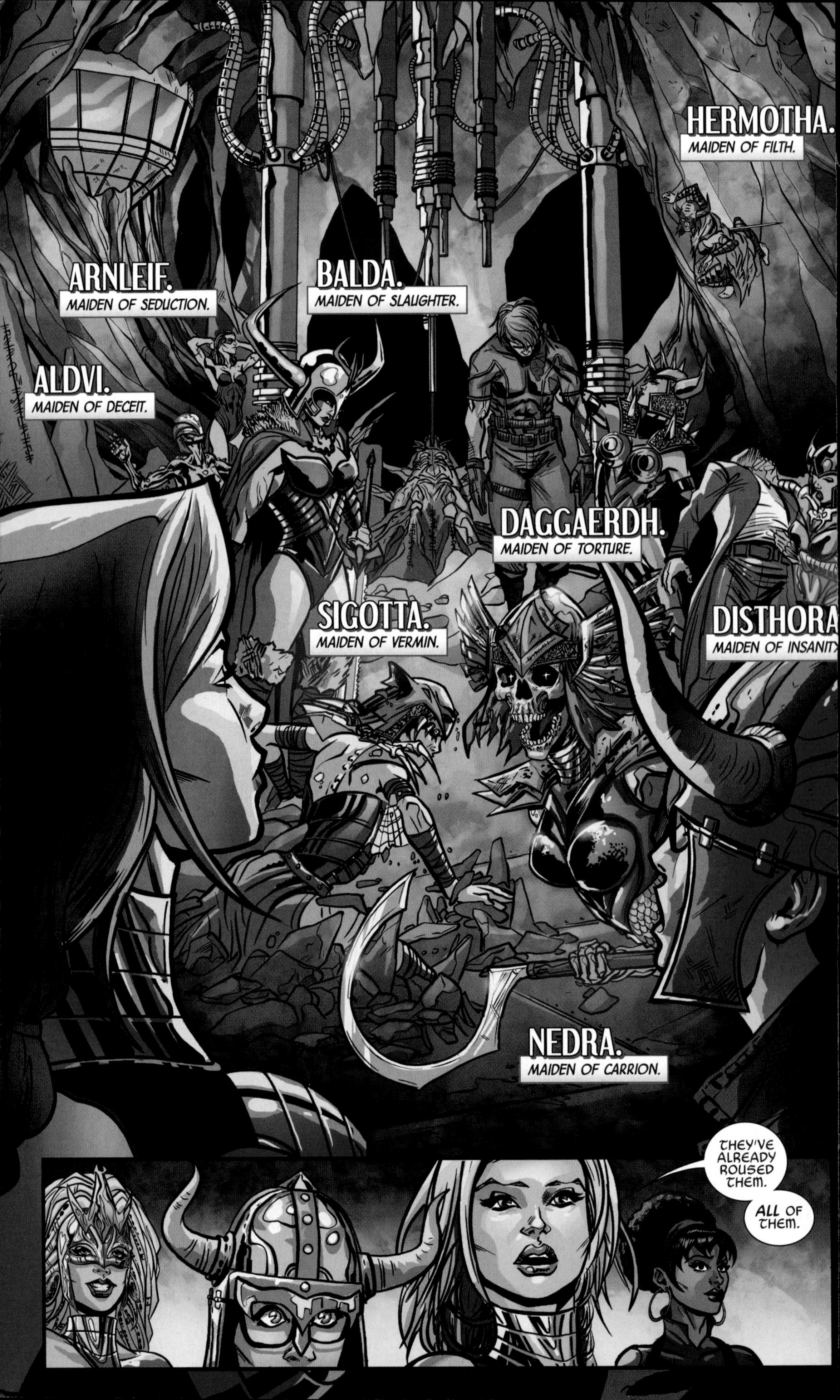

HERMOTHA.
MAIDEN OF FILTH.
ARNLEIF.
MAIDEN OF SEDUCTION.
BALDA.
MAIDEN OF SLAUGHTER.
ALDVI.
MAIDEN OF DECEIT.
DAGGAERDH.
MAIDEN OF TORTURE.
SIGOTTA.
MAIDEN OF VERMIN.
DISTHORA
MAIDEN OF INSANITY
NEDRA.
MAIDEN OF CARRION.
THEY'VE ALREADY ROUSED THEM.
ALL OF THEM.

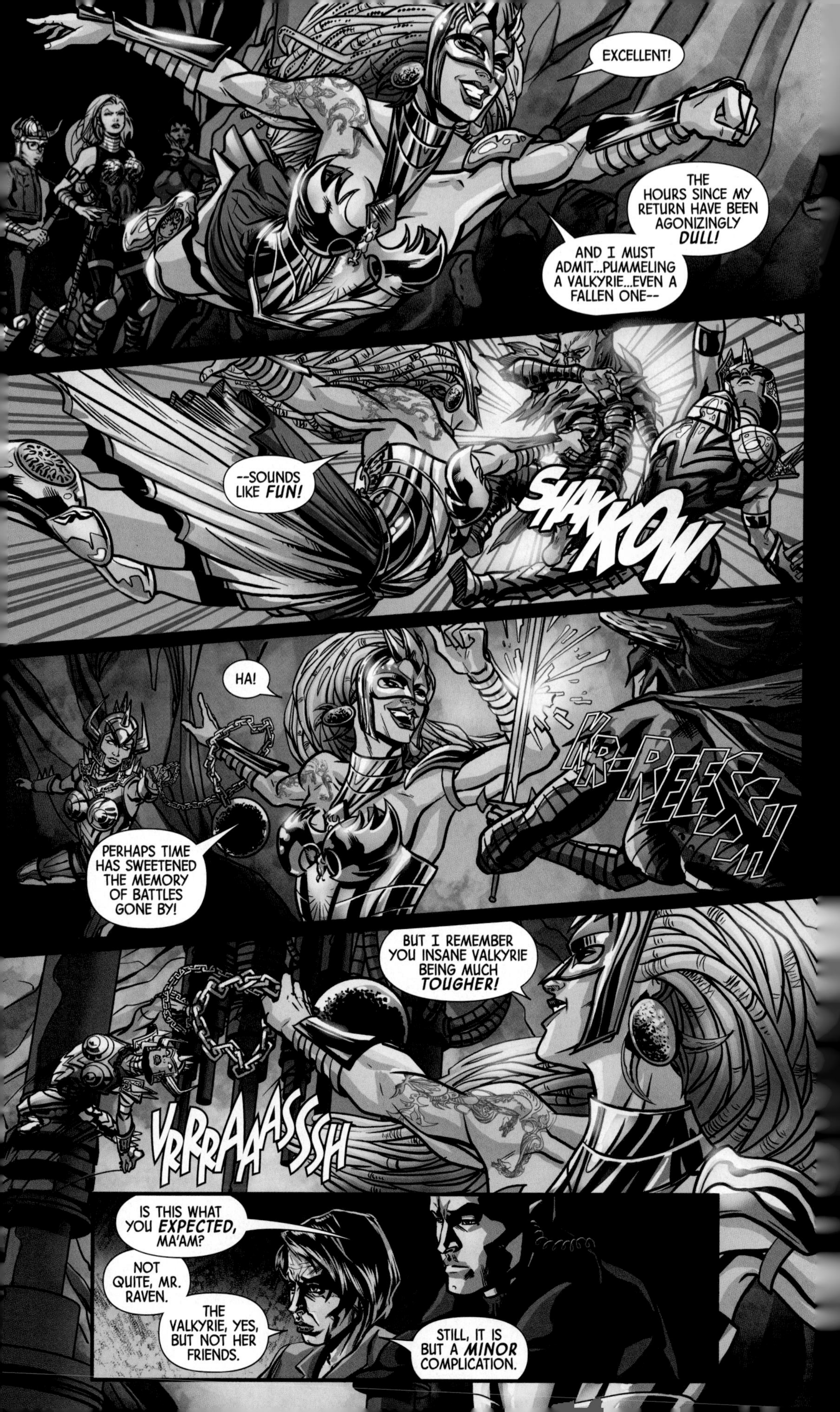
EXCELLENT!
THE HOURS SINCE MY RETURN HAVE BEEN AGONIZINGLY DULL!
AND I MUST ADMIT...PUMMELING A VALKYRIE...EVEN A FALLEN ONE--
--SOUNDS LIKE FUN!
SHAKOW
HA!
KR-REEEEECH
PERHAPS TIME HAS SWEETENED THE MEMORY OF BATTLES GONE BY!
BUT I REMEMBER YOU INSANE VALKYRIE BEING MUCH TOUGHER!
VRRRAAAASSSH
IS THIS WHAT YOU EXPECTED, MA'AM?
NOT QUITE, MR. RAVEN.
THE VALKYRIE, YES, BUT NOT HER FRIENDS.
STILL, IT IS BUT A MINOR COMPLICATION.

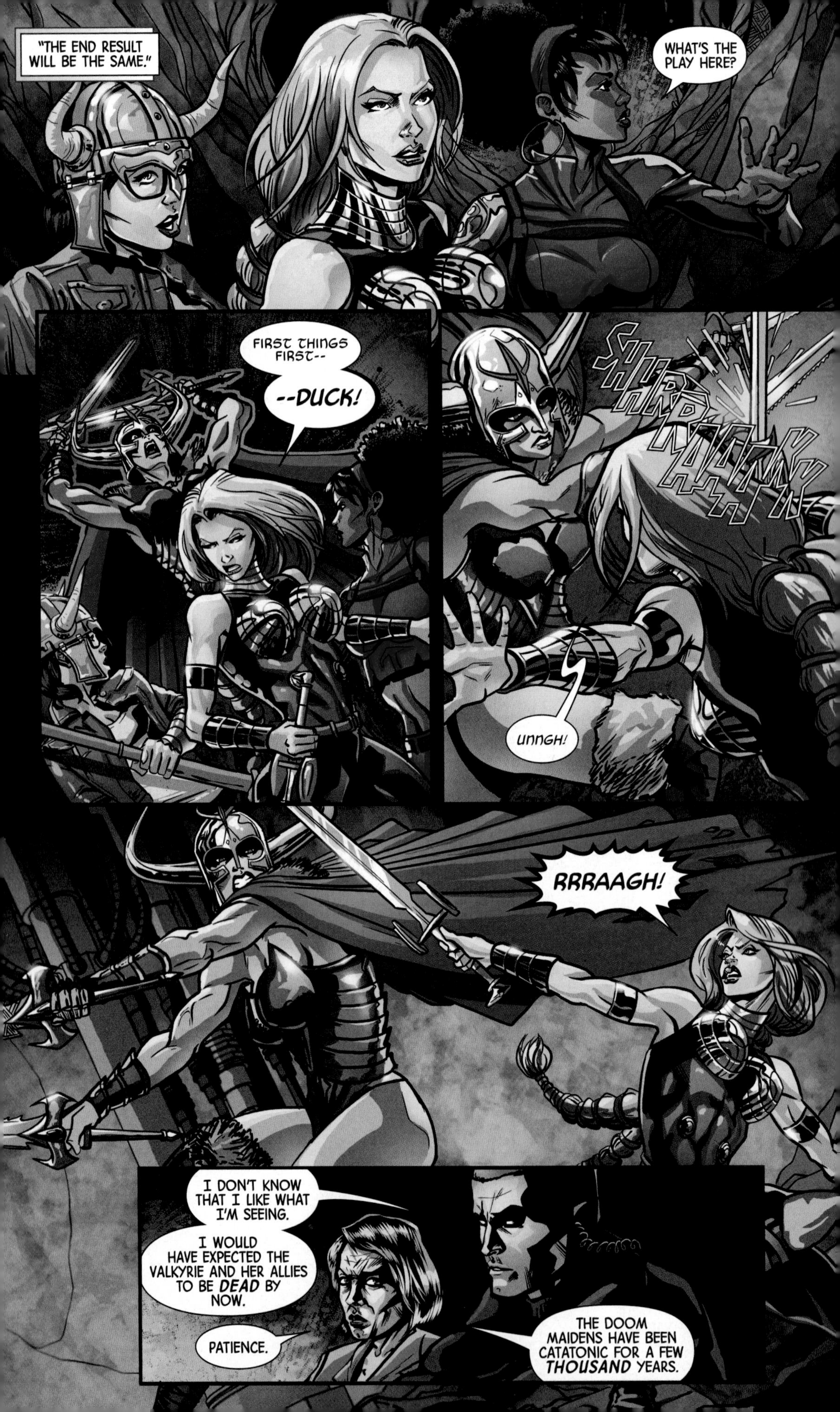
"THE END RESULT WILL BE THE SAME."
WHAT'S THE PLAY HERE?
FIRST THINGS FIRST--
--DUCK!
SHRAAAKK
UNNGH!
RRRAAGH!
I DON'T KNOW THAT I LIKE WHAT I'M SEEING.
I WOULD HAVE EXPECTED THE VALKYRIE AND HER ALLIES TO BE DEAD BY NOW.
PATIENCE.
THE DOOM MAIDENS HAVE BEEN CATATONIC FOR A FEW THOUSAND YEARS.

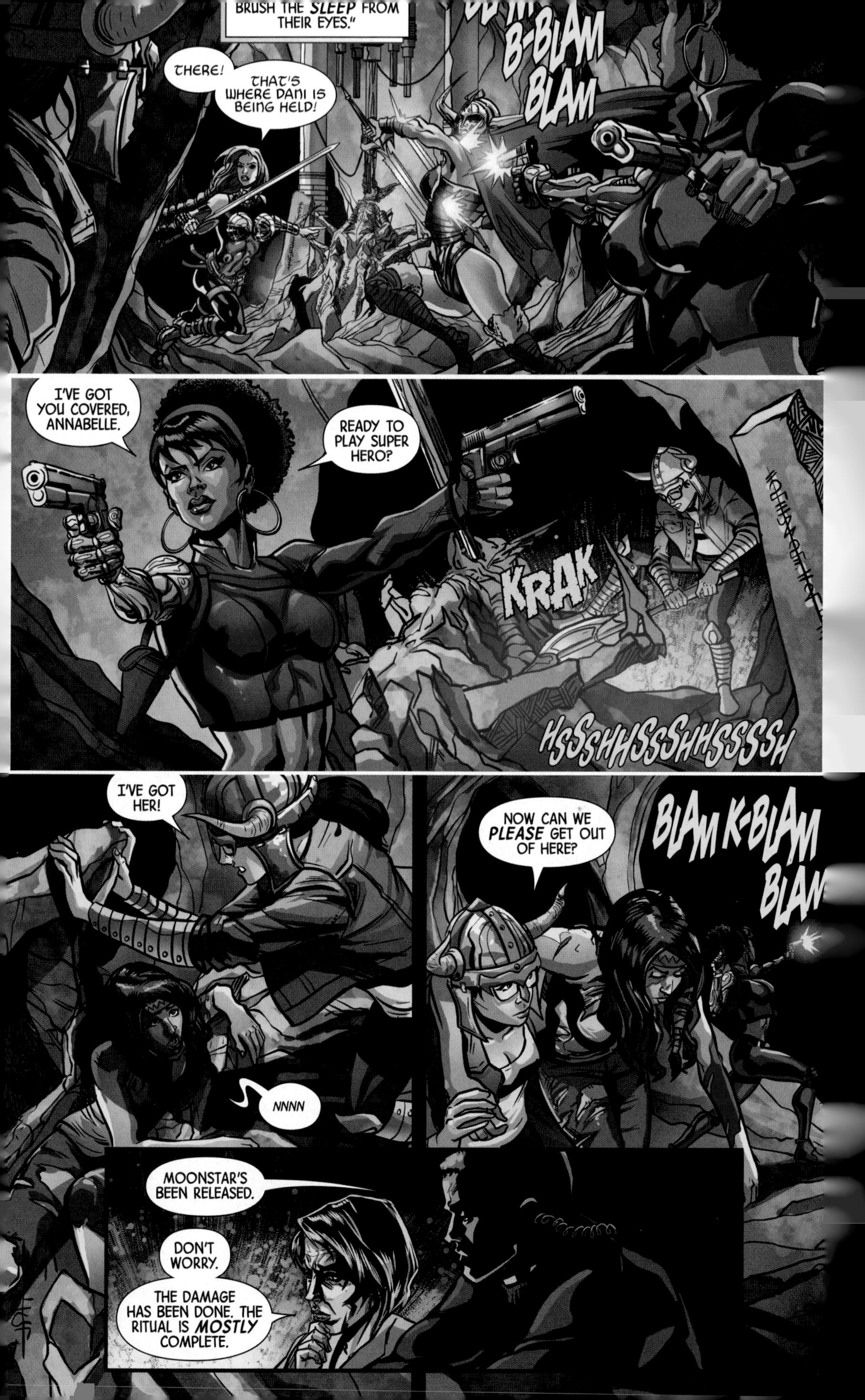
BRUSH THE SLEEP FROM THEIR EYES."
B-BLAM BLAM
THERE!
THAT'S WHERE DANI IS BEING HELD!
I'VE GOT YOU COVERED, ANNABELLE.
READY TO PLAY SUPER HERO?
KRAK
HSSSHHSSSHHSSSSH
I'VE GOT HER!
NNNN
NOW CAN WE PLEASE GET OUT OF HERE?
BLAM K-BLAM
MOONSTAR'S BEEN RELEASED.
DON'T WORRY.
THE DAMAGE HAS BEEN DONE. THE RITUAL IS MOSTLY COMPLETE.

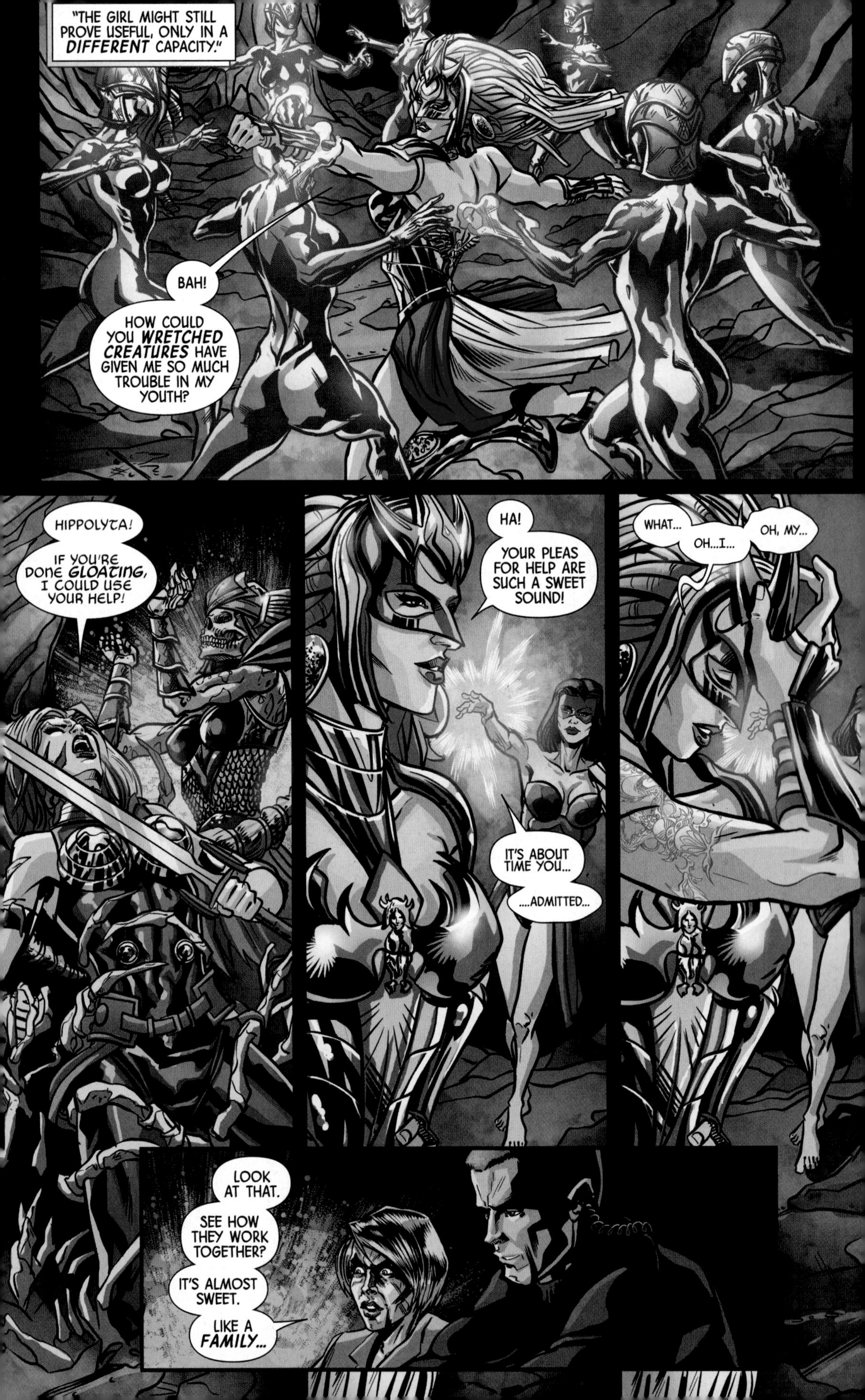
"THE GIRL MIGHT STILL PROVE USEFUL, ONLY IN A DIFFERENT CAPACITY."
BAH!
HOW COULD YOU WRETCHED CREATURES HAVE GIVEN ME SO MUCH TROUBLE IN MY YOUTH?
HIPPOLYTA!
IF YOU'RE DONE GLOATING, I COULD USE YOUR HELP!
HA!
YOUR PLEAS FOR HELP ARE SUCH A SWEET SOUND!
IT'S ABOUT TIME YOU...
....ADMITTED...
WHAT...
OH...I...
OH, MY...
LOOK AT THAT.
SEE HOW THEY WORK TOGETHER?
IT'S ALMOST SWEET.
LIKE A FAMILY...

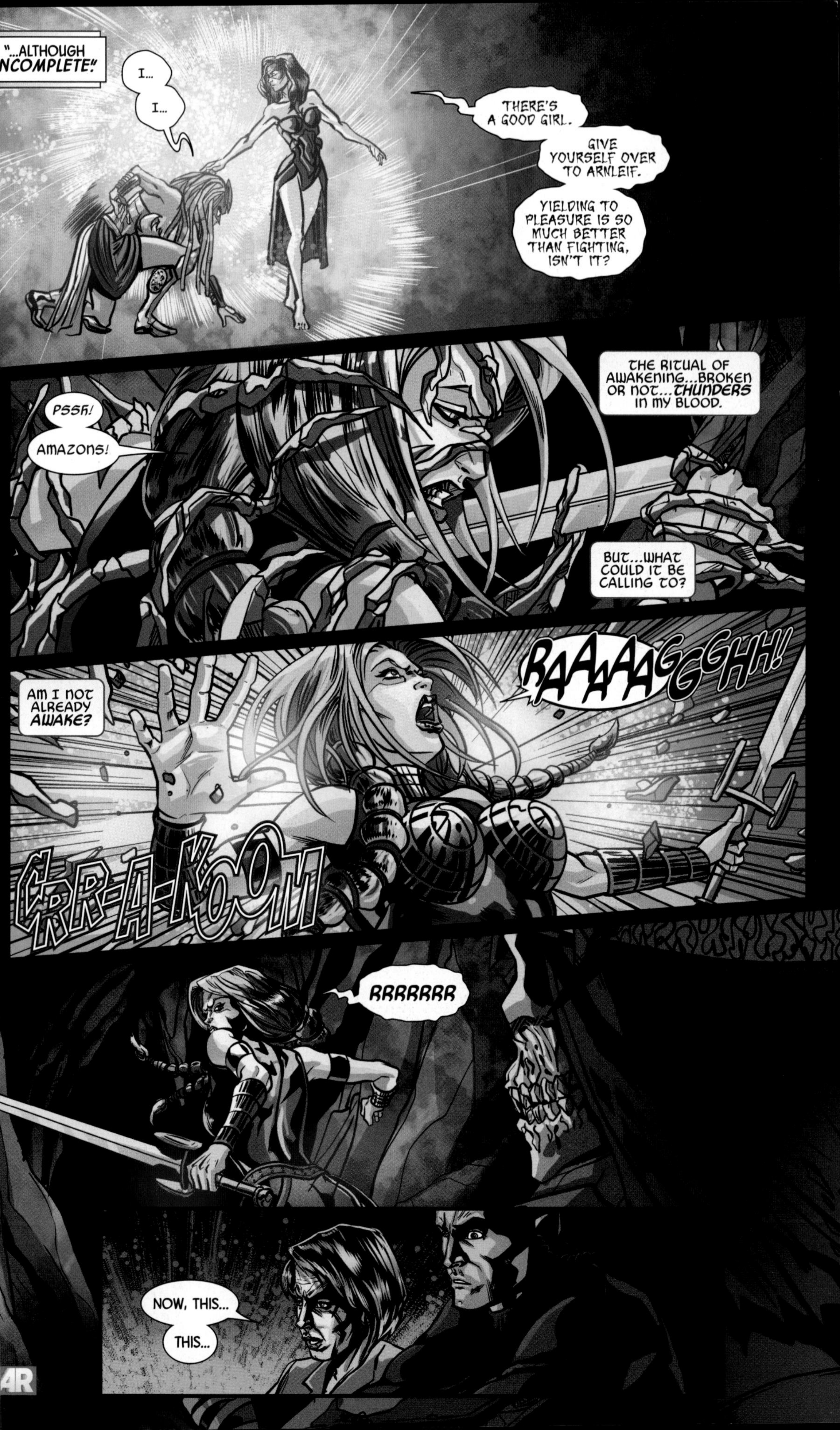
"...ALTHOUGH INCOMPLETE!"
I... I...
THERE'S A GOOD GIRL.
GIVE YOURSELF OVER TO ARNLEIF.
YIELDING TO PLEASURE IS SO MUCH BETTER THAN FIGHTING, ISN'T IT?
THE RITUAL OF AWAKENING...BROKEN OR NOT...THUNDERS IN MY BLOOD.
PSSH!
AMAZONS!
BUT...WHAT COULD IT BE CALLING TO?
AM I NOT ALREADY AWAKE?
RAAAAAGGGHH!
CRR-A-KOOM
RRRRRRR
NOW, THIS...
THIS...

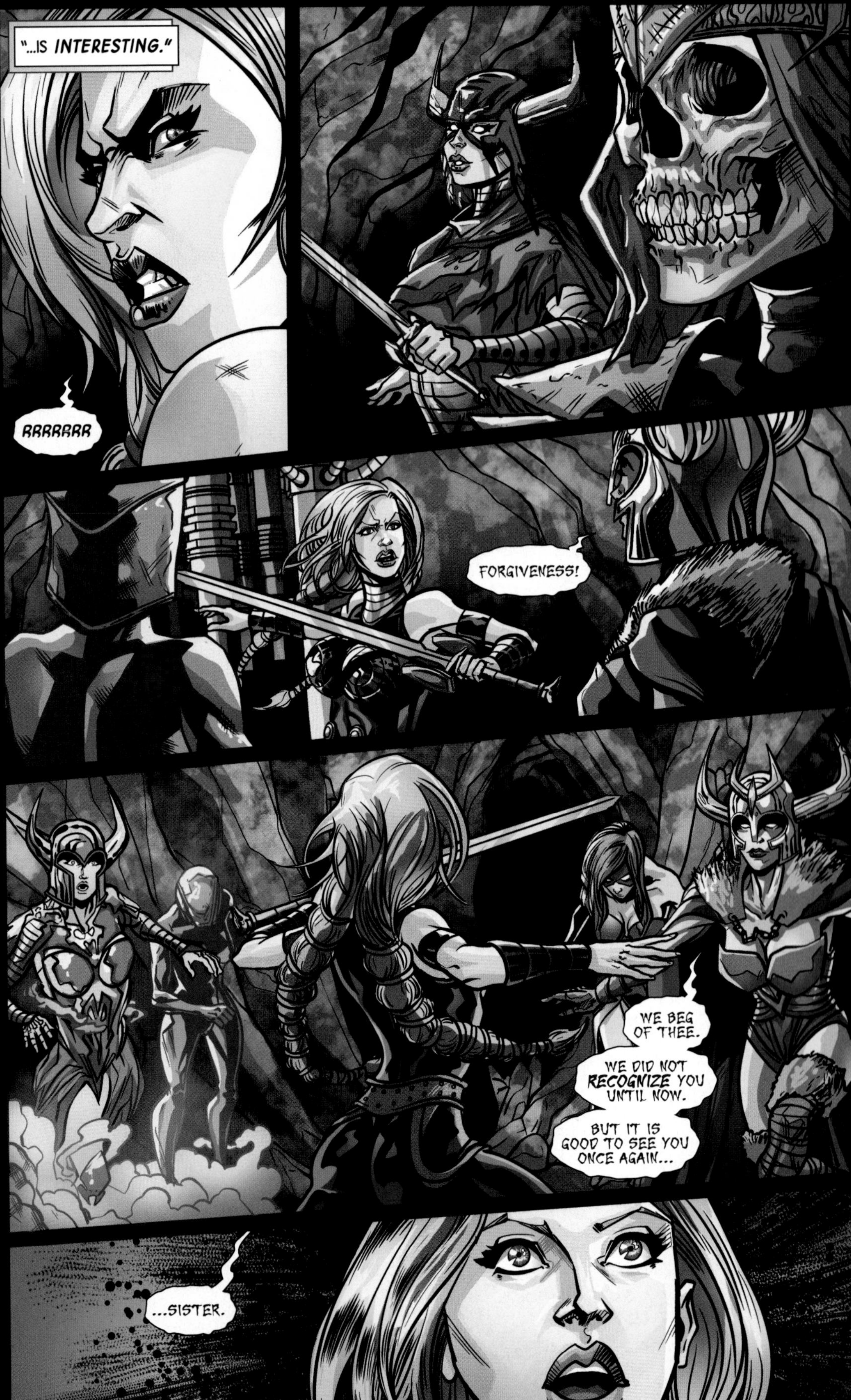
"...IS INTERESTING."
RRRRRRR
FORGIVENESS!
WE BEG OF THEE.
WE DID NOT RECOGNIZE YOU UNTIL NOW.
BUT IT IS GOOD TO SEE YOU ONCE AGAIN...
...SISTER.

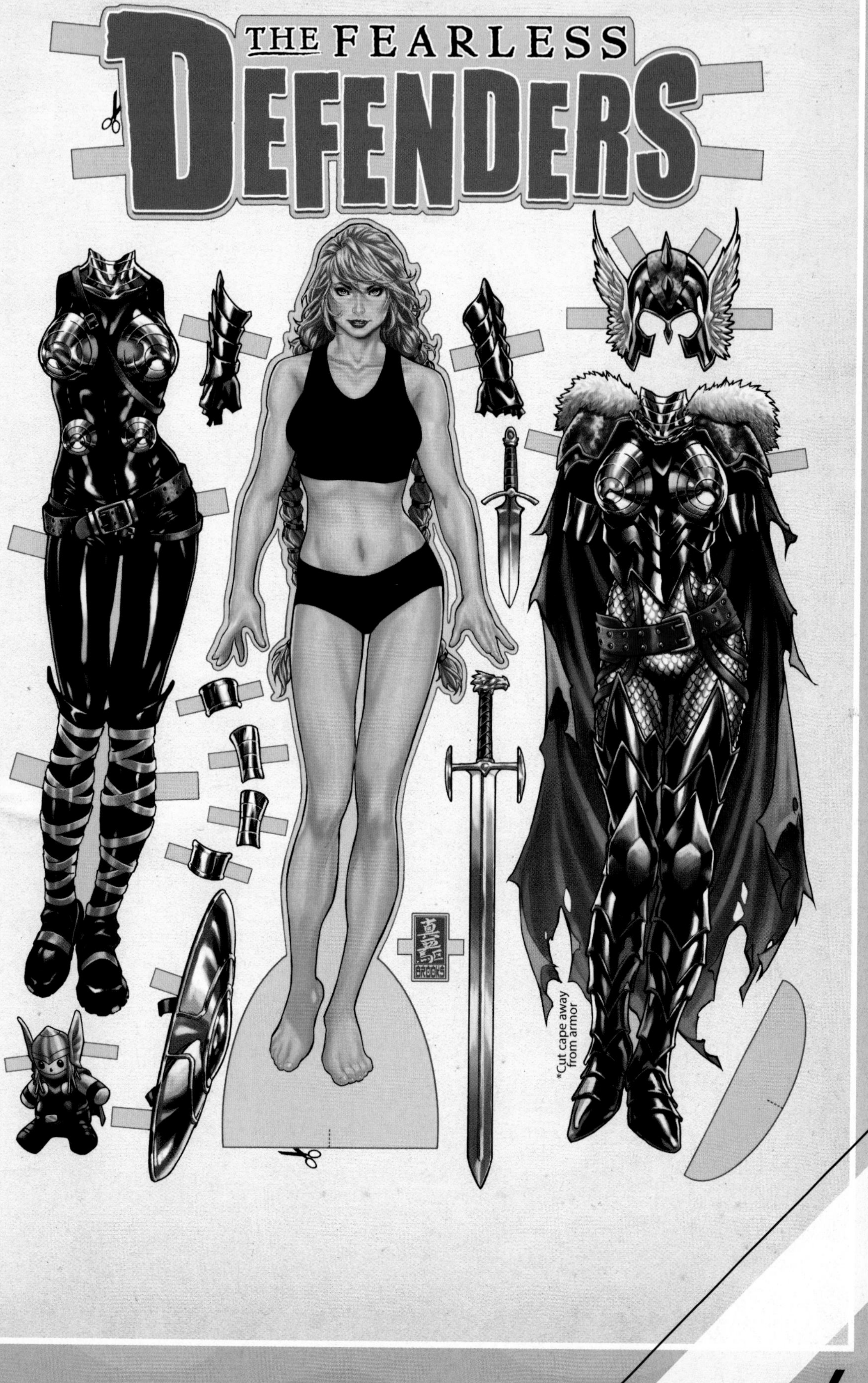
THE FEARLESS DEFENDERS
BROOKS
*Cut cape away from armor

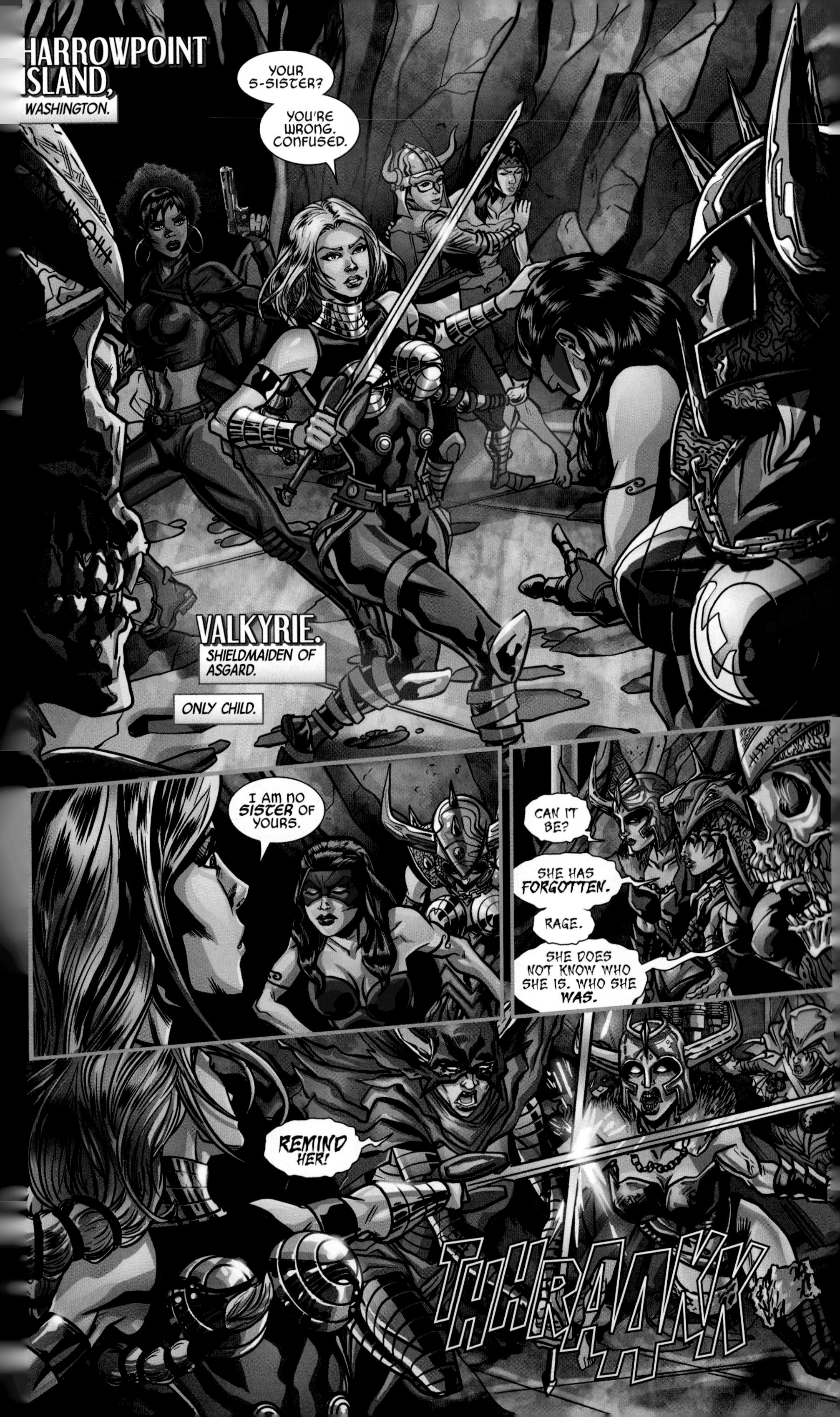
HARROWPOINT ISLAND, WASHINGTON.
YOUR S-SISTER?
YOU'RE WRONG. CONFUSED.
VALKYRIE.
SHIELDMAIDEN OF ASGARD.
ONLY CHILD.
I AM NO SISTER OF YOURS.
CAN IT BE?
SHE HAS FORGOTTEN.
RAGE.
SHE DOES NOT KNOW WHO SHE IS. WHO SHE WAS.
REMIND HER!
THRAAKK

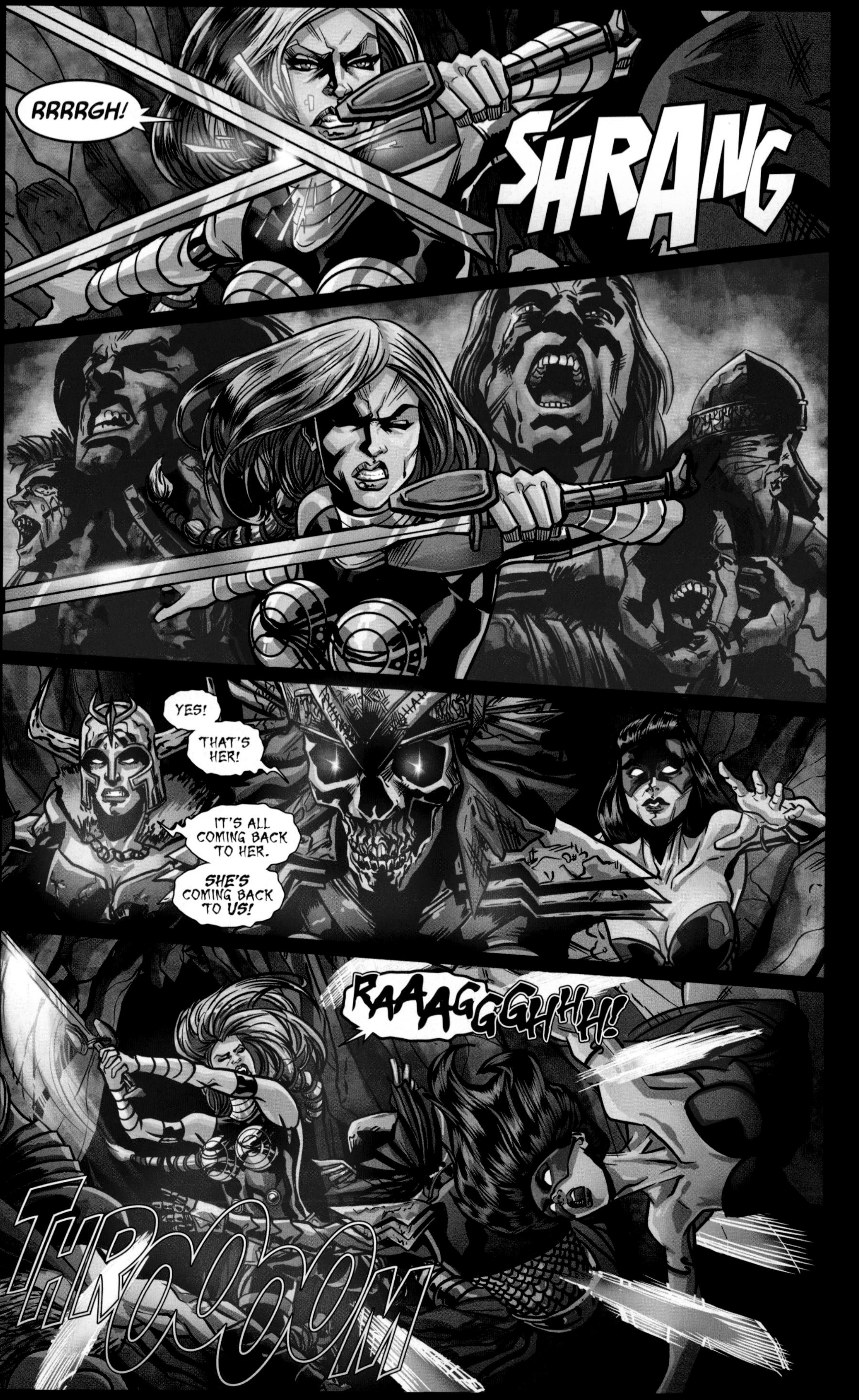
RRRRGH!
SHRANG
YES!
THAT'S HER!
IT'S ALL COMING BACK TO HER.
SHE'S COMING BACK TO US!
RAAAGGGHHH!
THROOOOM

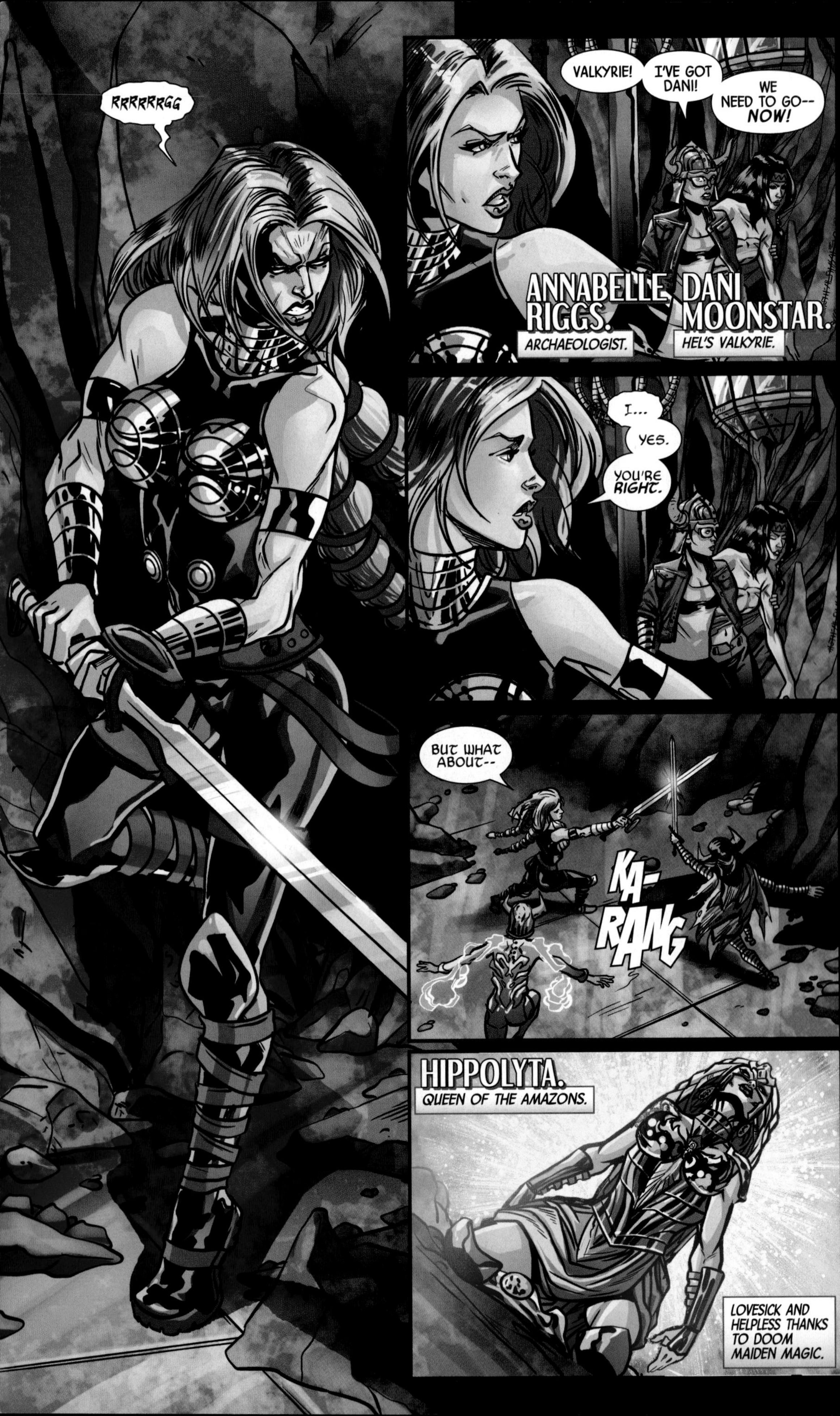
RRRRRRGG
VALKYRIE!
I'VE GOT DANI!
WE NEED TO GO-- NOW!
ANNABELLE RIGGS.
ARCHAEOLOGIST.
DANI MOONSTAR.
HEL'S VALKYRIE.
I...
YES.
YOU'RE RIGHT.
BUT WHAT ABOUT--
KA-RANG
HIPPOLYTA.
QUEEN OF THE AMAZONS.
LOVESICK AND HELPLESS THANKS TO DOOM MAIDEN MAGIC.

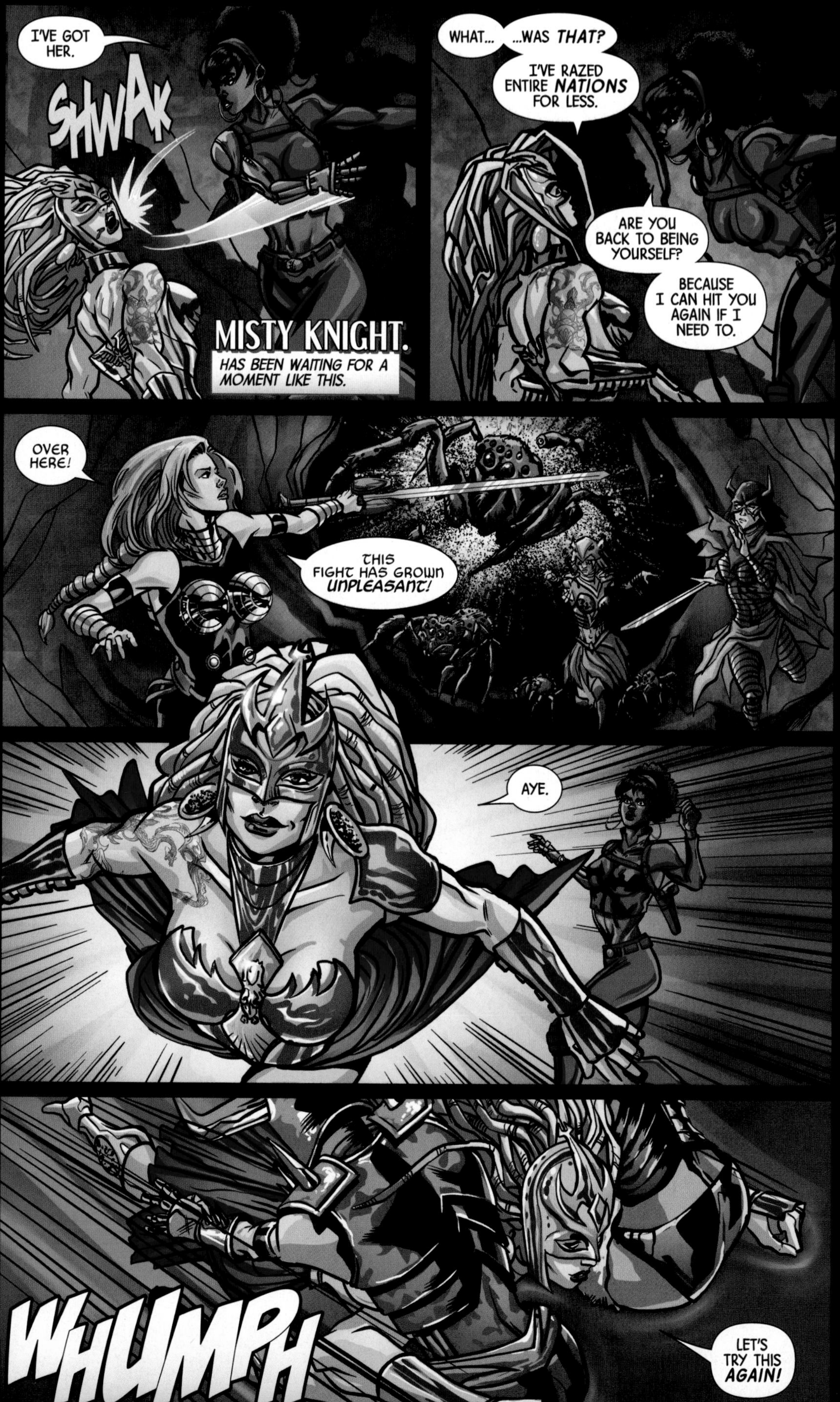
I'VE GOT HER.
SHWAK
MISTY KNIGHT.
HAS BEEN WAITING FOR A MOMENT LIKE THIS.
WHAT...
...WAS THAT?
I'VE RAZED ENTIRE NATIONS FOR LESS.
ARE YOU BACK TO BEING YOURSELF?
BECAUSE I CAN HIT YOU AGAIN IF I NEED TO.
OVER HERE!
THIS FIGHT HAS GROWN UNPLEASANT!
AYE.
WHUMPH
LET'S TRY THIS AGAIN!

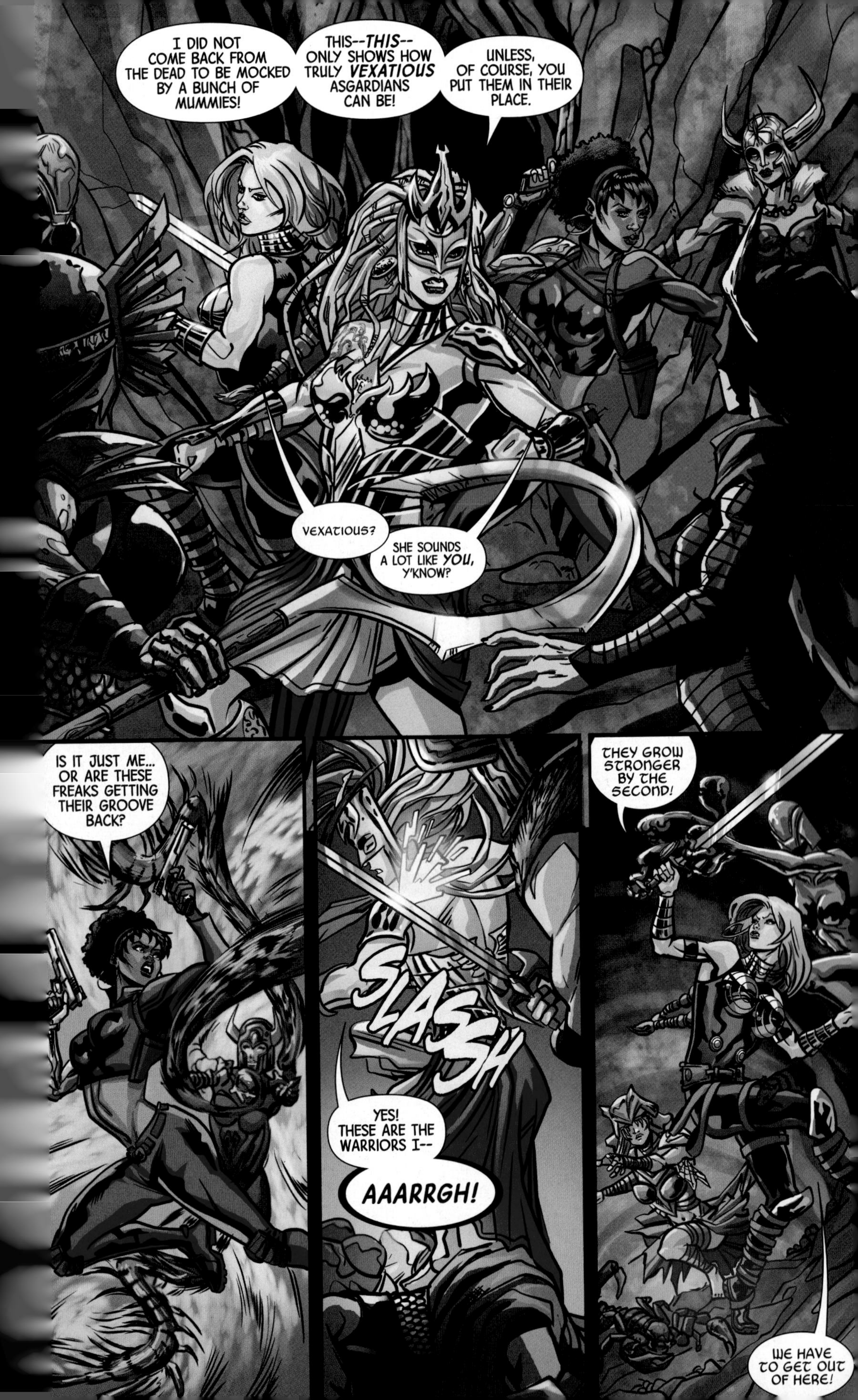
I DID NOT COME BACK FROM THE DEAD TO BE MOCKED BY A BUNCH OF MUMMIES!
THIS--THIS--ONLY SHOWS HOW TRULY VEXATIOUS ASGARDIANS CAN BE!
UNLESS, OF COURSE, YOU PUT THEM IN THEIR PLACE.
VEXATIOUS?
SHE SOUNDS A LOT LIKE YOU, Y'KNOW?
IS IT JUST ME... OR ARE THESE FREAKS GETTING THEIR GROOVE BACK?
SLASSH
YES! THESE ARE THE WARRIORS I--
AAARRGH!
THEY GROW STRONGER BY THE SECOND!
WE HAVE TO GET OUT OF HERE!

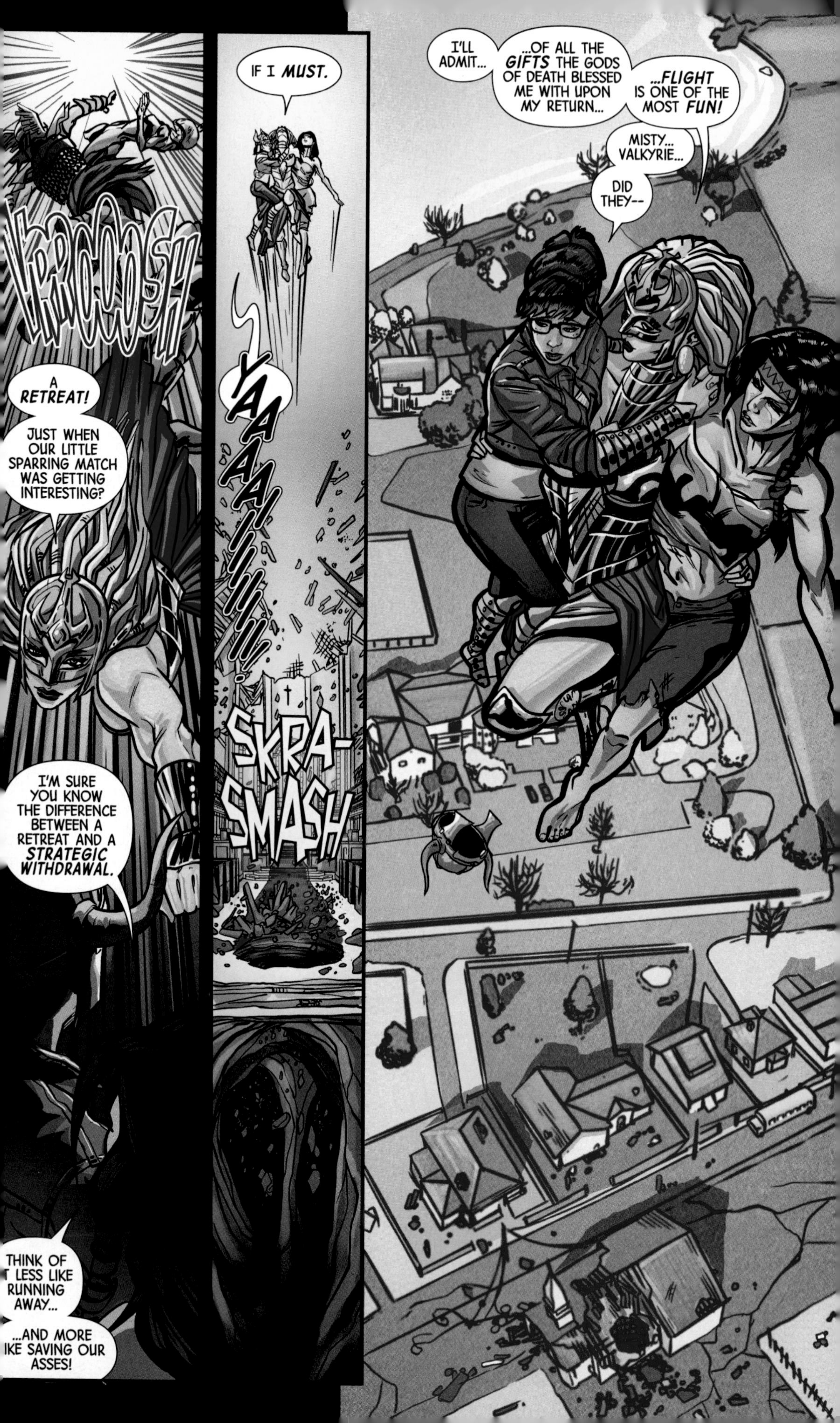

VRROOOSH
A RETREAT!
JUST WHEN OUR LITTLE SPARRING MATCH WAS GETTING INTERESTING?
I'M SURE YOU KNOW THE DIFFERENCE BETWEEN A RETREAT AND A STRATEGIC WITHDRAWAL.
THINK OF T LESS LIKE RUNNING AWAY...
...AND MORE IKE SAVING OUR ASSES!
IF I MUST.
YAAAIIIIIIII!!
SKRA-SMASH
I'LL ADMIT...
...OF ALL THE GIFTS THE GODS OF DEATH BLESSED ME WITH UPON MY RETURN...
...FLIGHT IS ONE OF THE MOST FUN!
MISTY... VALKYRIE...
DID THEY--

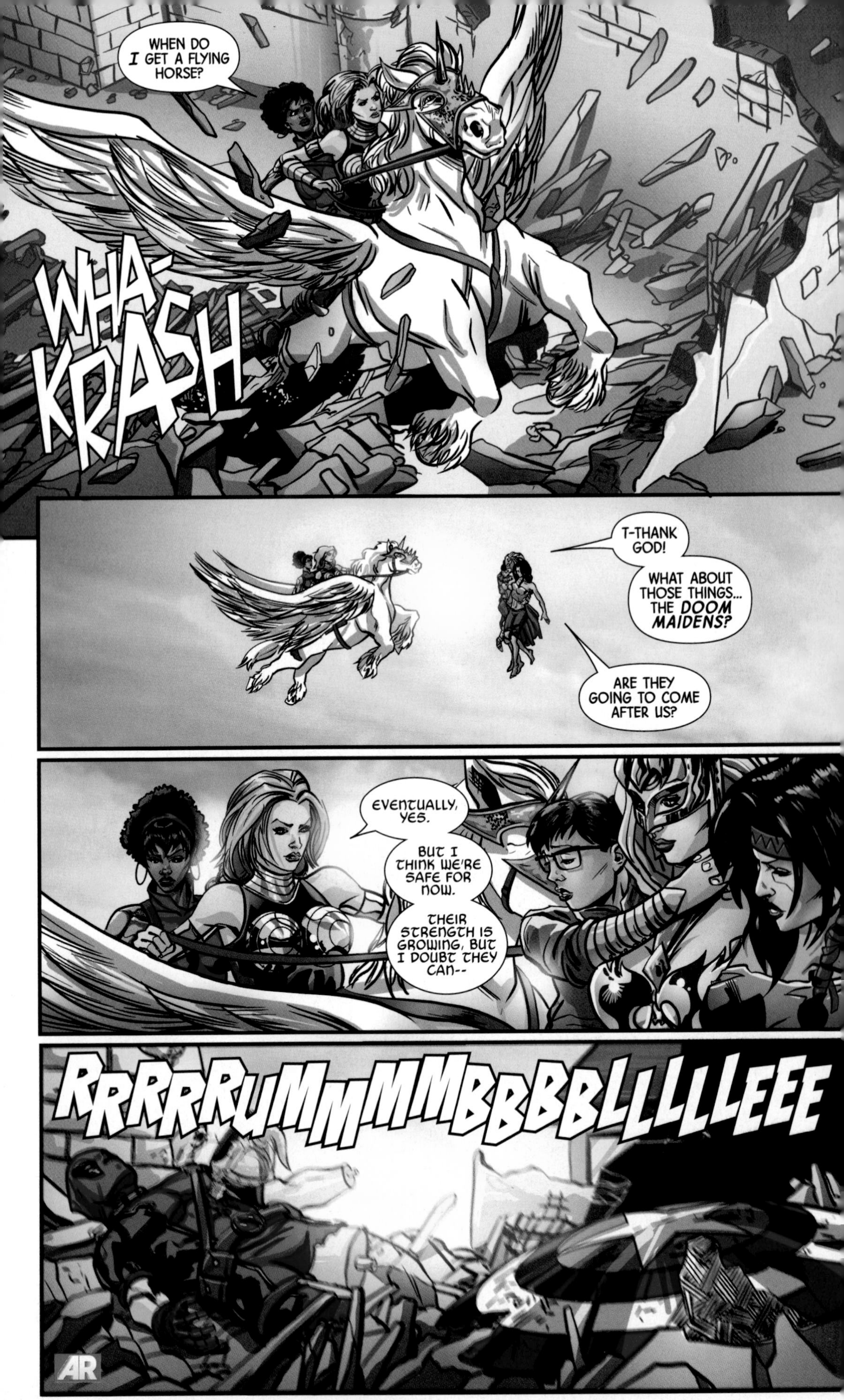
WHEN DO I GET A FLYING HORSE?
WHA-KRASH
T-THANK GOD!
WHAT ABOUT THOSE THINGS... THE DOOM MAIDENS?
ARE THEY GOING TO COME AFTER US?
EVENTUALLY, YES.
BUT I THINK WE'RE SAFE FOR NOW.
THEIR STRENGTH IS GROWING, BUT I DOUBT THEY CAN--
RRRRRUMMMMMBBBBLLLLLEEE

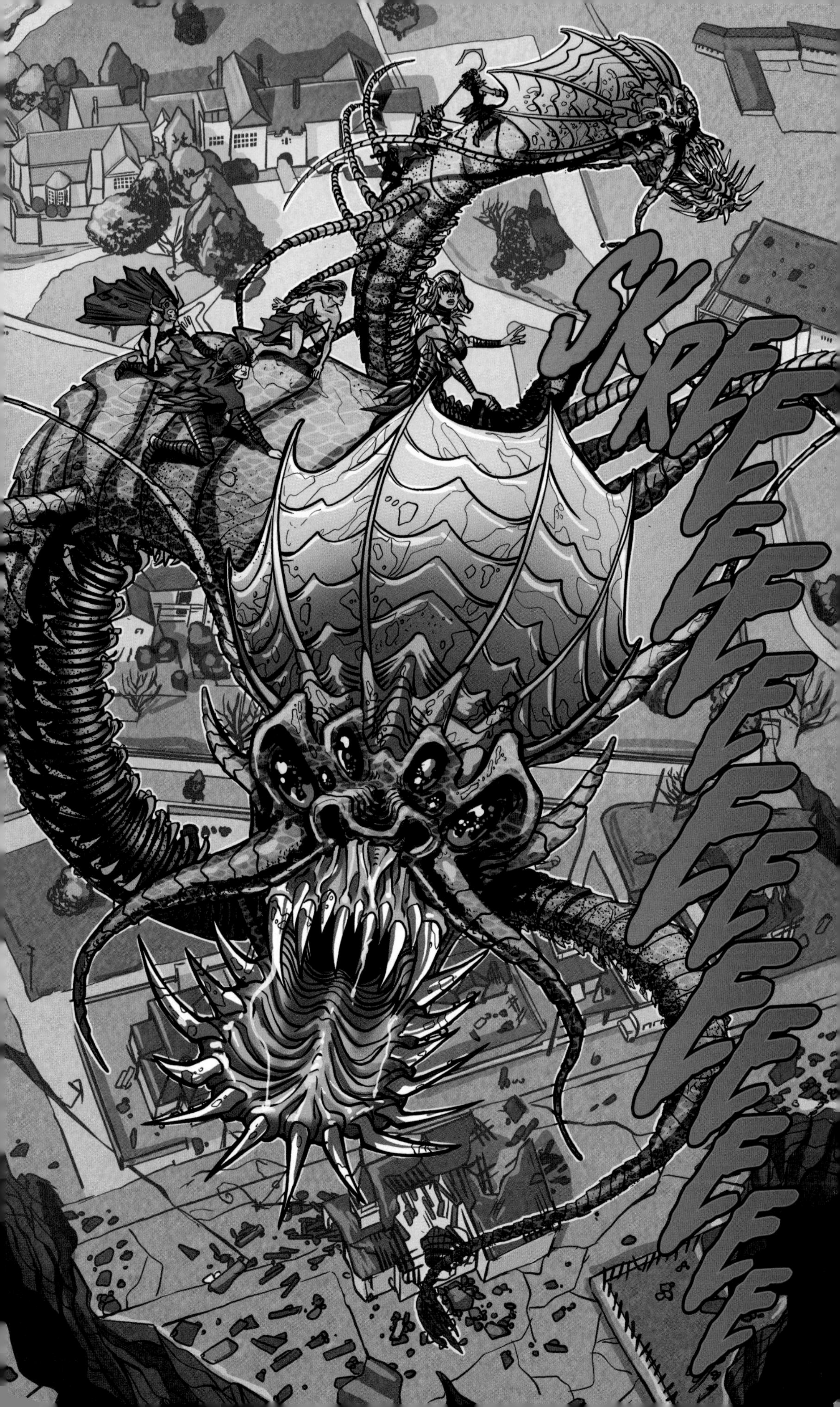
SKREEEEEEEEEEEEEE

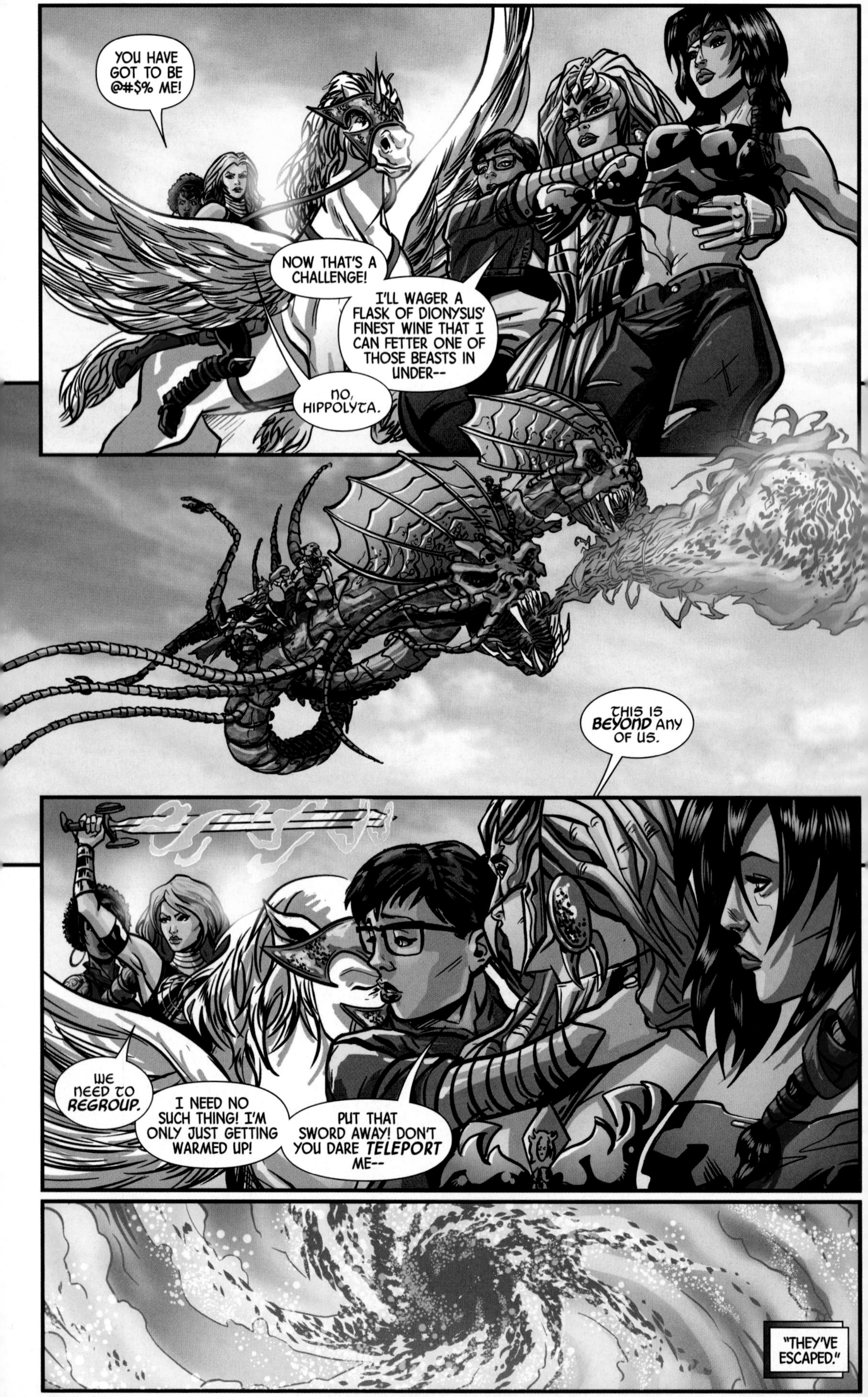
YOU HAVE GOT TO BE @#$% ME!
NOW THAT'S A CHALLENGE!
I'LL WAGER A FLASK OF DIONYSUS' FINEST WINE THAT I CAN FETTER ONE OF THOSE BEASTS IN UNDER--
NO, HIPPOLYTA.
THIS IS BEYOND ANY OF US.
WE NEED TO REGROUP.
I NEED NO SUCH THING! I'M ONLY JUST GETTING WARMED UP!
PUT THAT SWORD AWAY! DON'T YOU DARE TELEPORT ME--
"THEY'VE ESCAPED."

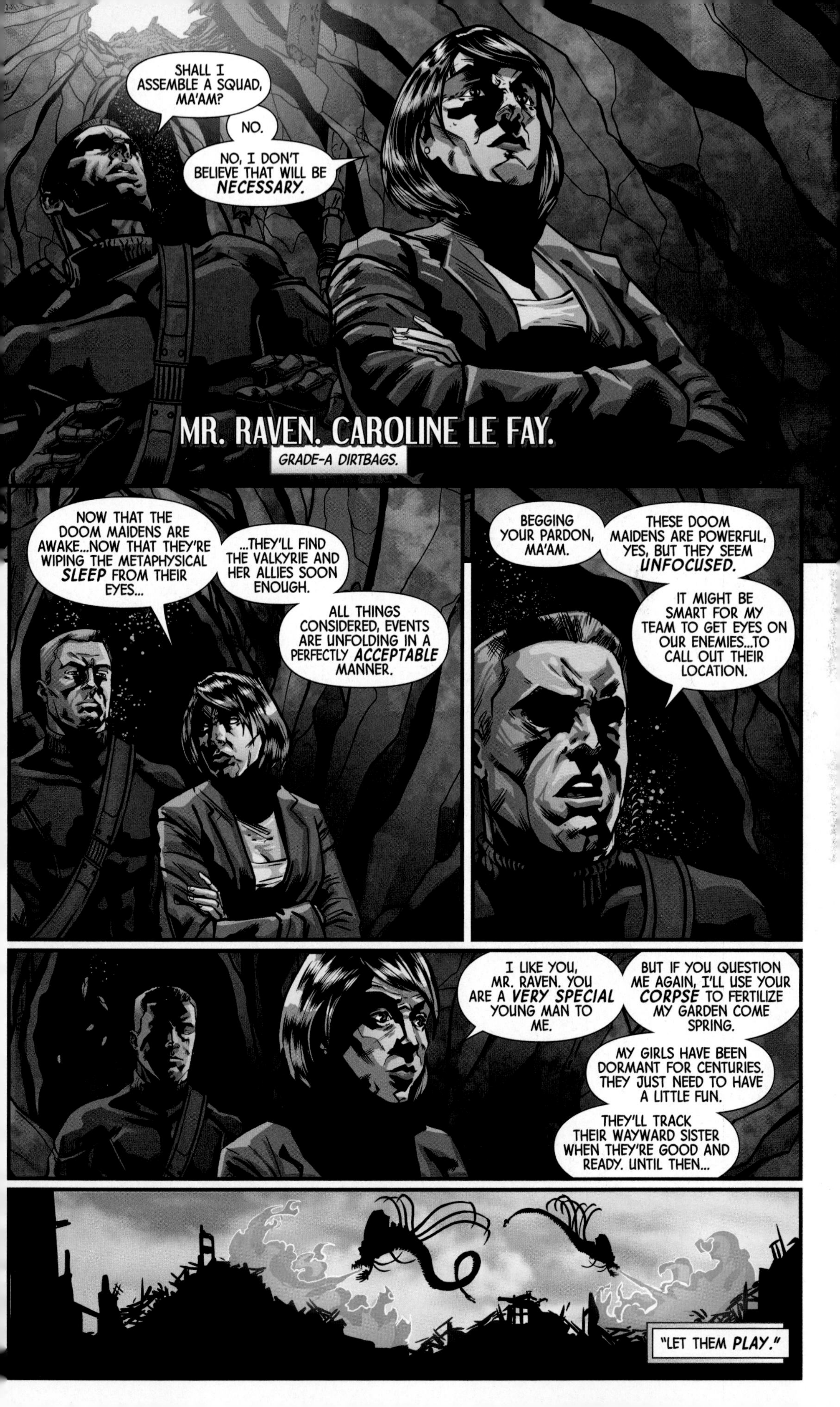
SHALL I ASSEMBLE A SQUAD, MA'AM?
NO.
NO, I DON'T BELIEVE THAT WILL BE NECESSARY.
MR. RAVEN. CAROLINE LE FAY.
GRADE-A DIRTBAGS.
NOW THAT THE DOOM MAIDENS ARE AWAKE...NOW THAT THEY'RE WIPING THE METAPHYSICAL SLEEP FROM THEIR EYES...
...THEY'LL FIND THE VALKYRIE AND HER ALLIES SOON ENOUGH.
ALL THINGS CONSIDERED, EVENTS ARE UNFOLDING IN A PERFECTLY ACCEPTABLE MANNER.
BEGGING YOUR PARDON, MA'AM.
THESE DOOM MAIDENS ARE POWERFUL, YES, BUT THEY SEEM UNFOCUSED.
IT MIGHT BE SMART FOR MY TEAM TO GET EYES ON OUR ENEMIES...TO CALL OUT THEIR LOCATION.
I LIKE YOU, MR. RAVEN. YOU ARE A VERY SPECIAL YOUNG MAN TO ME.
BUT IF YOU QUESTION ME AGAIN, I'LL USE YOUR CORPSE TO FERTILIZE MY GARDEN COME SPRING.
MY GIRLS HAVE BEEN DORMANT FOR CENTURIES. THEY JUST NEED TO HAVE A LITTLE FUN.
THEY'LL TRACK THEIR WAYWARD SISTER WHEN THEY'RE GOOD AND READY. UNTIL THEN...
"LET THEM PLAY."

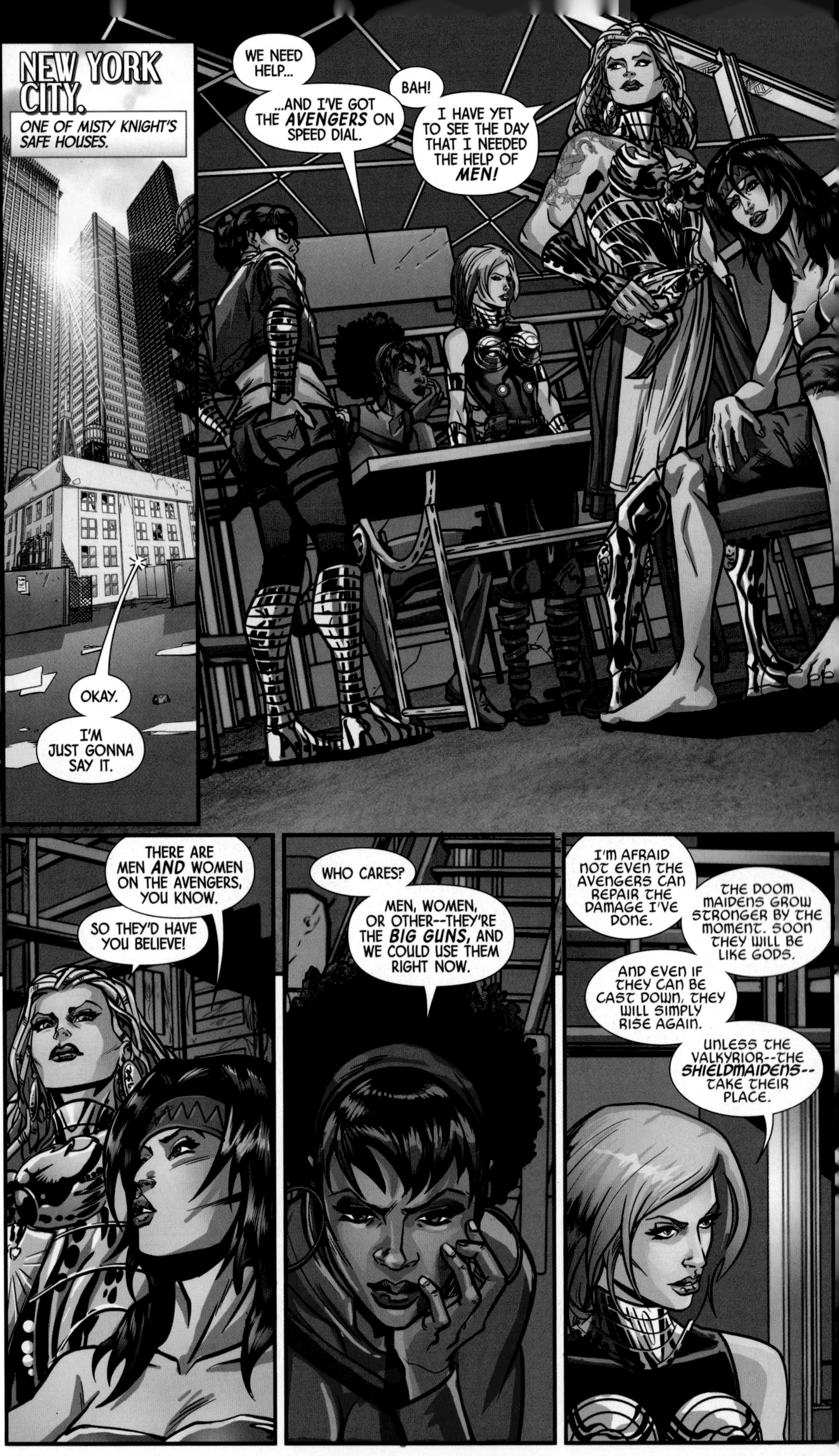
NEW YORK CITY.
ONE OF MISTY KNIGHT'S SAFE HOUSES.
OKAY.
I'M JUST GONNA SAY IT.
WE NEED HELP...
...AND I'VE GOT THE AVENGERS ON SPEED DIAL.
BAH!
I HAVE YET TO SEE THE DAY THAT I NEEDED THE HELP OF MEN!
THERE ARE MEN AND WOMEN ON THE AVENGERS, YOU KNOW.
SO THEY'D HAVE YOU BELIEVE!
WHO CARES?
MEN, WOMEN, OR OTHER--THEY'RE THE BIG GUNS, AND WE COULD USE THEM RIGHT NOW.
I'M AFRAID NOT EVEN THE AVENGERS CAN REPAIR THE DAMAGE I'VE DONE.
THE DOOM MAIDENS GROW STRONGER BY THE MOMENT. SOON THEY WILL BE LIKE GODS.
AND EVEN IF THEY CAN BE CAST DOWN, THEY WILL SIMPLY RISE AGAIN.
UNLESS THE VALKYRIOR--THE SHIELDMAIDENS--TAKE THEIR PLACE.

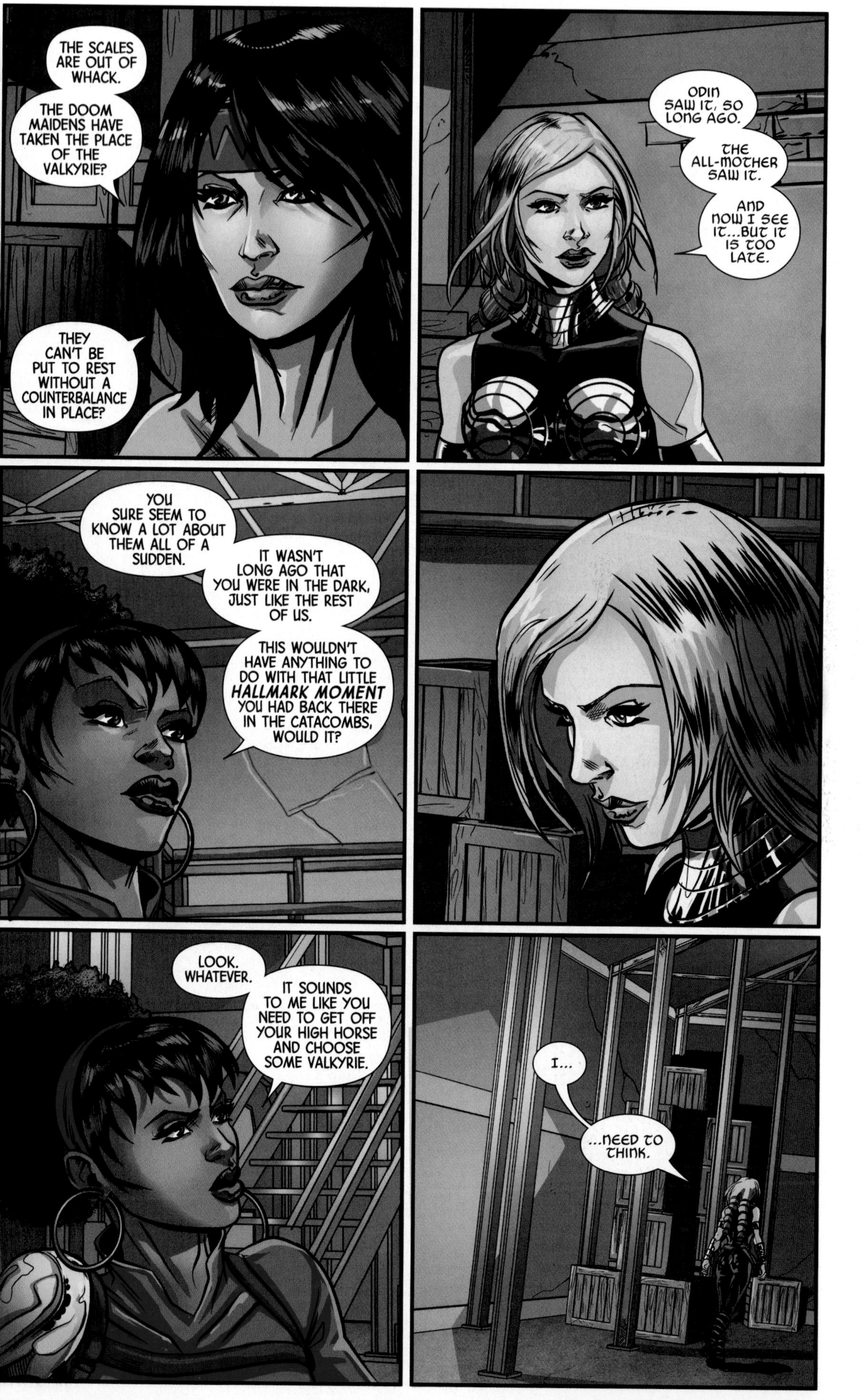
THE SCALES ARE OUT OF WHACK.
THE DOOM MAIDENS HAVE TAKEN THE PLACE OF THE VALKYRIE?
THEY CAN'T BE PUT TO REST WITHOUT A COUNTERBALANCE IN PLACE?
ODIN SAW IT, SO LONG AGO.
THE ALL-MOTHER SAW IT.
AND NOW I SEE IT...BUT IT IS TOO LATE.
YOU SURE SEEM TO KNOW A LOT ABOUT THEM ALL OF A SUDDEN.
IT WASN'T LONG AGO THAT YOU WERE IN THE DARK, JUST LIKE THE REST OF US.
THIS WOULDN'T HAVE ANYTHING TO DO WITH THAT LITTLE *HALLMARK MOMENT* YOU HAD BACK THERE IN THE CATACOMBS, WOULD IT?
LOOK. WHATEVER.
IT SOUNDS TO ME LIKE YOU NEED TO GET OFF YOUR HIGH HORSE AND CHOOSE SOME VALKYRIE.
I...
...NEED TO THINK.

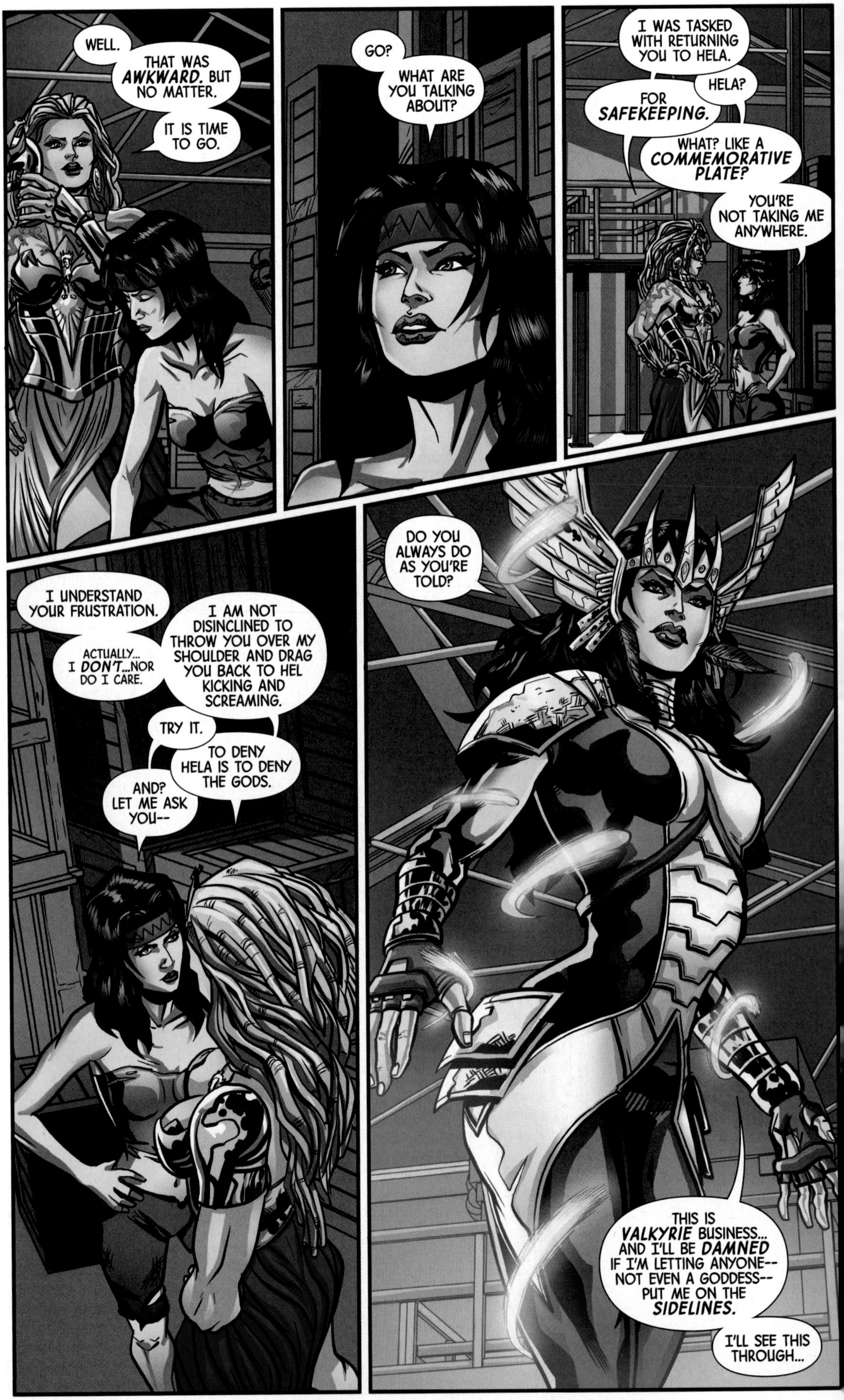
WELL.
THAT WAS AWKWARD. BUT NO MATTER.
IT IS TIME TO GO.
GO?
WHAT ARE YOU TALKING ABOUT?
I WAS TASKED WITH RETURNING YOU TO HELA.
HELA?
FOR SAFEKEEPING.
WHAT? LIKE A COMMEMORATIVE PLATE?
YOU'RE NOT TAKING ME ANYWHERE.
I UNDERSTAND YOUR FRUSTRATION.
ACTUALLY... I DON'T...NOR DO I CARE.
I AM NOT DISINCLINED TO THROW YOU OVER MY SHOULDER AND DRAG YOU BACK TO HEL KICKING AND SCREAMING.
TRY IT.
TO DENY HELA IS TO DENY THE GODS.
AND? LET ME ASK YOU--
DO YOU ALWAYS DO AS YOU'RE TOLD?
THIS IS VALKYRIE BUSINESS... AND I'LL BE DAMNED IF I'M LETTING ANYONE-- NOT EVEN A GODDESS-- PUT ME ON THE SIDELINES.
I'LL SEE THIS THROUGH...

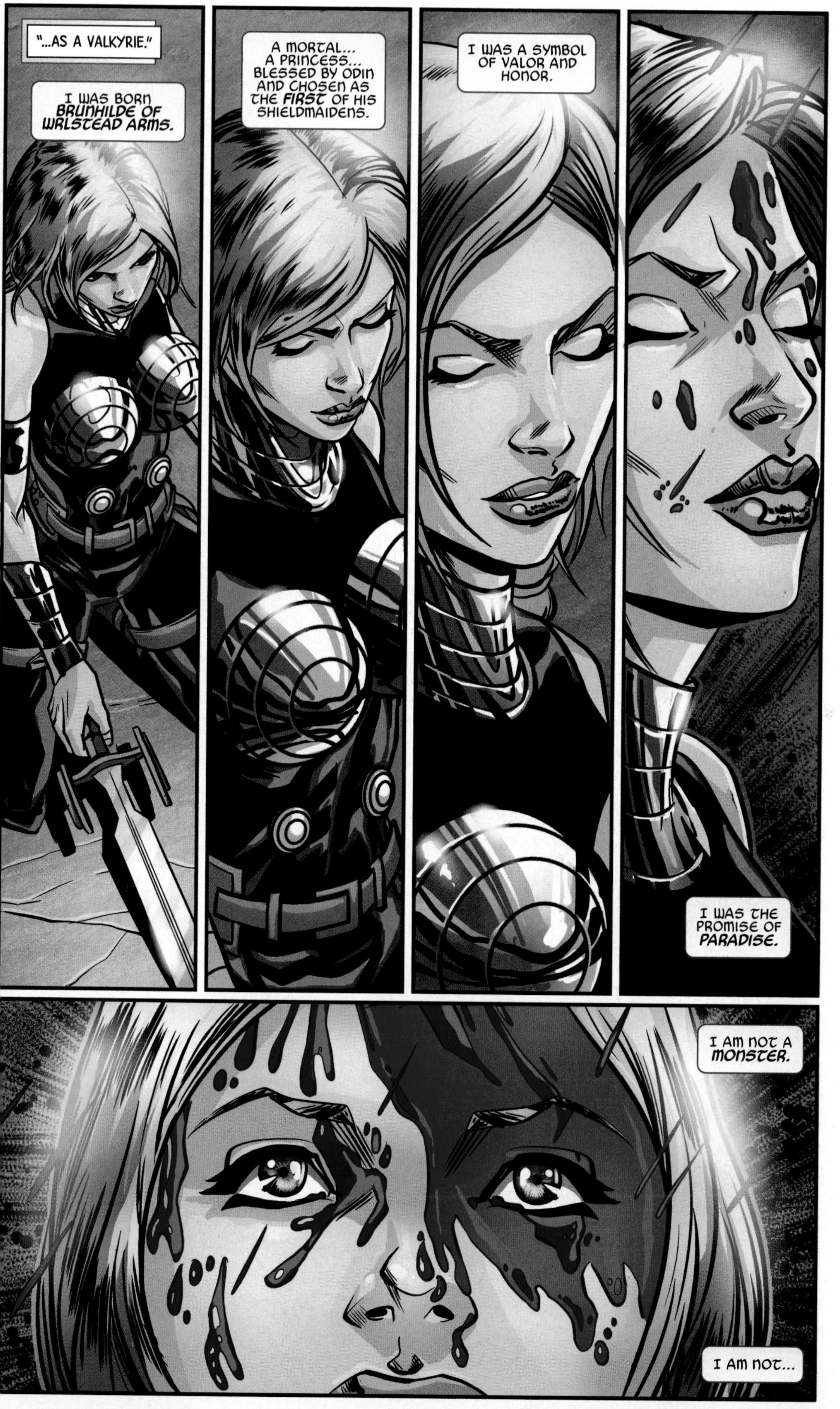
"...AS A VALKYRIE."
I WAS BORN BRUNHILDE OF WRLSTEAD ARMS.
A MORTAL... A PRINCESS... BLESSED BY ODIN AND CHOSEN AS THE FIRST OF HIS SHIELDMAIDENS.
I WAS A SYMBOL OF VALOR AND HONOR.
I WAS THE PROMISE OF PARADISE.
I AM NOT A MONSTER.
I AM NOT...

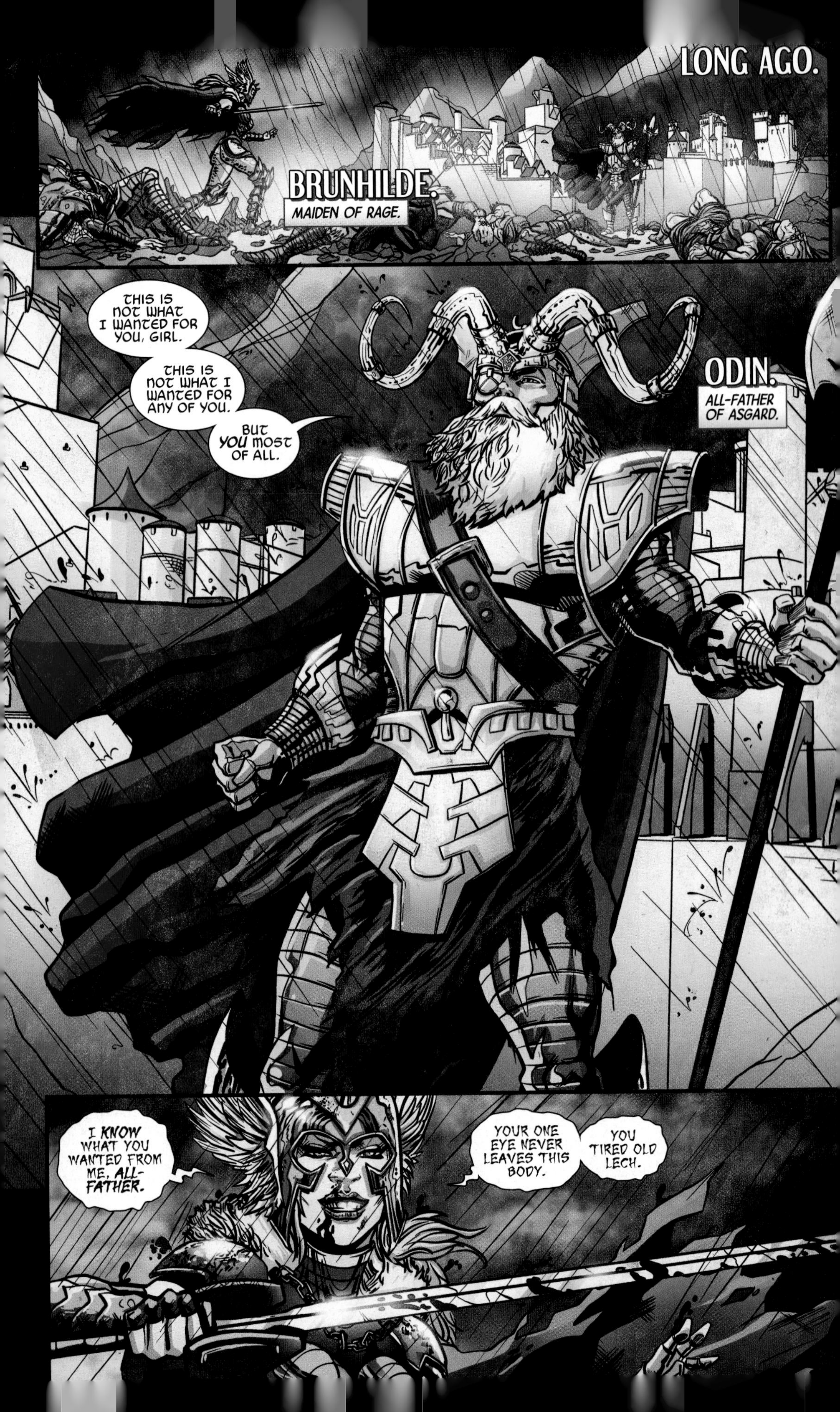
LONG AGO.
BRUNHILDE.
MAIDEN OF RAGE.
THIS IS NOT WHAT I WANTED FOR YOU, GIRL.
THIS IS NOT WHAT I WANTED FOR ANY OF YOU.
BUT YOU MOST OF ALL.
ODIN.
ALL-FATHER OF ASGARD.
I KNOW WHAT YOU WANTED FROM ME, ALL-FATHER.
YOUR ONE EYE NEVER LEAVES THIS BODY.
YOU TIRED OLD LECH.

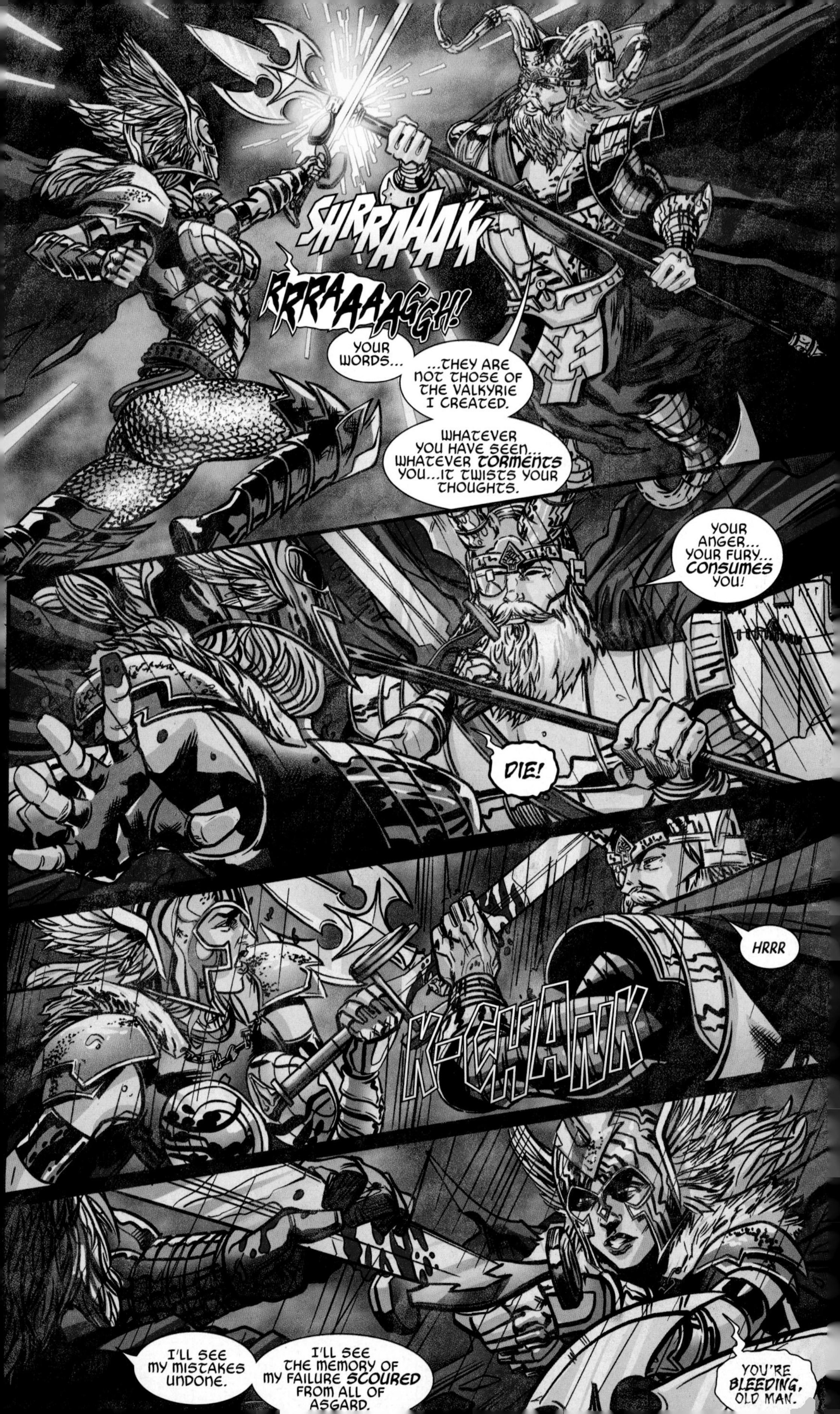
SHRRAAAKK
RRRAAAAGGH!
YOUR WORDS...
...THEY ARE NOT THOSE OF THE VALKYRIE I CREATED.
WHATEVER YOU HAVE SEEN... WHATEVER **TORMENTS** YOU...IT TWISTS YOUR THOUGHTS.
YOUR ANGER... YOUR FURY... **CONSUMES** YOU!
DIE!
HRRR
K-CHANK
I'LL SEE MY MISTAKES UNDONE.
I'LL SEE THE MEMORY OF MY FAILURE **SCOURED** FROM ALL OF ASGARD.
YOU'RE **BLEEDING,** OLD MAN.

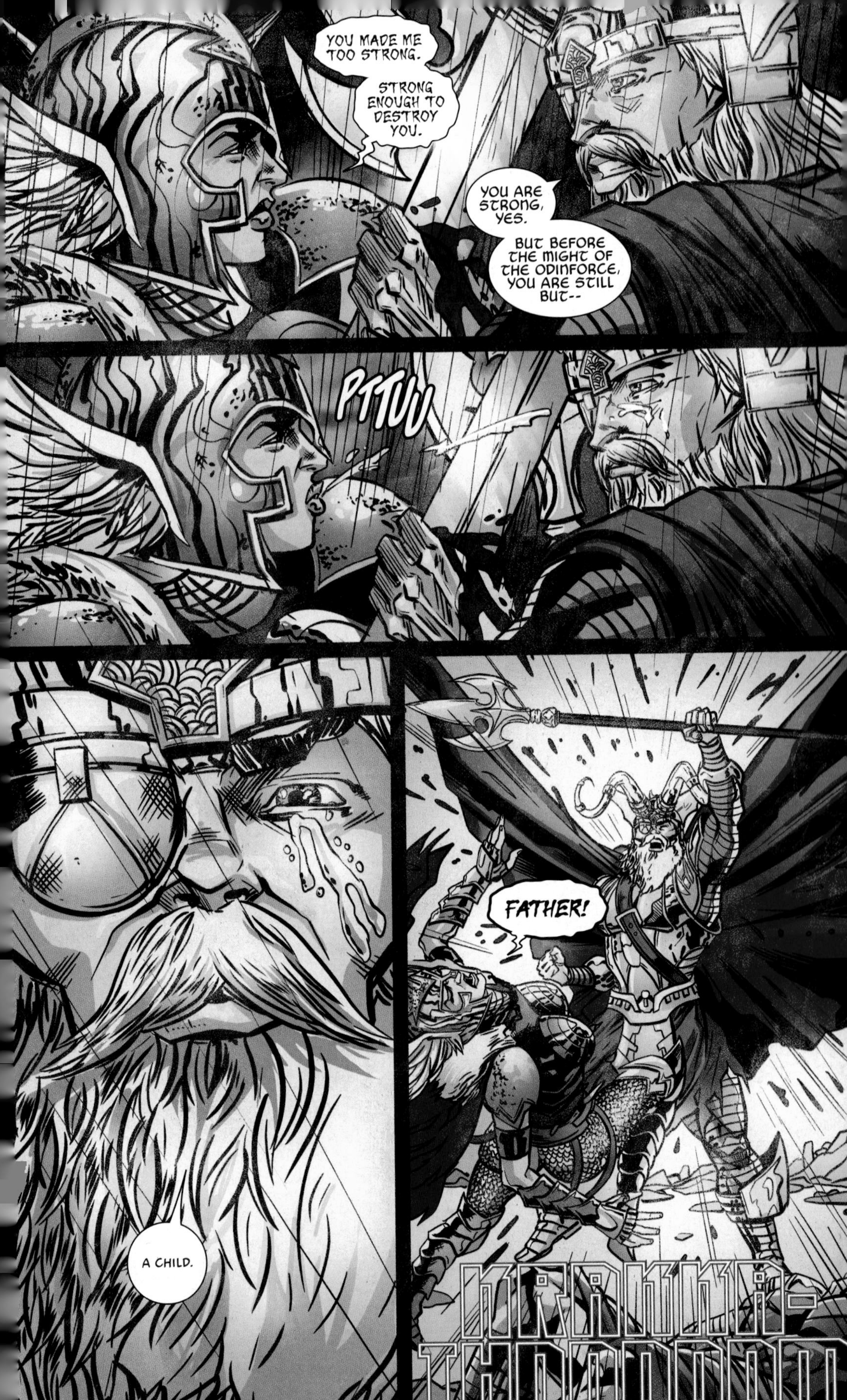
YOU MADE ME TOO STRONG.
STRONG ENOUGH TO DESTROY YOU.
YOU ARE STRONG, YES.
BUT BEFORE THE MIGHT OF THE ODINFORCE, YOU ARE STILL BUT--
PTTUU
A CHILD.
FATHER!

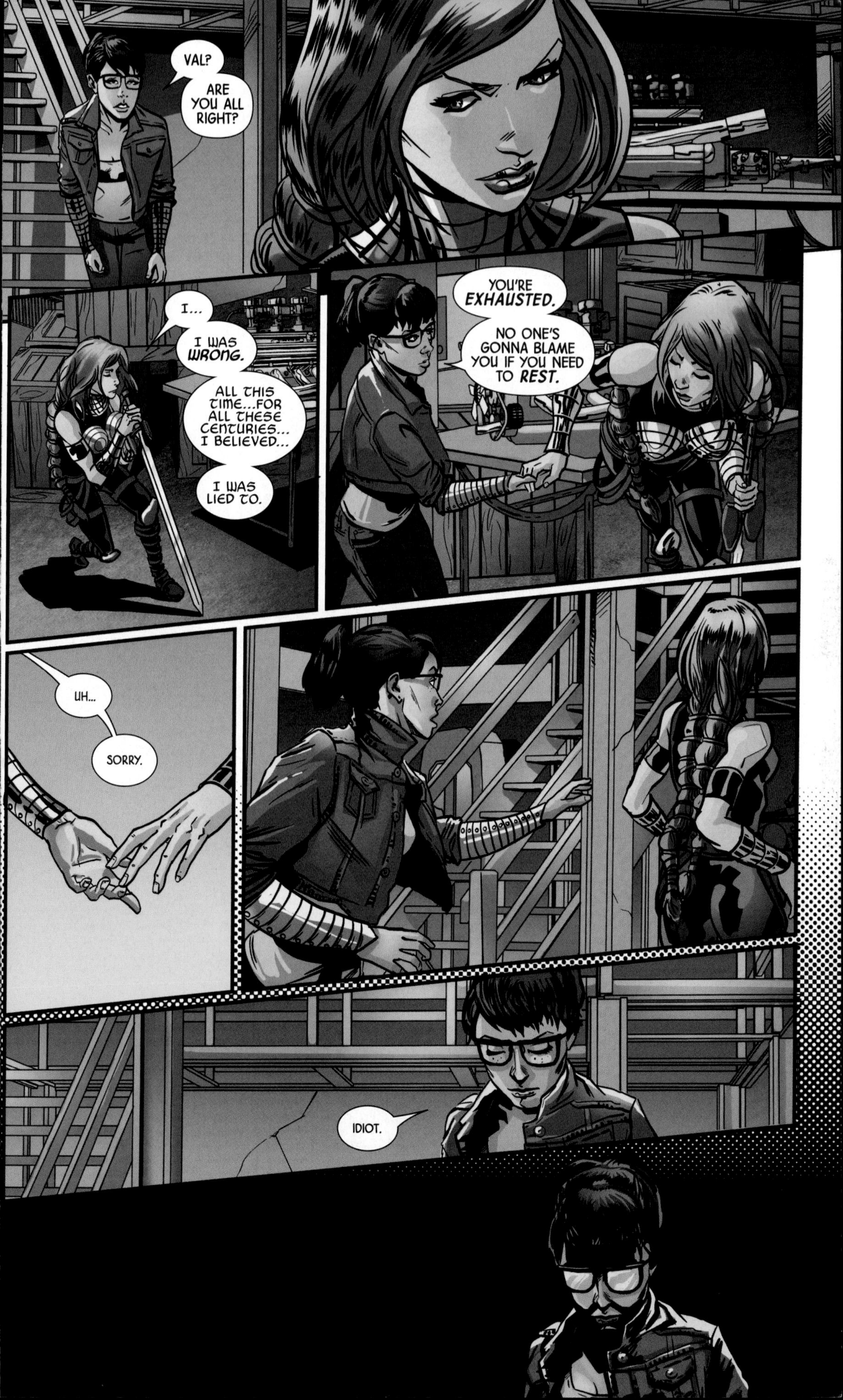
VAL?
ARE YOU ALL RIGHT?
I...
I WAS WRONG.
ALL THIS TIME...FOR ALL THESE CENTURIES... I BELIEVED...
I WAS LIED TO.
YOU'RE EXHAUSTED.
NO ONE'S GONNA BLAME YOU IF YOU NEED TO REST.
UH...
SORRY.
IDIOT.

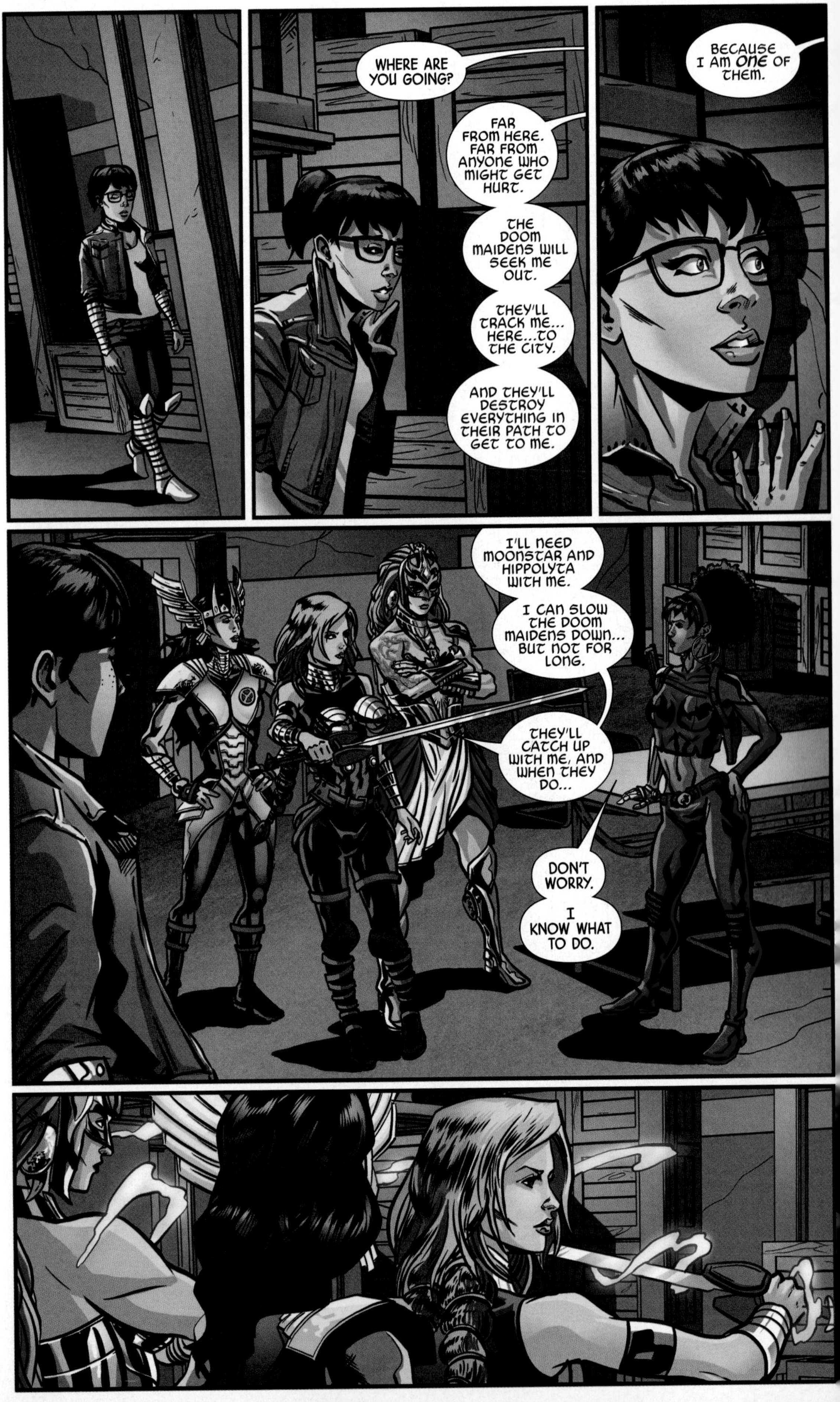
WHERE ARE YOU GOING?
FAR FROM HERE. FAR FROM ANYONE WHO MIGHT GET HURT.
THE DOOM MAIDENS WILL SEEK ME OUT.
THEY'LL TRACK ME... HERE...TO THE CITY.
AND THEY'LL DESTROY EVERYTHING IN THEIR PATH TO GET TO ME.
BECAUSE I AM ONE OF THEM.
I'LL NEED MOONSTAR AND HIPPOLYTA WITH ME.
I CAN SLOW THE DOOM MAIDENS DOWN... BUT NOT FOR LONG.
THEY'LL CATCH UP WITH ME, AND WHEN THEY DO...
DON'T WORRY.
I KNOW WHAT TO DO.

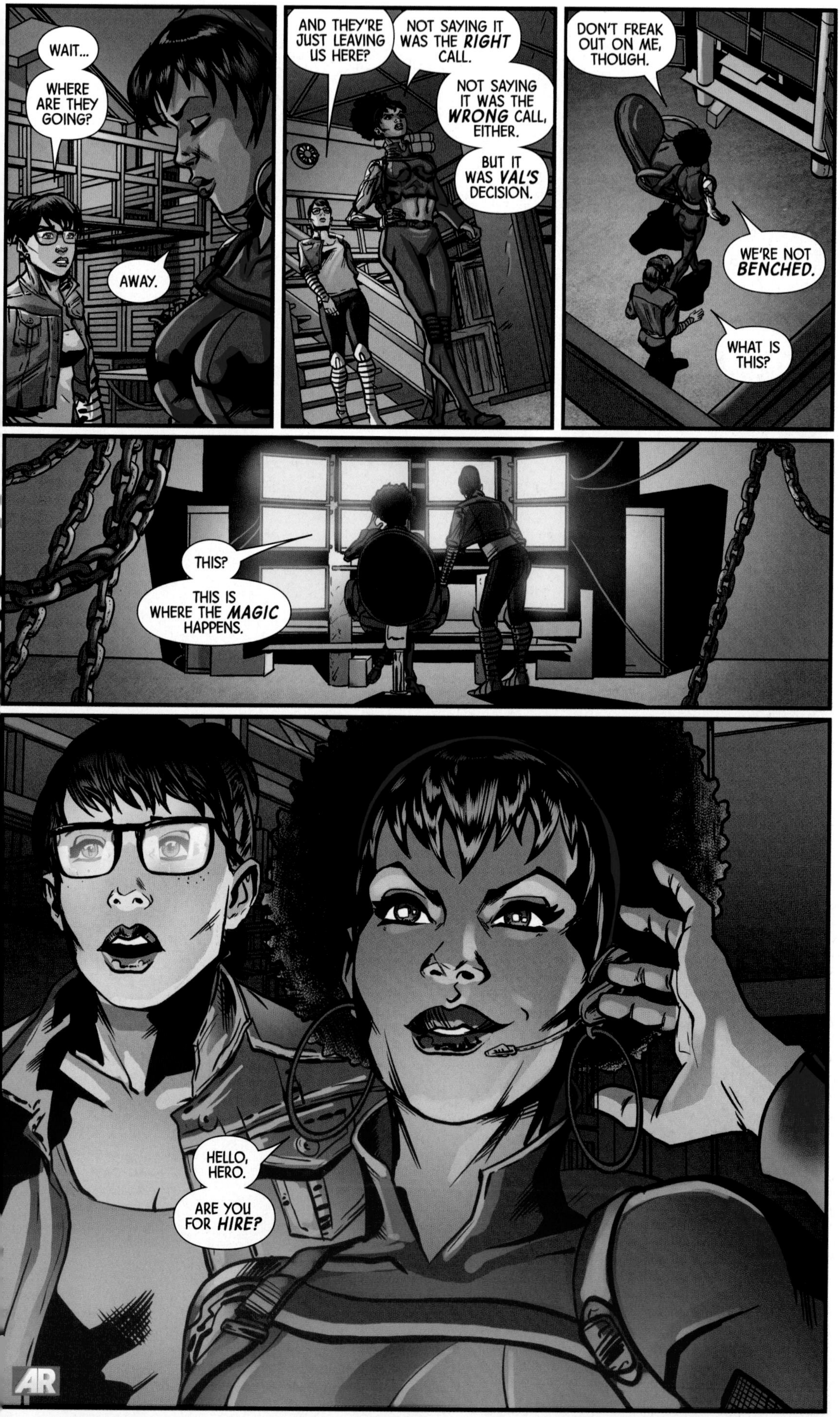
WAIT...
WHERE ARE THEY GOING?
AWAY.
AND THEY'RE JUST LEAVING US HERE?
NOT SAYING IT WAS THE RIGHT CALL.
NOT SAYING IT WAS THE WRONG CALL, EITHER.
BUT IT WAS VAL'S DECISION.
DON'T FREAK OUT ON ME, THOUGH.
WE'RE NOT BENCHED.
WHAT IS THIS?
THIS?
THIS IS WHERE THE MAGIC HAPPENS.
HELLO, HERO.
ARE YOU FOR HIRE?
AR

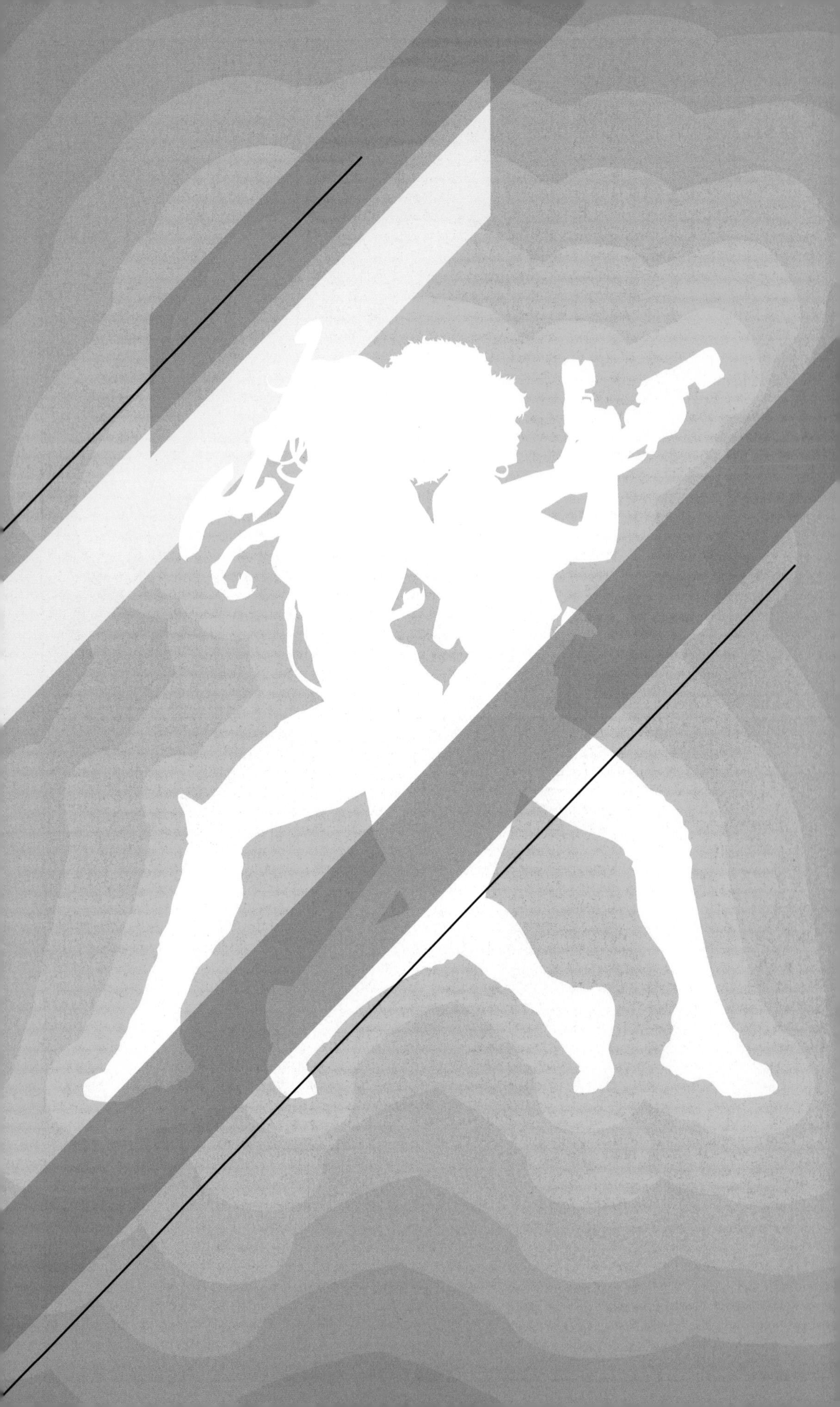

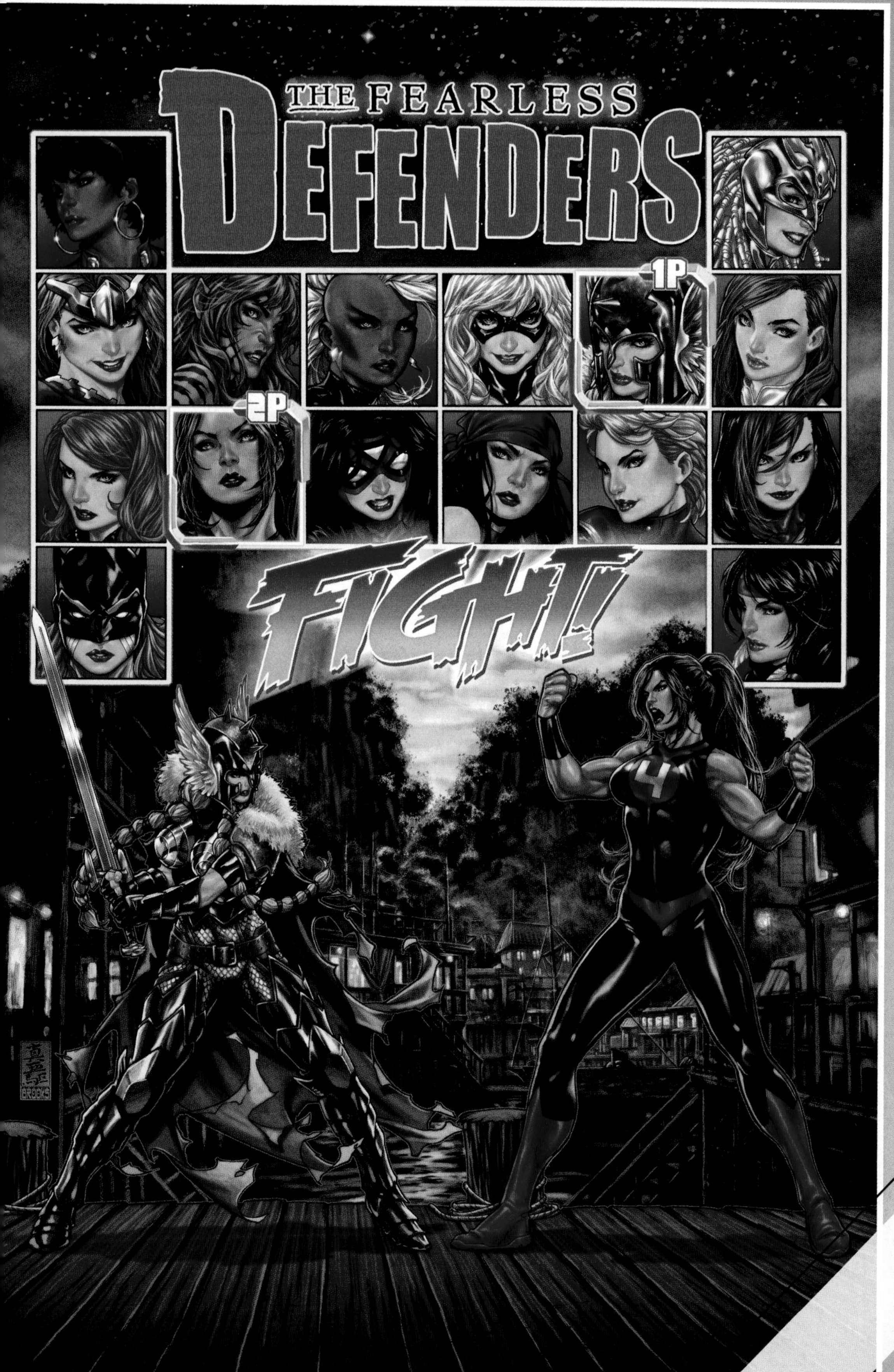
THE FEARLESS
DEFENDERS
1P
2P
FIGHT!
BROOKS

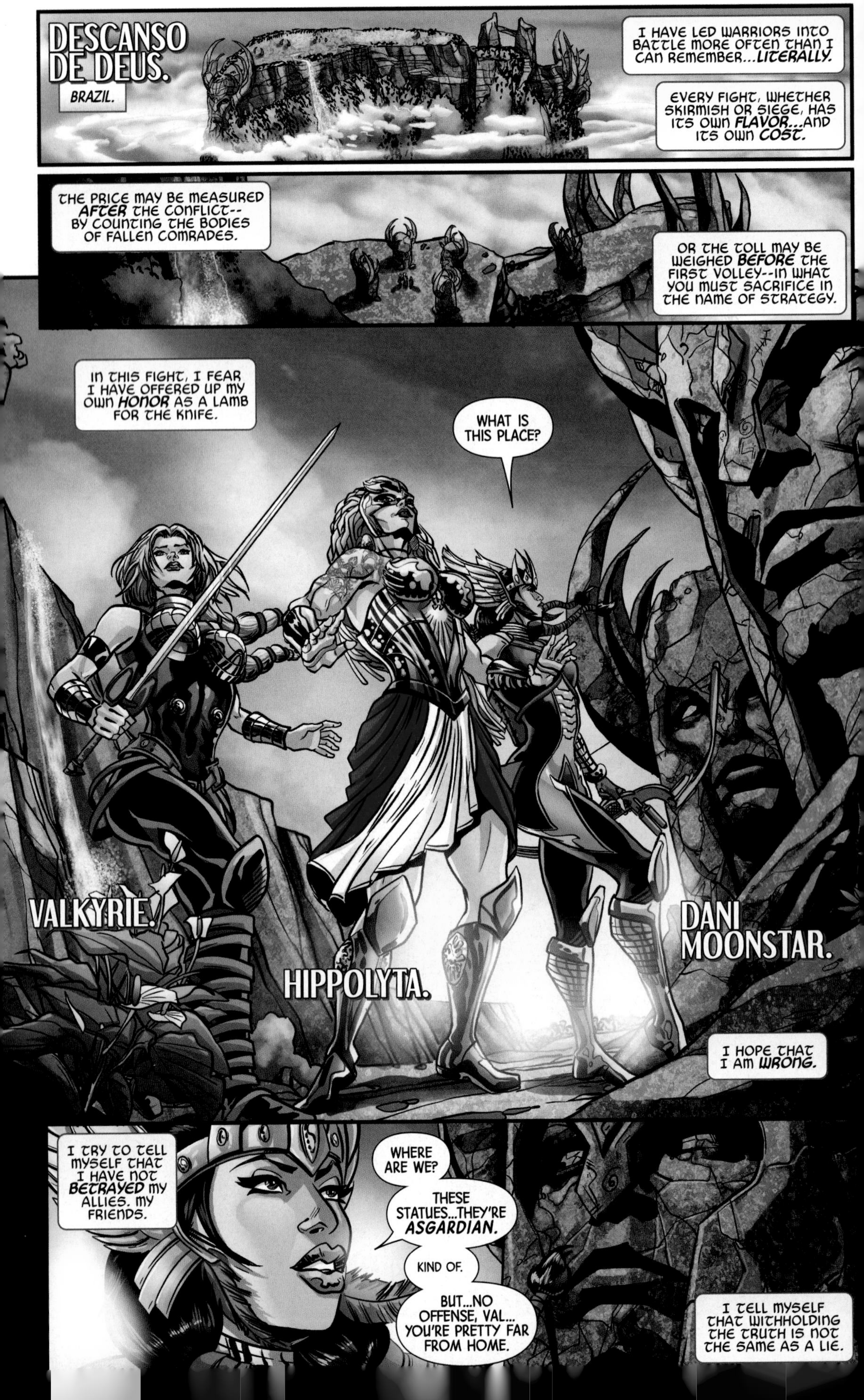
DESCANSO DE DEUS.
BRAZIL.
I HAVE LED WARRIORS INTO BATTLE MORE OFTEN THAN I CAN REMEMBER...LITERALLY.
EVERY FIGHT, WHETHER SKIRMISH OR SIEGE, HAS ITS OWN FLAVOR...AND ITS OWN COST.
THE PRICE MAY BE MEASURED AFTER THE CONFLICT--BY COUNTING THE BODIES OF FALLEN COMRADES.
OR THE TOLL MAY BE WEIGHED BEFORE THE FIRST VOLLEY--IN WHAT YOU MUST SACRIFICE IN THE NAME OF STRATEGY.
IN THIS FIGHT, I FEAR I HAVE OFFERED UP MY OWN HONOR AS A LAMB FOR THE KNIFE.
WHAT IS THIS PLACE?
VALKYRIE.
HIPPOLYTA.
DANI MOONSTAR.
I HOPE THAT I AM WRONG.
I TRY TO TELL MYSELF THAT I HAVE NOT BETRAYED MY ALLIES. MY FRIENDS.
WHERE ARE WE?
THESE STATUES...THEY'RE ASGARDIAN.
KIND OF.
BUT...NO OFFENSE, VAL... YOU'RE PRETTY FAR FROM HOME.
I TELL MYSELF THAT WITHHOLDING THE TRUTH IS NOT THE SAME AS A LIE.

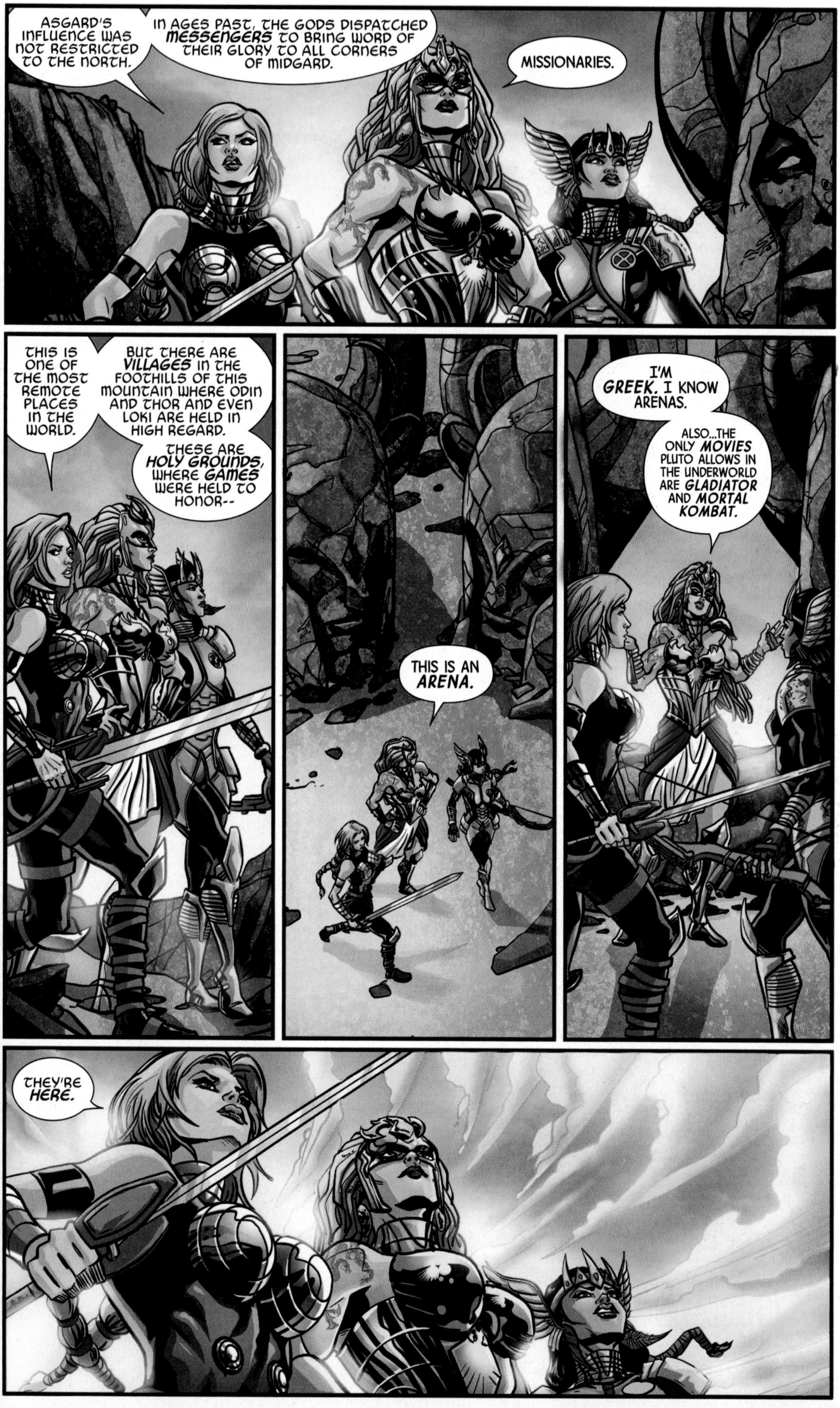
ASGARD'S INFLUENCE WAS NOT RESTRICTED TO THE NORTH.
IN AGES PAST, THE GODS DISPATCHED MESSENGERS TO BRING WORD OF THEIR GLORY TO ALL CORNERS OF MIDGARD.
MISSIONARIES.
THIS IS ONE OF THE MOST REMOTE PLACES IN THE WORLD.
BUT THERE ARE VILLAGES IN THE FOOTHILLS OF THIS MOUNTAIN WHERE ODIN AND THOR AND EVEN LOKI ARE HELD IN HIGH REGARD.
THESE ARE HOLY GROUNDS, WHERE GAMES WERE HELD TO HONOR--
THIS IS AN ARENA.
I'M GREEK. I KNOW ARENAS.
ALSO...THE ONLY MOVIES PLUTO ALLOWS IN THE UNDERWORLD ARE GLADIATOR AND MORTAL KOMBAT.
THEY'RE HERE.

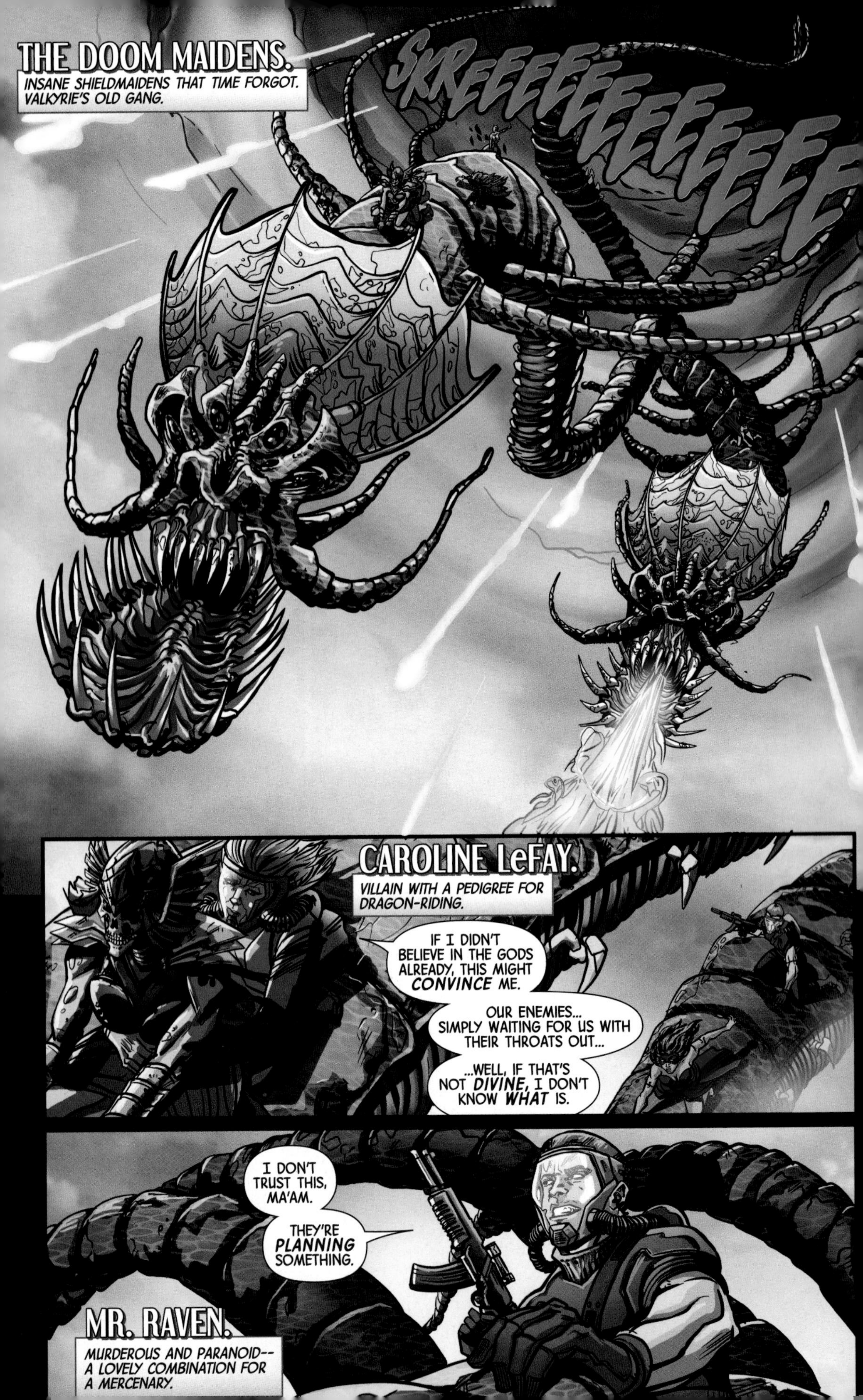
THE DOOM MAIDENS.
INSANE SHIELDMAIDENS THAT TIME FORGOT. VALKYRIE'S OLD GANG.
SKREEEEEEEEEEEE
CAROLINE LeFAY.
VILLAIN WITH A PEDIGREE FOR DRAGON-RIDING.
IF I DIDN'T BELIEVE IN THE GODS ALREADY, THIS MIGHT CONVINCE ME.
OUR ENEMIES... SIMPLY WAITING FOR US WITH THEIR THROATS OUT...
...WELL, IF THAT'S NOT DIVINE, I DON'T KNOW WHAT IS.
I DON'T TRUST THIS, MA'AM.
THEY'RE PLANNING SOMETHING.
MR. RAVEN.
MURDEROUS AND PARANOID-- A LOVELY COMBINATION FOR A MERCENARY.

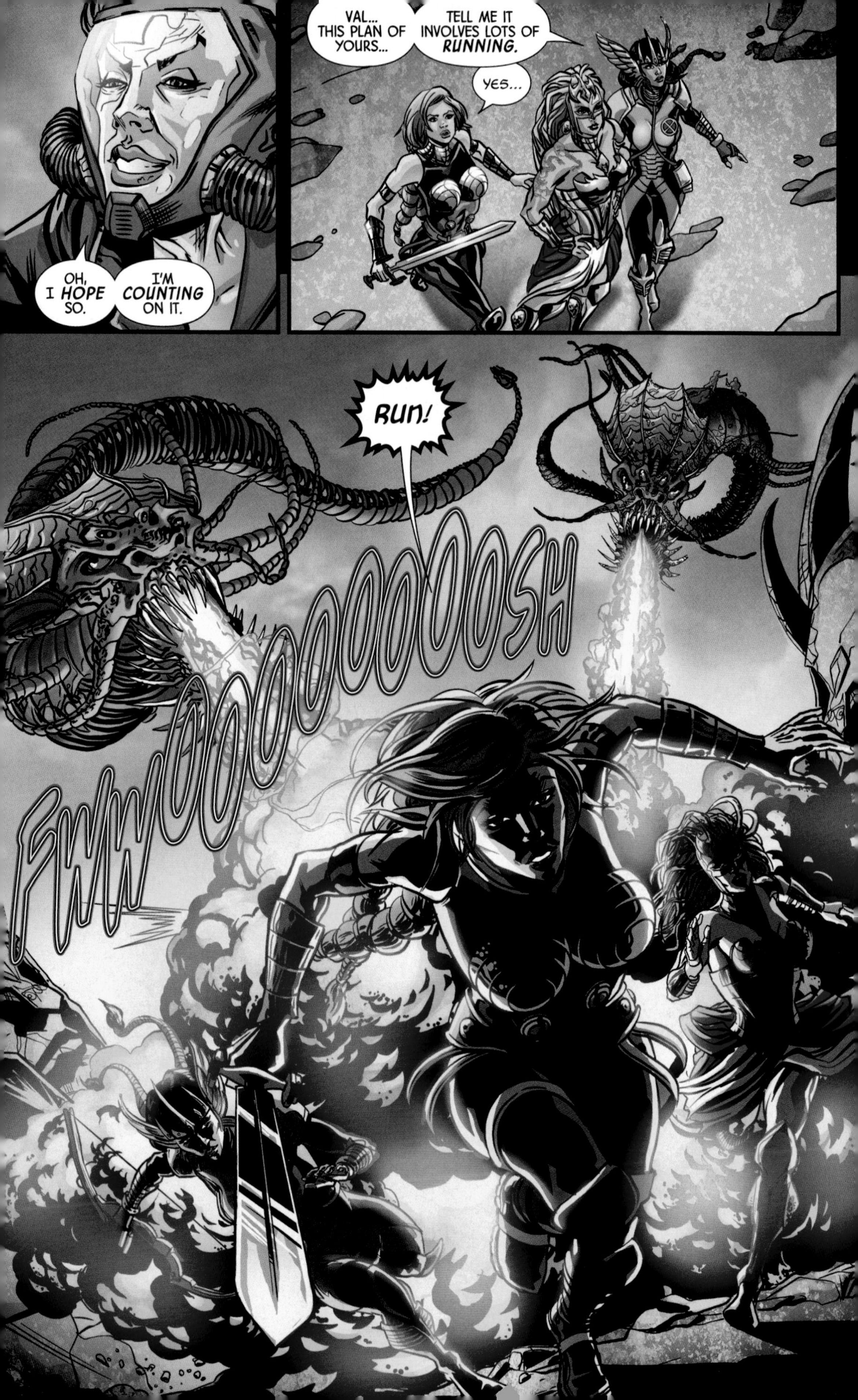
VAL... THIS PLAN OF YOURS...
TELL ME IT INVOLVES LOTS OF RUNNING.
YES...
OH, I HOPE SO.
I'M COUNTING ON IT.
RUN!
FWWOOOOOOOOOOSH

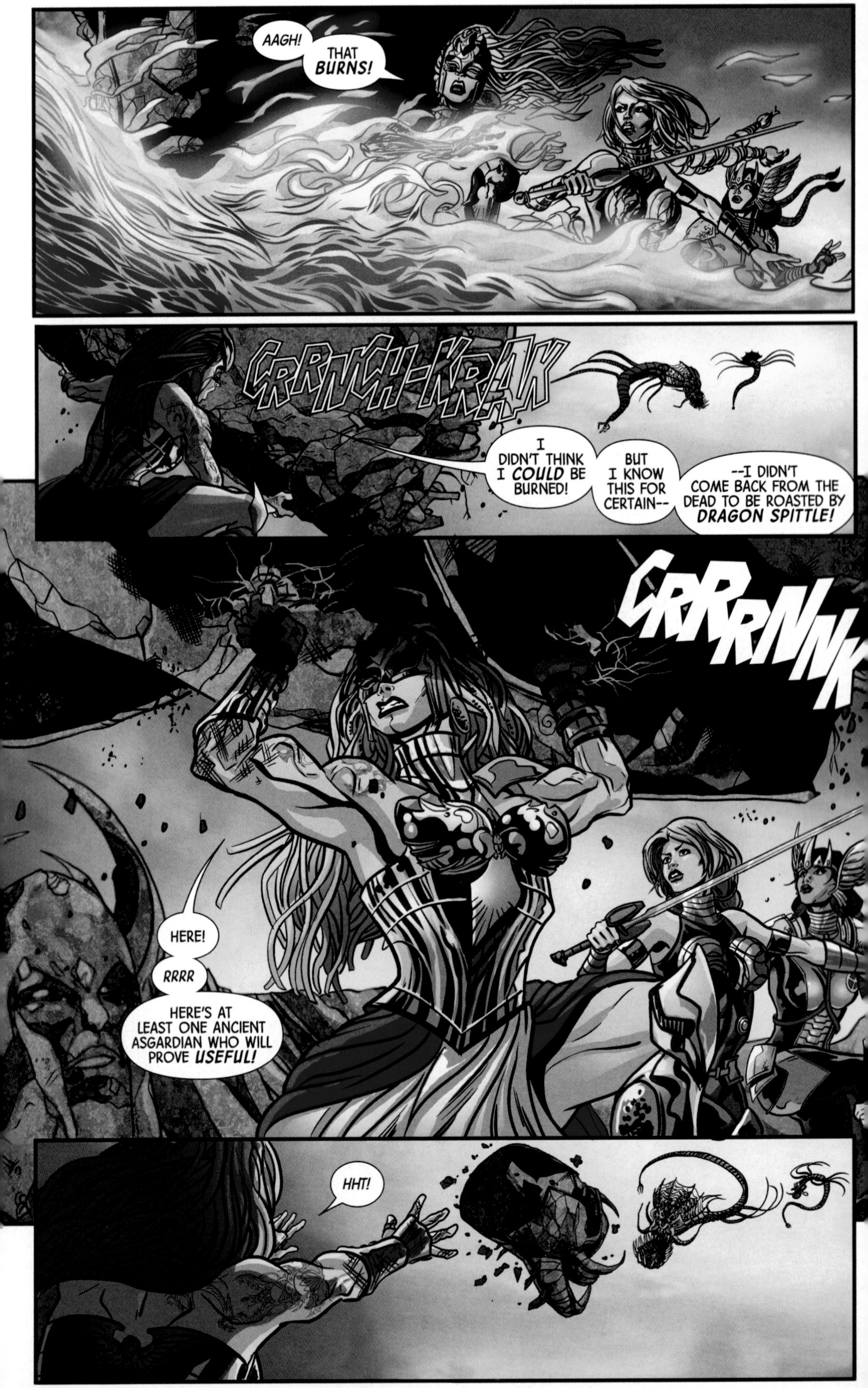

AAGH!
THAT BURNS!
CRRNCH-KRAK
I DIDN'T THINK I COULD BE BURNED!
BUT I KNOW THIS FOR CERTAIN--
--I DIDN'T COME BACK FROM THE DEAD TO BE ROASTED BY DRAGON SPITTLE!
CRRRNNK
HERE!
RRRR
HERE'S AT LEAST ONE ANCIENT ASGARDIAN WHO WILL PROVE USEFUL!
HHT!

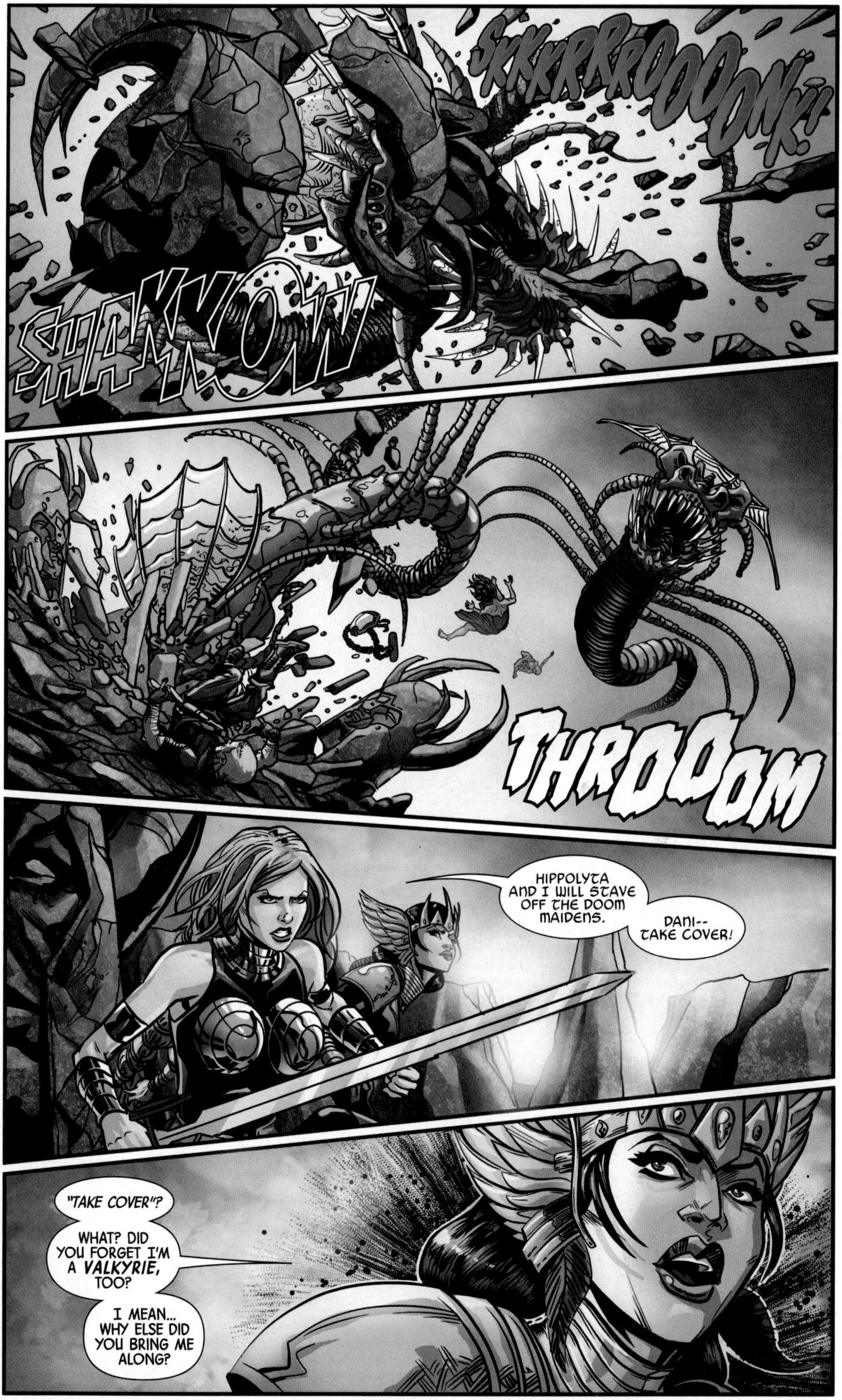

SKKKRRROOOOONK!!
SHAKNOW
THROOOM
HIPPOLYTA AND I WILL STAVE OFF THE DOOM MAIDENS.
DANI-- TAKE COVER!
"TAKE COVER"?
WHAT? DID YOU FORGET I'M A VALKYRIE, TOO?
I MEAN... WHY ELSE DID YOU BRING ME ALONG?

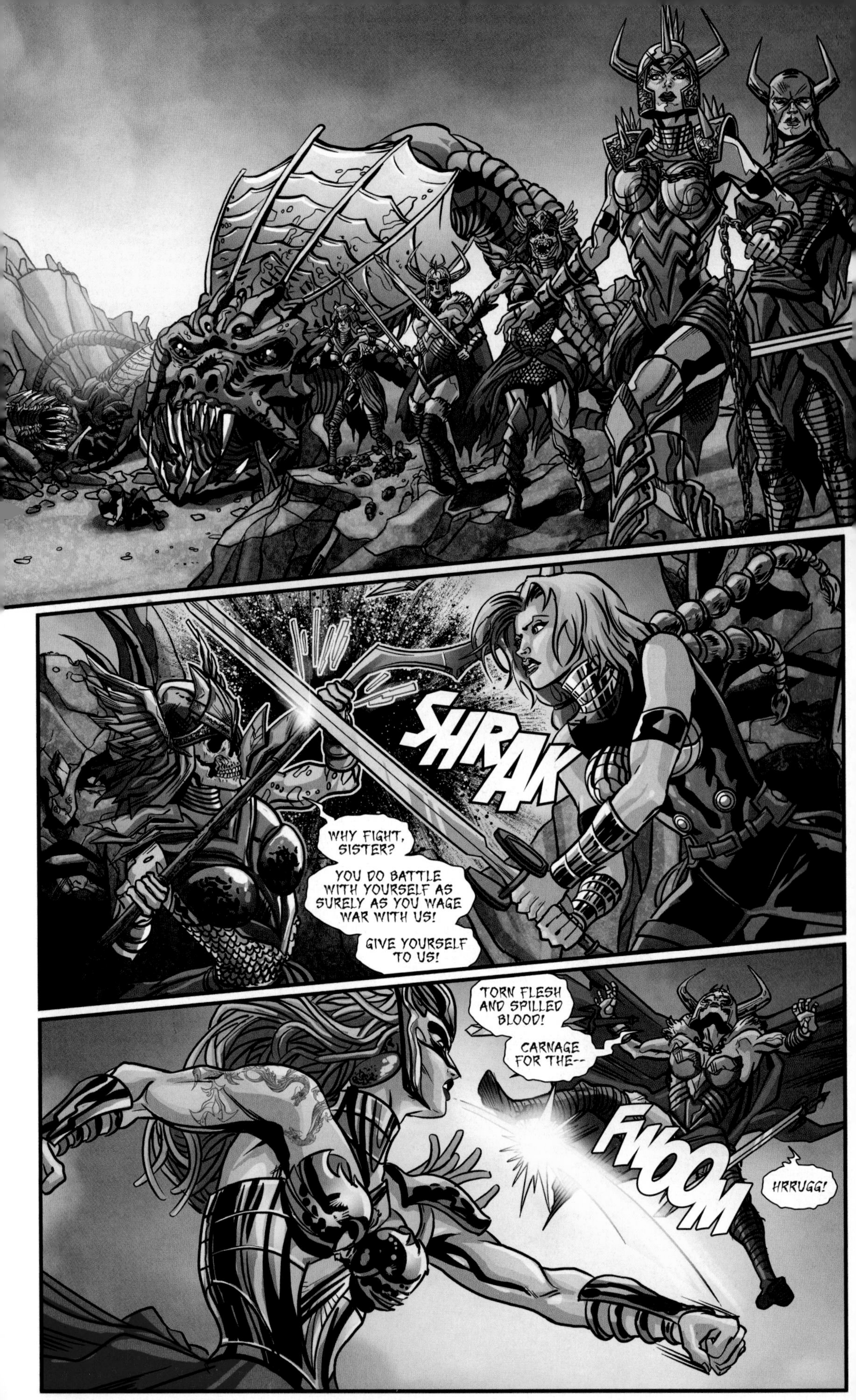
SHRAK
WHY FIGHT, SISTER?
YOU DO BATTLE WITH YOURSELF AS SURELY AS YOU WAGE WAR WITH US!
GIVE YOURSELF TO US!
TORN FLESH AND SPILLED BLOOD!
CARNAGE FOR THE--
FWOOM
HRRUGG!

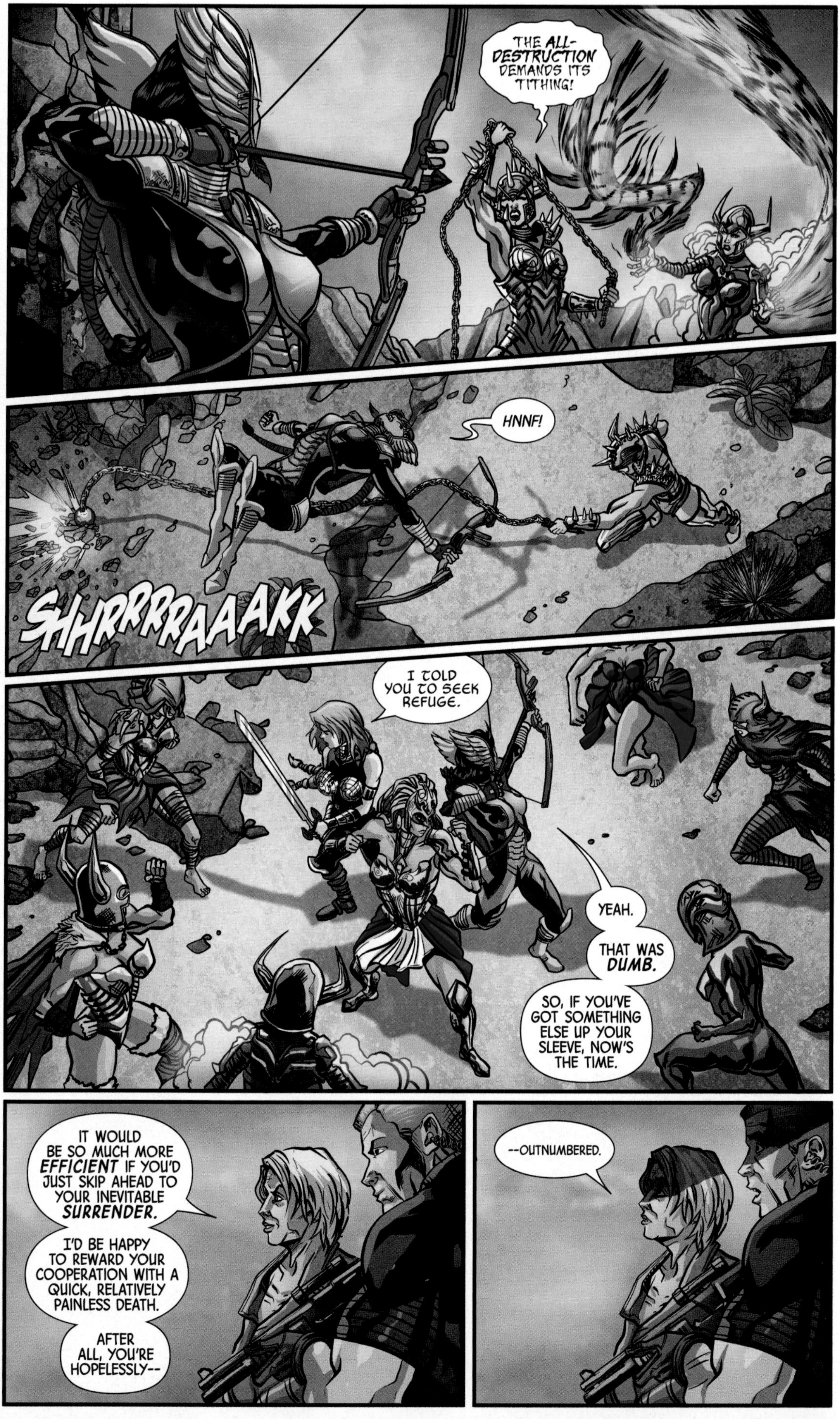
THE ALL-DESTRUCTION DEMANDS ITS TITHING!
HNNF!
SHHRRRRAAAKK
I TOLD YOU TO SEEK REFUGE.
YEAH.
THAT WAS DUMB.
SO, IF YOU'VE GOT SOMETHING ELSE UP YOUR SLEEVE, NOW'S THE TIME.
IT WOULD BE SO MUCH MORE EFFICIENT IF YOU'D JUST SKIP AHEAD TO YOUR INEVITABLE SURRENDER.
I'D BE HAPPY TO REWARD YOUR COOPERATION WITH A QUICK, RELATIVELY PAINLESS DEATH.
AFTER ALL, YOU'RE HOPELESSLY--
--OUTNUMBERED.

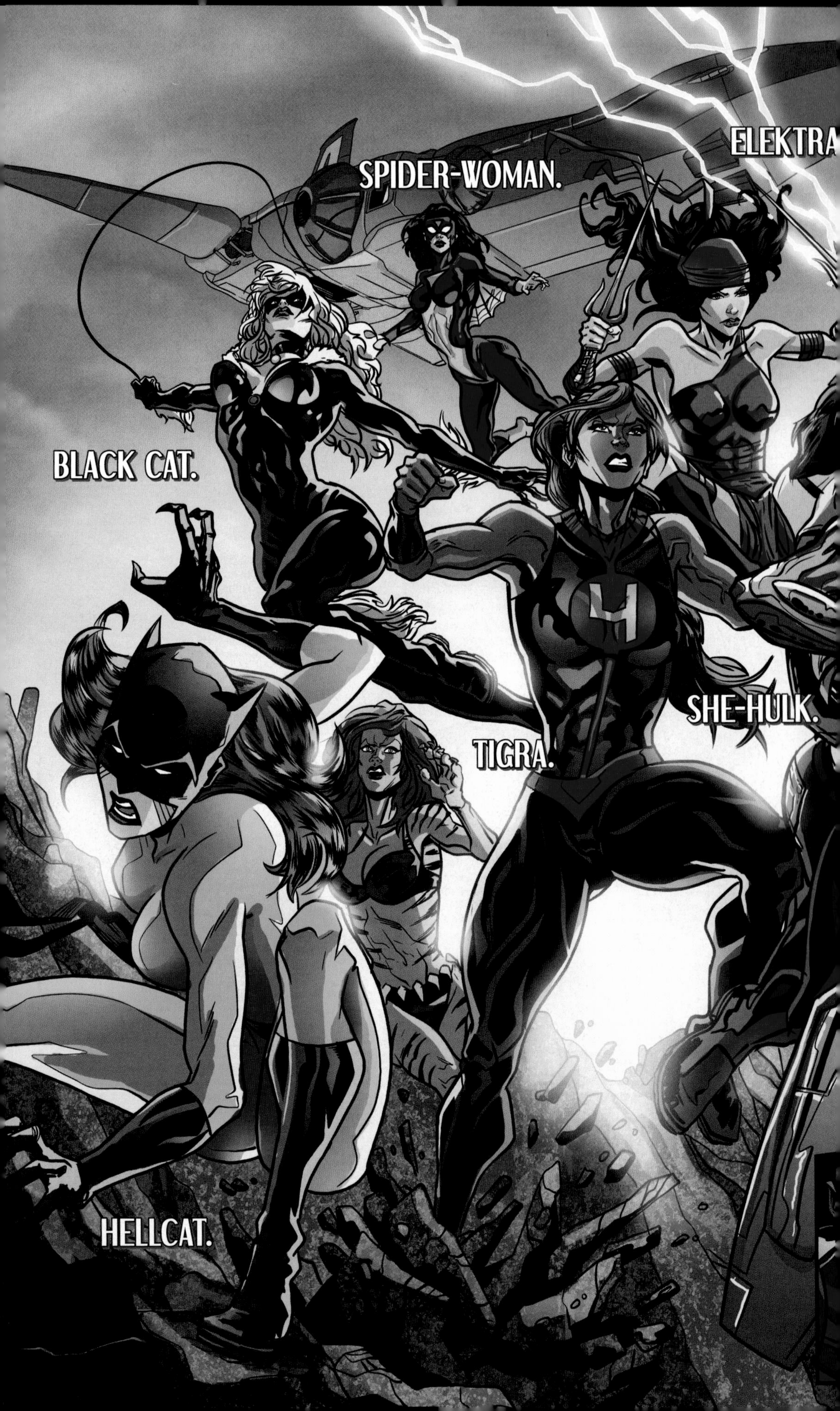

SPIDER-WOMAN.
ELEKTRA
BLACK CAT.
SHE-HULK.
TIGRA.
HELLCAT.

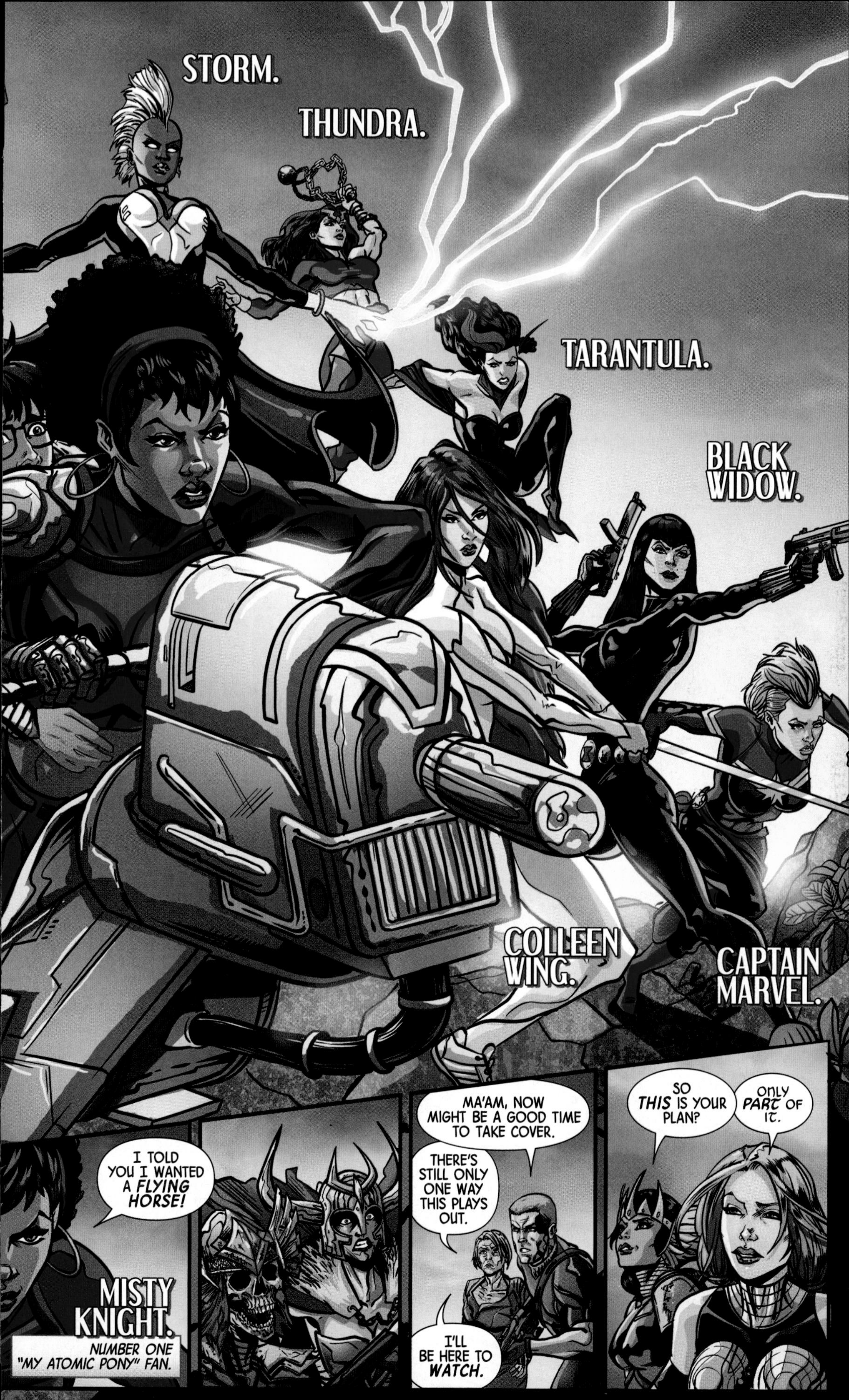
STORM.
THUNDRA.
TARANTULA.
BLACK WIDOW.
COLLEEN WING.
CAPTAIN MARVEL.
I TOLD YOU I WANTED A *FLYING HORSE!*
MISTY KNIGHT.
NUMBER ONE "MY ATOMIC PONY" FAN.
MA'AM, NOW MIGHT BE A GOOD TIME TO TAKE COVER.
THERE'S STILL ONLY ONE WAY THIS PLAYS OUT.
I'LL BE HERE TO *WATCH.*
SO *THIS* IS YOUR PLAN?
ONLY *PART* OF IT.

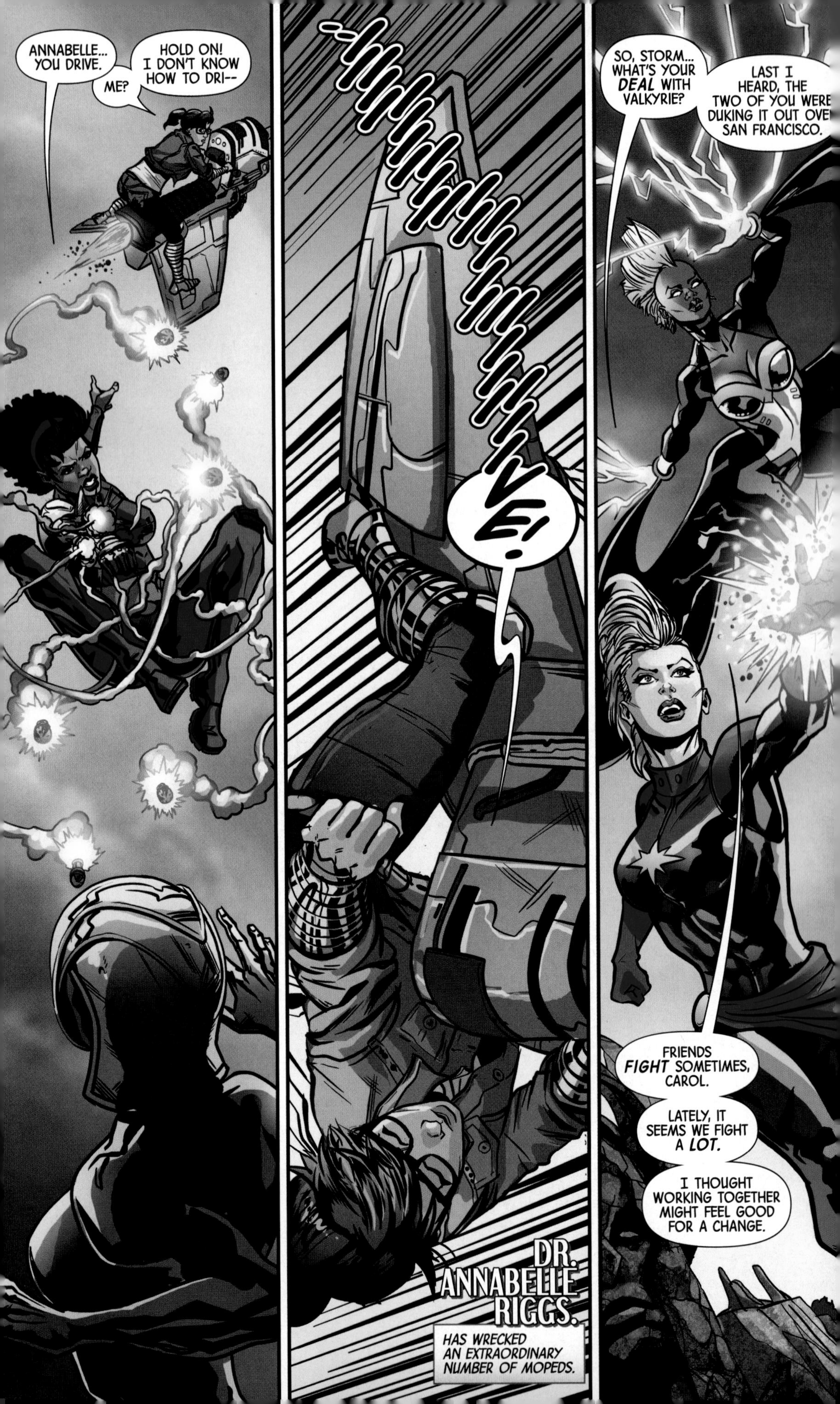
ANNABELLE... YOU DRIVE.
ME?
HOLD ON! I DON'T KNOW HOW TO DRI--
--WHHHHHHHHHHHHHHHHHHHHHHHHHHHHHVE!
SO, STORM... WHAT'S YOUR DEAL WITH VALKYRIE?
LAST I HEARD, THE TWO OF YOU WERE DUKING IT OUT OVER SAN FRANCISCO.
FRIENDS FIGHT SOMETIMES, CAROL.
LATELY, IT SEEMS WE FIGHT A LOT.
I THOUGHT WORKING TOGETHER MIGHT FEEL GOOD FOR A CHANGE.
DR. ANNABELLE RIGGS.
HAS WRECKED AN EXTRAORDINARY NUMBER OF MOPEDS.

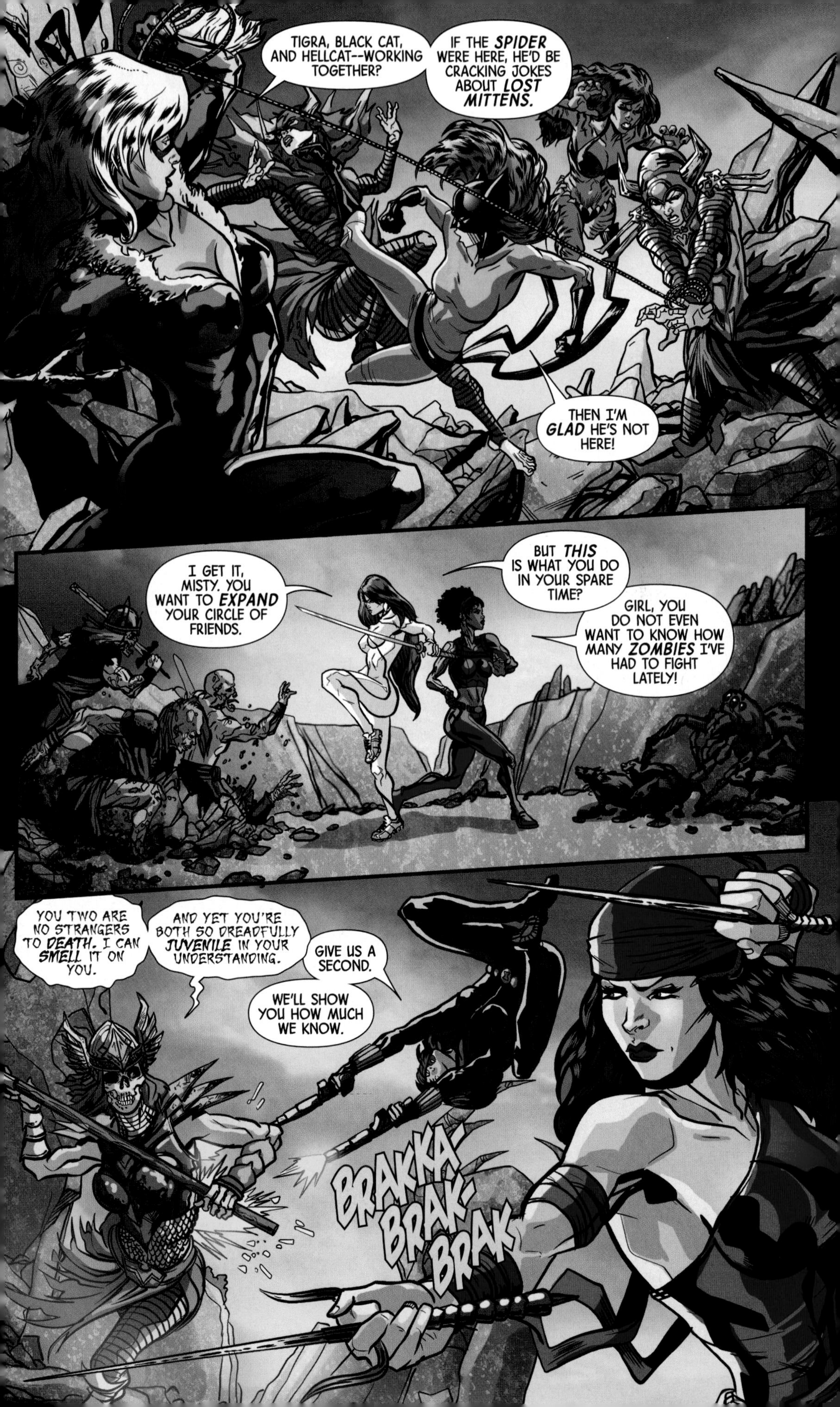
TIGRA, BLACK CAT, AND HELLCAT--WORKING TOGETHER?
IF THE SPIDER WERE HERE, HE'D BE CRACKING JOKES ABOUT LOST MITTENS.
THEN I'M GLAD HE'S NOT HERE!
I GET IT, MISTY. YOU WANT TO EXPAND YOUR CIRCLE OF FRIENDS.
BUT THIS IS WHAT YOU DO IN YOUR SPARE TIME?
GIRL, YOU DO NOT EVEN WANT TO KNOW HOW MANY ZOMBIES I'VE HAD TO FIGHT LATELY!
YOU TWO ARE NO STRANGERS TO DEATH. I CAN SMELL IT ON YOU.
AND YET YOU'RE BOTH SO DREADFULLY JUVENILE IN YOUR UNDERSTANDING.
GIVE US A SECOND.
WE'LL SHOW YOU HOW MUCH WE KNOW.
BRAKKA-BRAK-BRAK

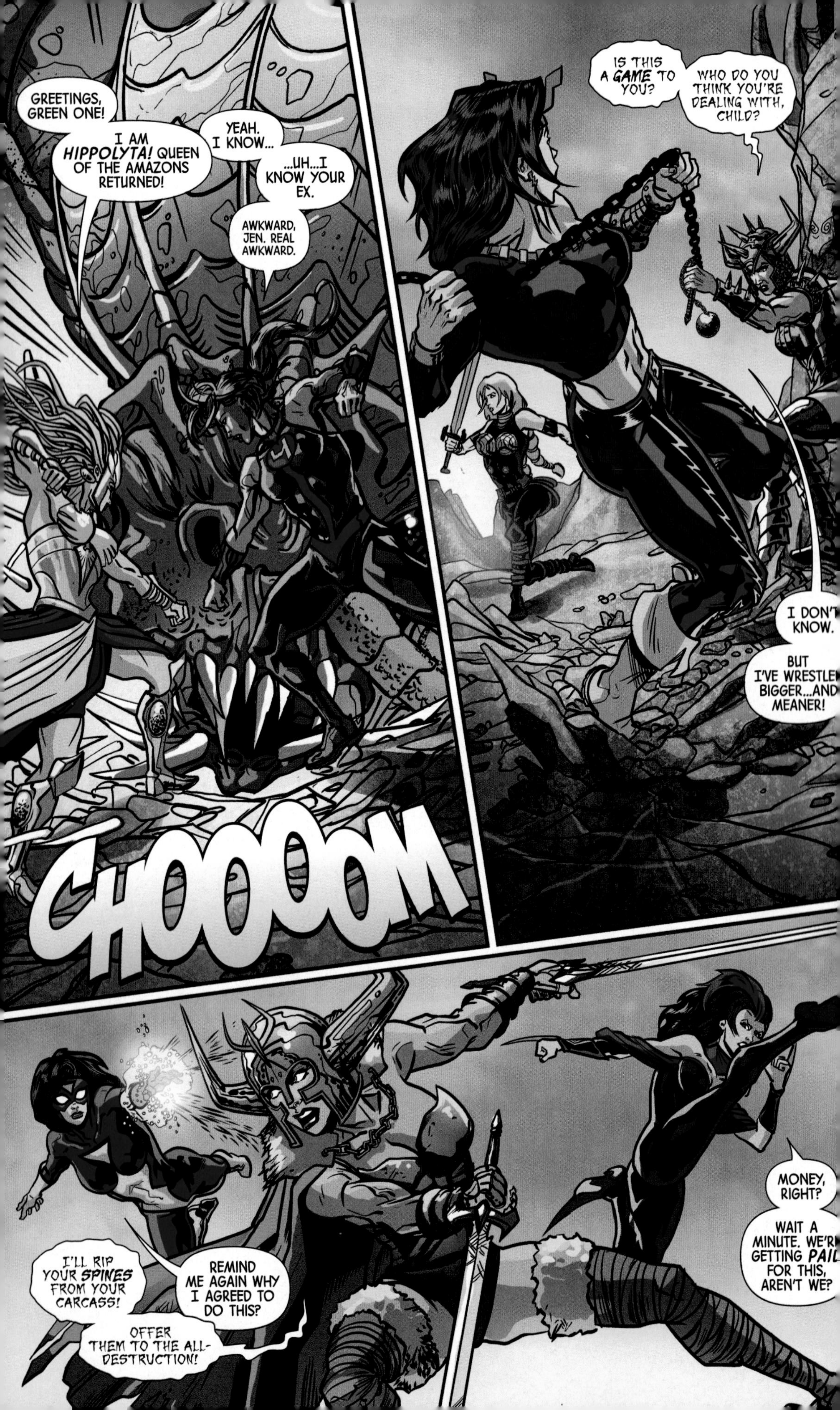
GREETINGS, GREEN ONE!
I AM HIPPOLYTA! QUEEN OF THE AMAZONS RETURNED!
YEAH. I KNOW...
...UH...I KNOW YOUR EX.
AWKWARD, JEN. REAL AWKWARD.
CHOOOOM
IS THIS A GAME TO YOU?
WHO DO YOU THINK YOU'RE DEALING WITH, CHILD?
I DON'T KNOW.
BUT I'VE WRESTLE BIGGER...AND MEANER!
I'LL RIP YOUR SPINES FROM YOUR CARCASS!
OFFER THEM TO THE ALL-DESTRUCTION!
REMIND ME AGAIN WHY I AGREED TO DO THIS?
MONEY, RIGHT?
WAIT A MINUTE. WE'R GETTING PAI FOR THIS, AREN'T WE?

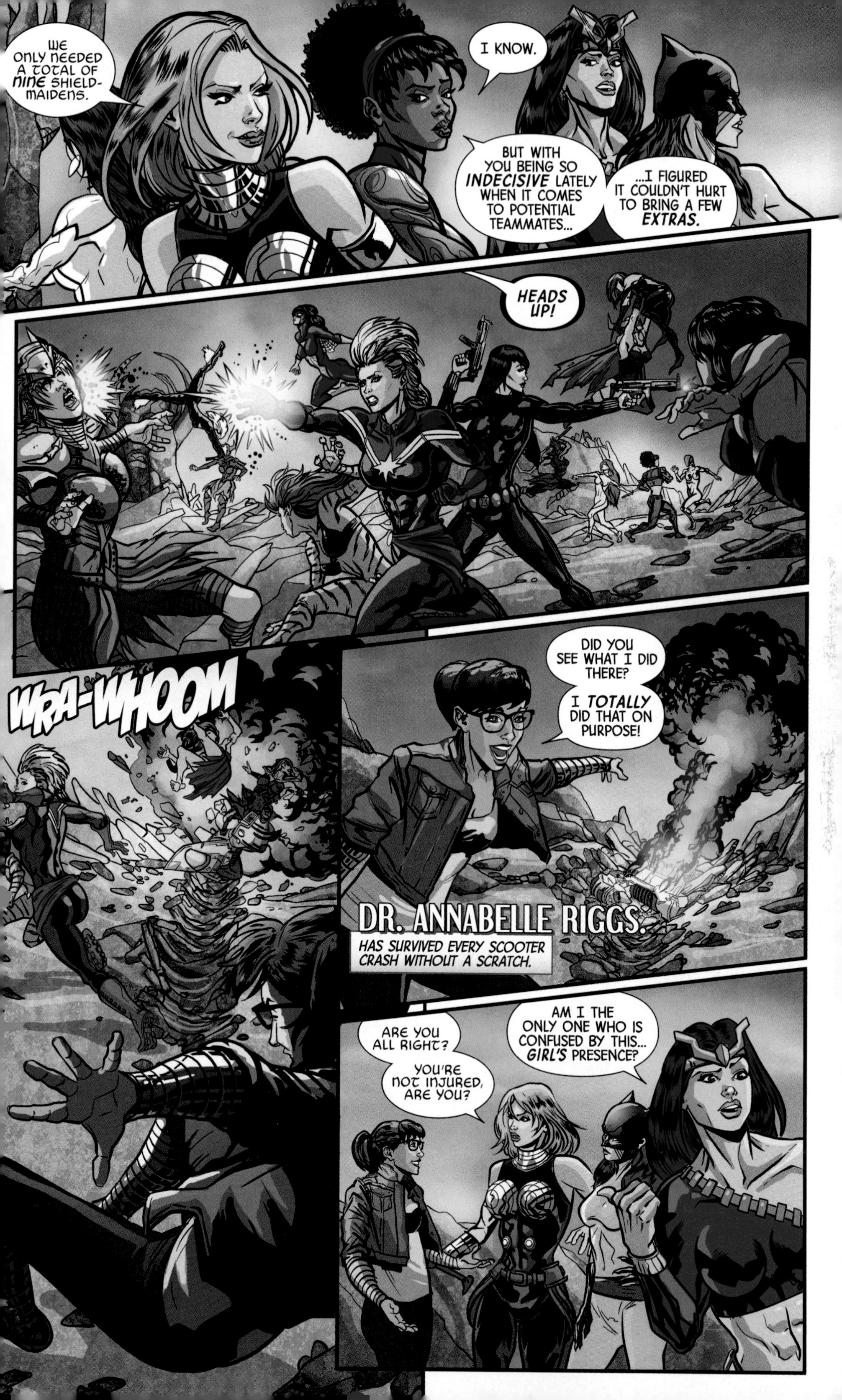

WE ONLY NEEDED A TOTAL OF NINE SHIELD-MAIDENS.
I KNOW.
BUT WITH YOU BEING SO INDECISIVE LATELY WHEN IT COMES TO POTENTIAL TEAMMATES...
...I FIGURED IT COULDN'T HURT TO BRING A FEW EXTRAS.
HEADS UP!
WRA-WHOOM
DID YOU SEE WHAT I DID THERE?
I TOTALLY DID THAT ON PURPOSE!
DR. ANNABELLE RIGGS.
HAS SURVIVED EVERY SCOOTER CRASH WITHOUT A SCRATCH.
ARE YOU ALL RIGHT?
YOU'RE NOT INJURED, ARE YOU?
AM I THE ONLY ONE WHO IS CONFUSED BY THIS... GIRL'S PRESENCE?

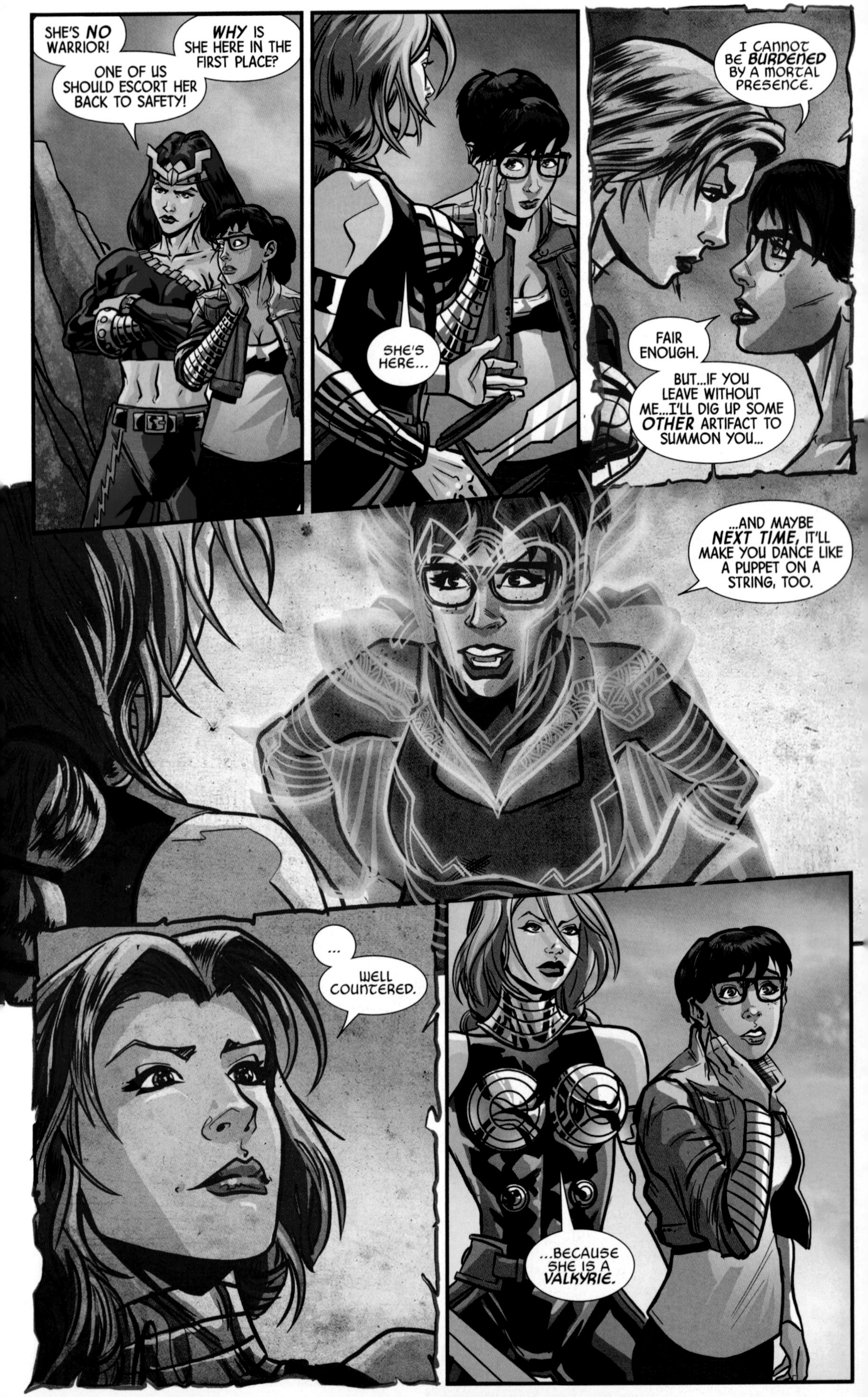
SHE'S NO WARRIOR!
WHY IS SHE HERE IN THE FIRST PLACE?
ONE OF US SHOULD ESCORT HER BACK TO SAFETY!
SHE'S HERE...
I CANNOT BE BURDENED BY A MORTAL PRESENCE.
FAIR ENOUGH.
BUT...IF YOU LEAVE WITHOUT ME...I'LL DIG UP SOME OTHER ARTIFACT TO SUMMON YOU...
...AND MAYBE NEXT TIME, IT'LL MAKE YOU DANCE LIKE A PUPPET ON A STRING, TOO.
...
WELL COUNTERED.
...BECAUSE SHE IS A VALKYRIE.

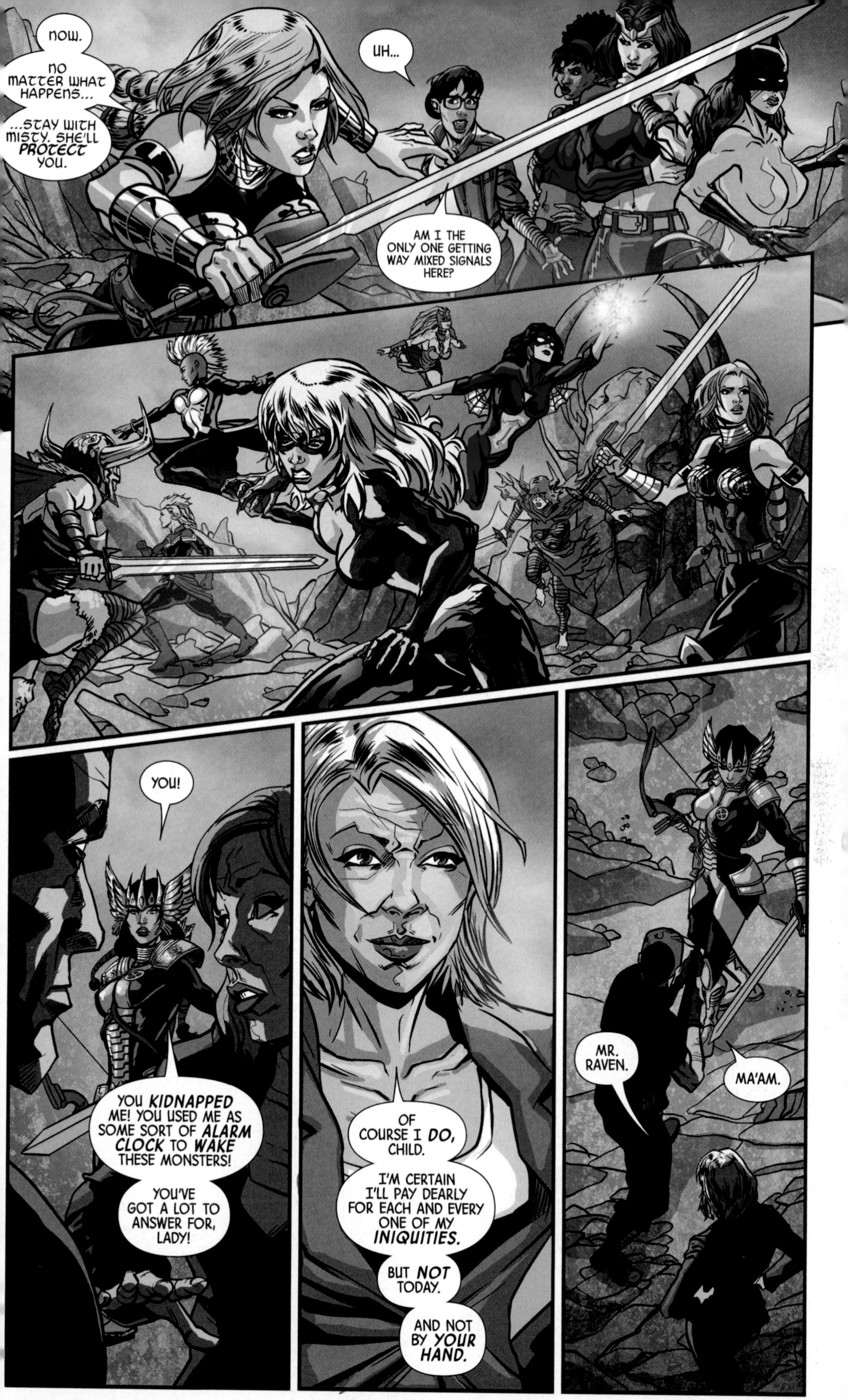

NOW.
NO MATTER WHAT HAPPENS...
...STAY WITH MISTY. SHE'LL PROTECT YOU.
UH...
AM I THE ONLY ONE GETTING WAY MIXED SIGNALS HERE?
YOU!
YOU KIDNAPPED ME! YOU USED ME AS SOME SORT OF ALARM CLOCK TO WAKE THESE MONSTERS!
YOU'VE GOT A LOT TO ANSWER FOR, LADY!
OF COURSE I DO, CHILD.
I'M CERTAIN I'LL PAY DEARLY FOR EACH AND EVERY ONE OF MY INIQUITIES.
BUT NOT TODAY.
AND NOT BY YOUR HAND.
MR. RAVEN.
MA'AM.

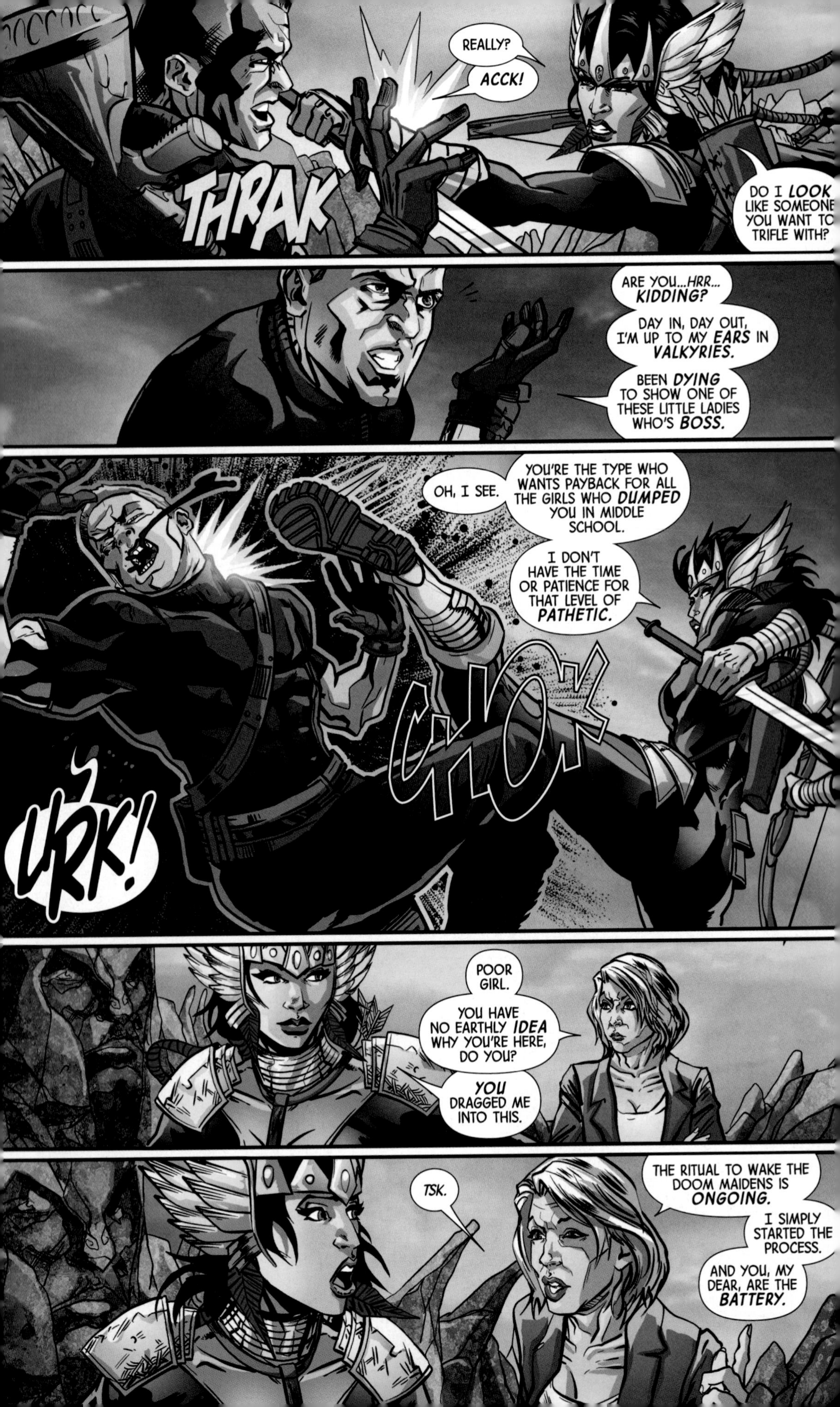
REALLY?
ACCK!
THRAK
DO I LOOK LIKE SOMEONE YOU WANT TO TRIFLE WITH?
ARE YOU...HRR... KIDDING?
DAY IN, DAY OUT, I'M UP TO MY EARS IN VALKYRIES.
BEEN DYING TO SHOW ONE OF THESE LITTLE LADIES WHO'S BOSS.
OH, I SEE.
YOU'RE THE TYPE WHO WANTS PAYBACK FOR ALL THE GIRLS WHO DUMPED YOU IN MIDDLE SCHOOL.
I DON'T HAVE THE TIME OR PATIENCE FOR THAT LEVEL OF PATHETIC.
CHOK
URK!
POOR GIRL.
YOU HAVE NO EARTHLY IDEA WHY YOU'RE HERE, DO YOU?
YOU DRAGGED ME INTO THIS.
TSK.
THE RITUAL TO WAKE THE DOOM MAIDENS IS ONGOING.
I SIMPLY STARTED THE PROCESS.
AND YOU, MY DEAR, ARE THE BATTERY.

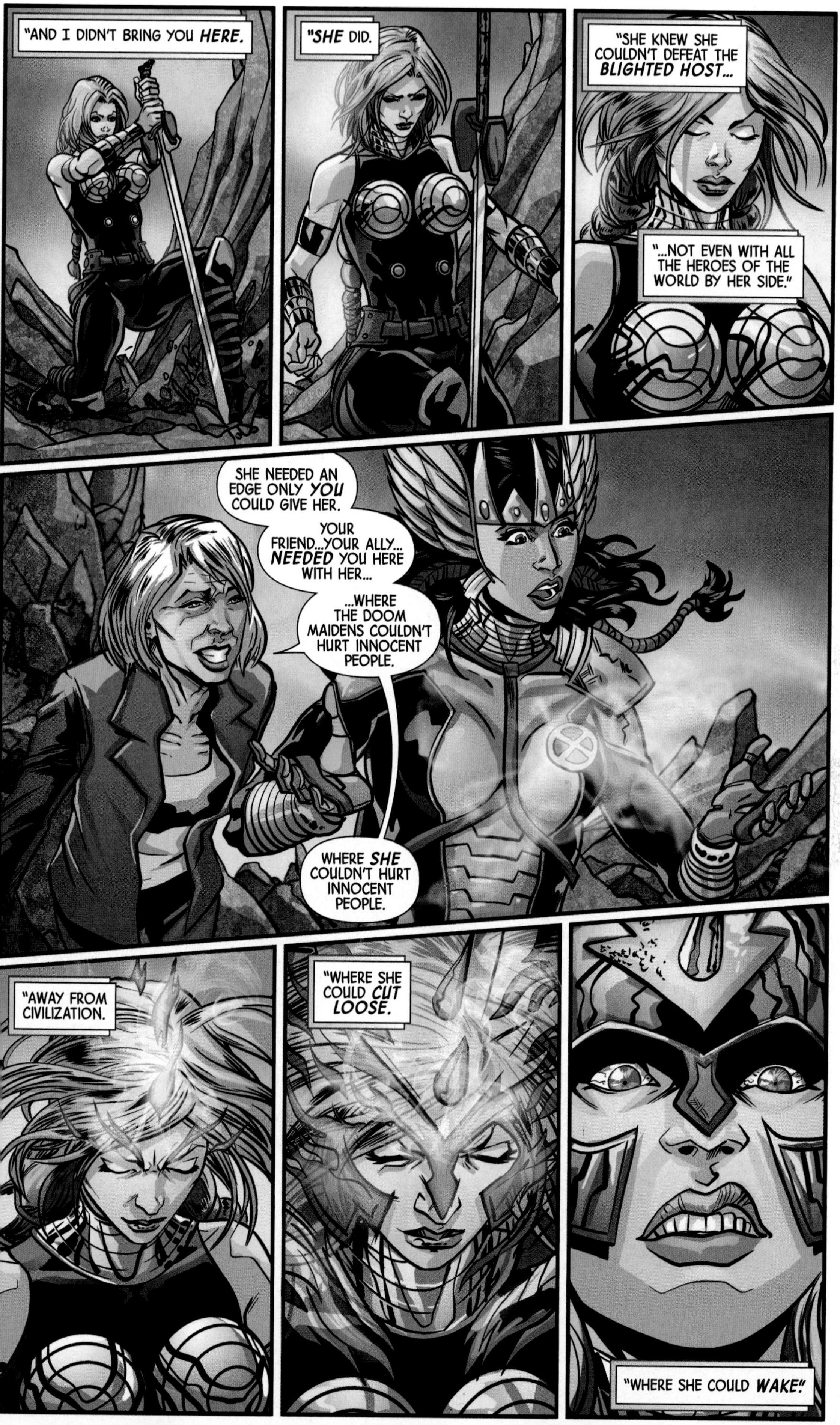
"AND I DIDN'T BRING YOU HERE.
"SHE DID.
"SHE KNEW SHE COULDN'T DEFEAT THE BLIGHTED HOST...
"...NOT EVEN WITH ALL THE HEROES OF THE WORLD BY HER SIDE."
SHE NEEDED AN EDGE ONLY YOU COULD GIVE HER.
YOUR FRIEND...YOUR ALLY... NEEDED YOU HERE WITH HER...
...WHERE THE DOOM MAIDENS COULDN'T HURT INNOCENT PEOPLE.
WHERE SHE COULDN'T HURT INNOCENT PEOPLE.
"AWAY FROM CIVILIZATION.
"WHERE SHE COULD CUT LOOSE.
"WHERE SHE COULD WAKE!"

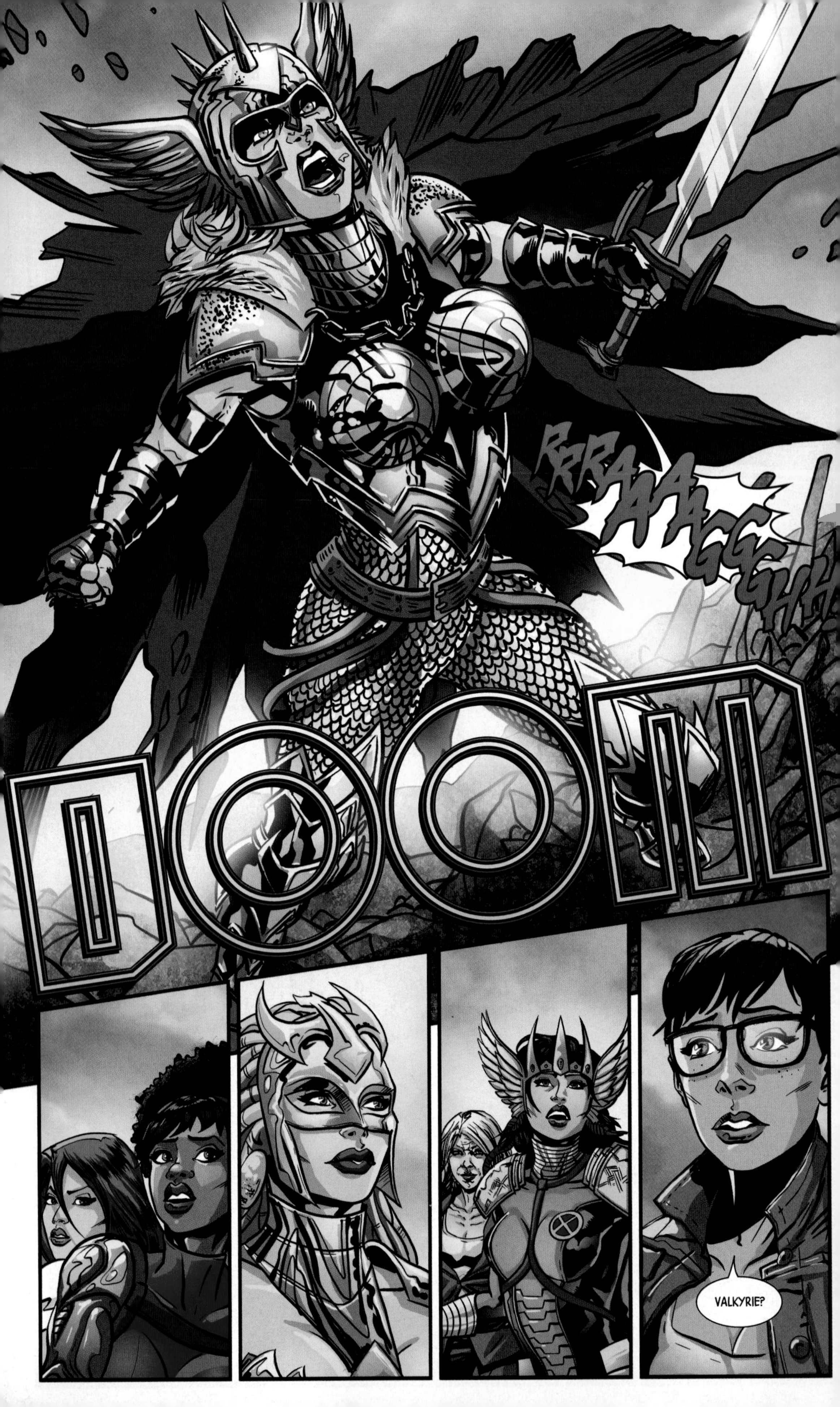
RRRAAAAGGGHH
DOOM
VALKYRIE?

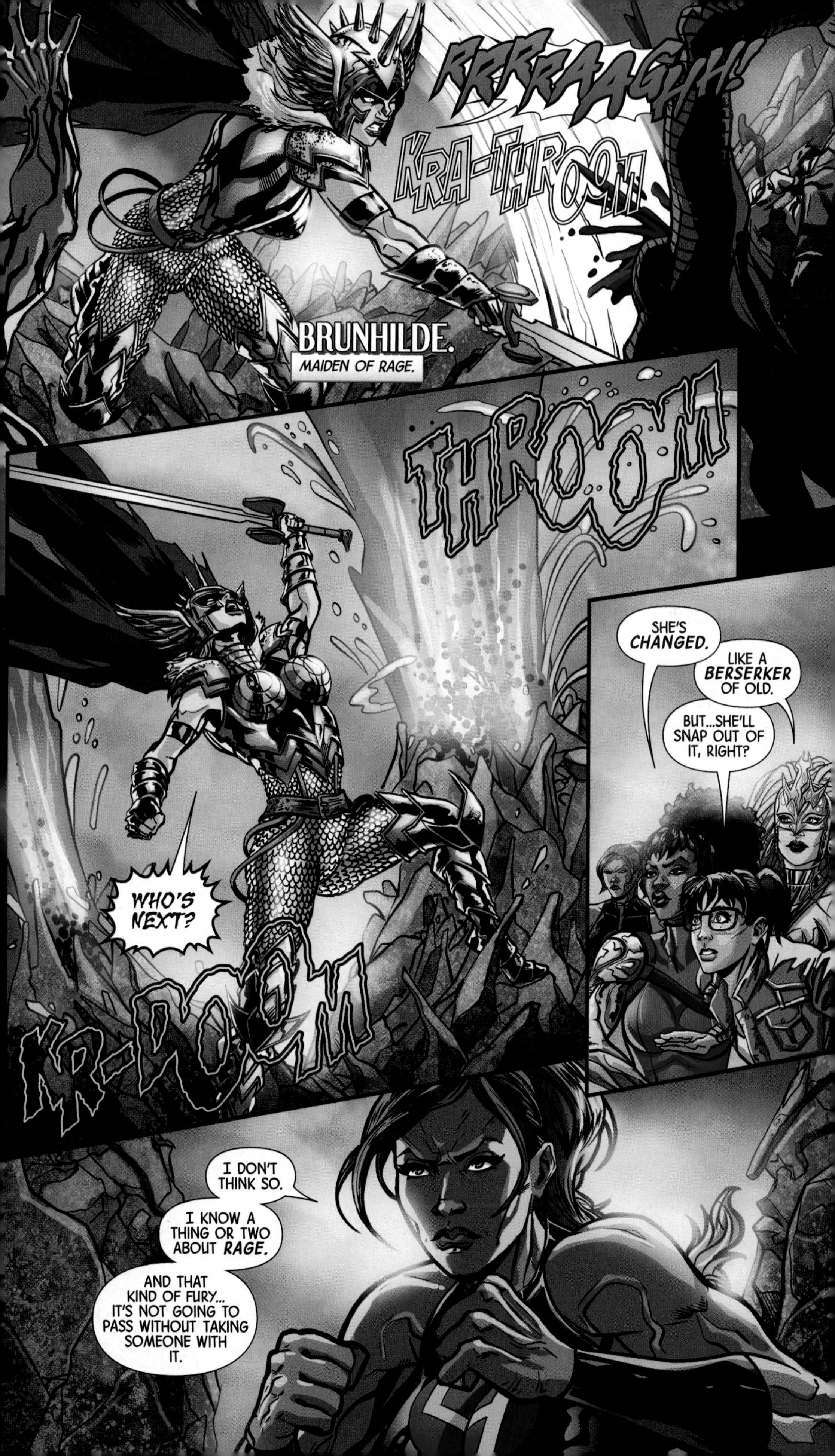
RRRRAAAGHH!
KRA-THROOM
BRUNHILDE.
MAIDEN OF RAGE.
THROOM
WHO'S NEXT?
KR-DOOM
SHE'S CHANGED.
LIKE A BERSERKER OF OLD.
BUT...SHE'LL SNAP OUT OF IT, RIGHT?
I DON'T THINK SO.
I KNOW A THING OR TWO ABOUT RAGE.
AND THAT KIND OF FURY... IT'S NOT GOING TO PASS WITHOUT TAKING SOMEONE WITH IT.

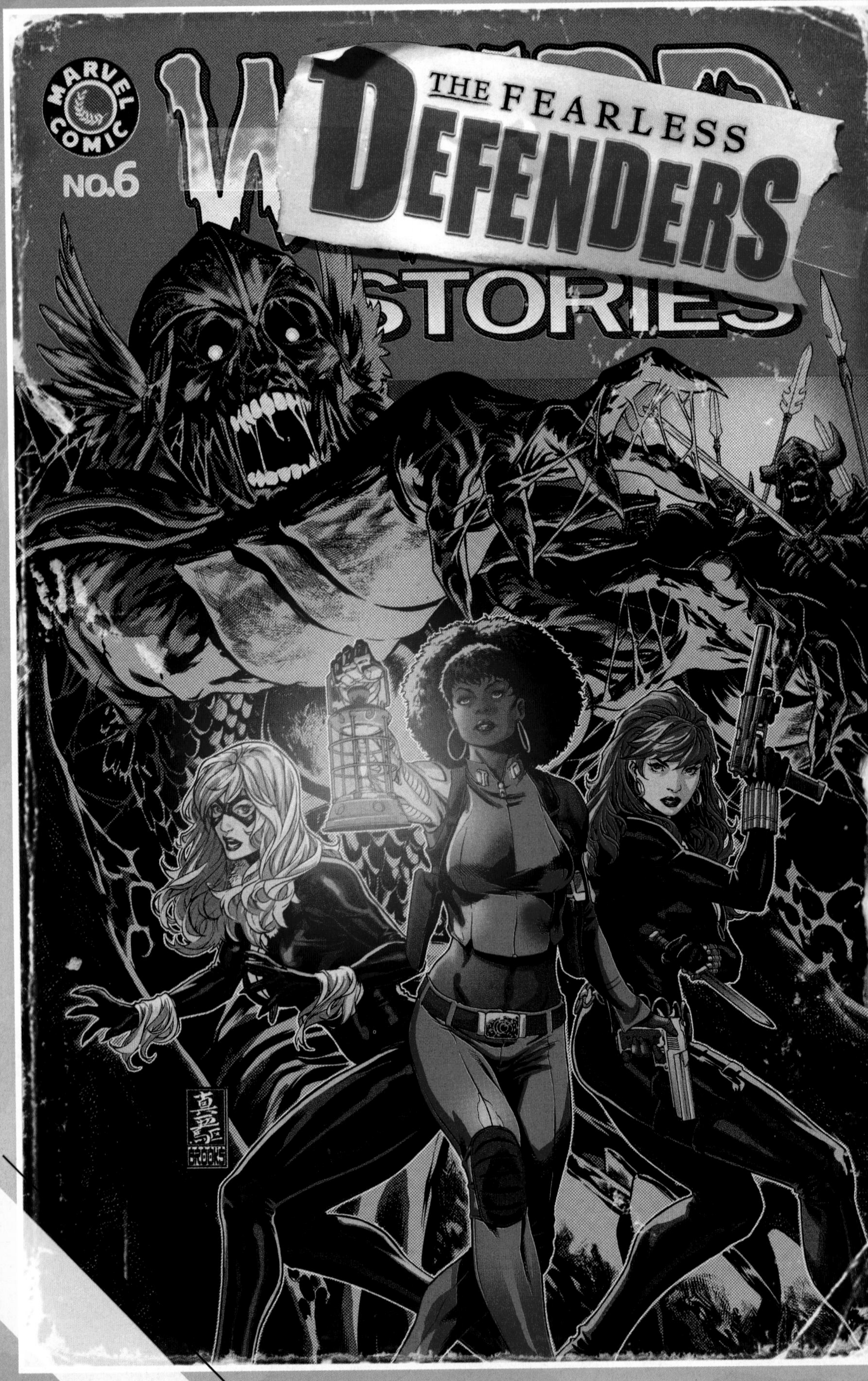
MARVEL COMIC
NO.6
THE FEARLESS
DEFENDERS
STORIES
BROOKS

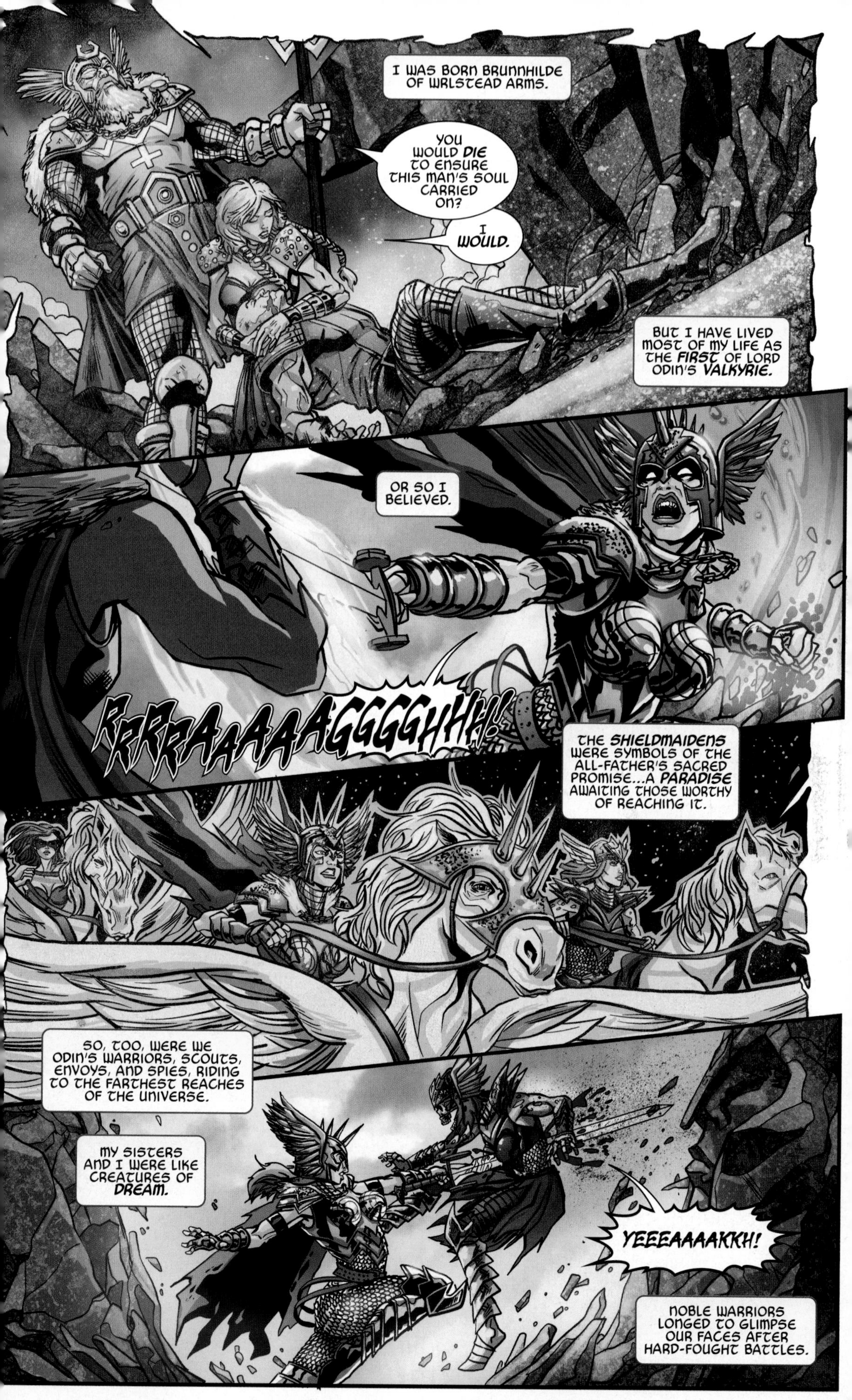
I WAS BORN BRUNNHILDE OF WRLSTEAD ARMS.
YOU WOULD DIE TO ENSURE THIS MAN'S SOUL CARRIED ON?
I WOULD.
BUT I HAVE LIVED MOST OF MY LIFE AS THE FIRST OF LORD ODIN'S VALKYRIE.
OR SO I BELIEVED.
RRRRAAAAAAGGGGHHH!
THE SHIELDMAIDENS WERE SYMBOLS OF THE ALL-FATHER'S SACRED PROMISE...A PARADISE AWAITING THOSE WORTHY OF REACHING IT.
SO, TOO, WERE WE ODIN'S WARRIORS, SCOUTS, ENVOYS, AND SPIES, RIDING TO THE FARTHEST REACHES OF THE UNIVERSE.
MY SISTERS AND I WERE LIKE CREATURES OF DREAM.
YEEEAAAAKKH!
NOBLE WARRIORS LONGED TO GLIMPSE OUR FACES AFTER HARD-FOUGHT BATTLES.

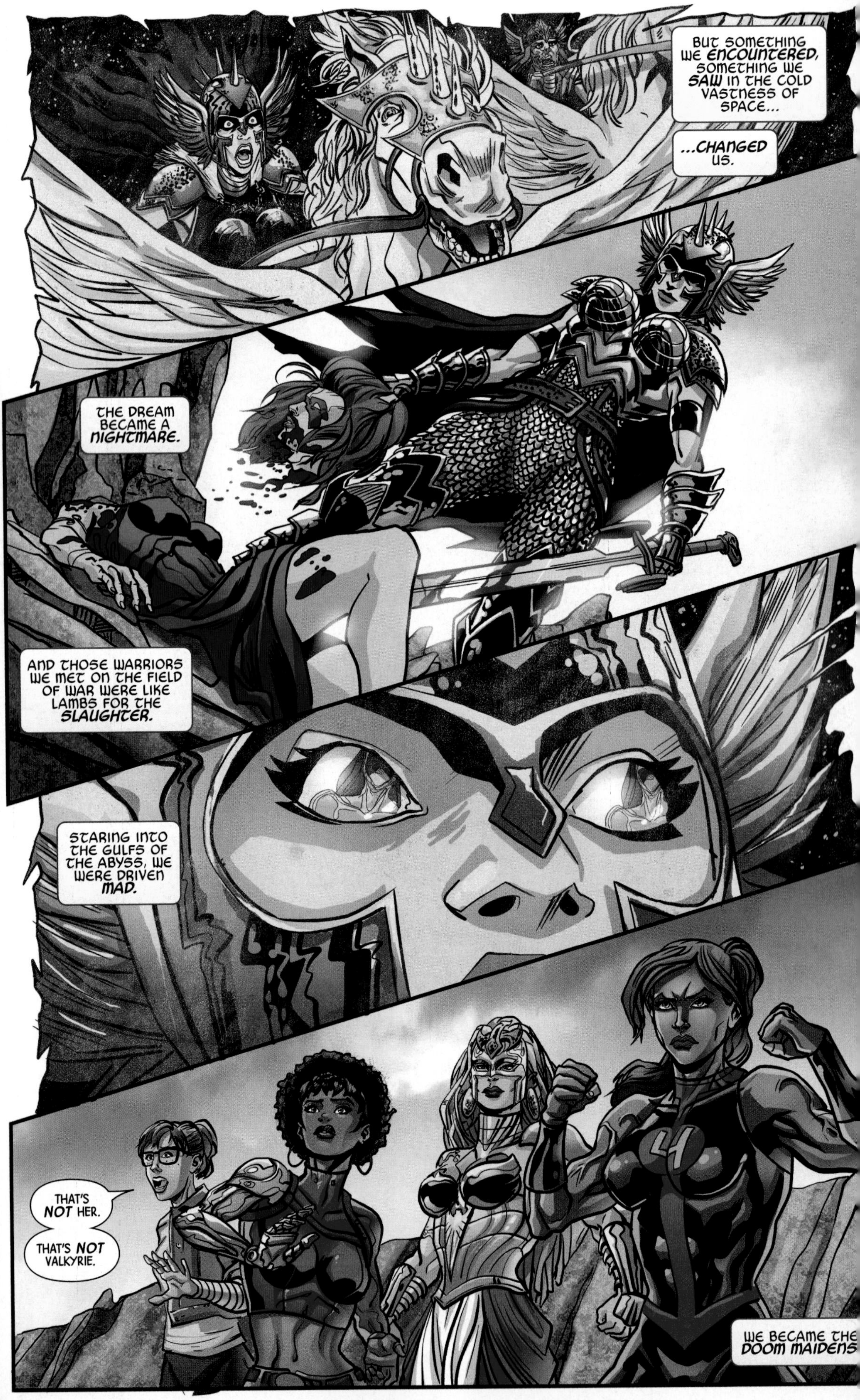

BUT SOMETHING WE ENCOUNTERED, SOMETHING WE SAW IN THE COLD VASTNESS OF SPACE...
...CHANGED US.
THE DREAM BECAME A NIGHTMARE.
AND THOSE WARRIORS WE MET ON THE FIELD OF WAR WERE LIKE LAMBS FOR THE SLAUGHTER.
STARING INTO THE GULFS OF THE ABYSS, WE WERE DRIVEN MAD.
THAT'S NOT HER.
THAT'S NOT VALKYRIE.
WE BECAME THE DOOM MAIDENS

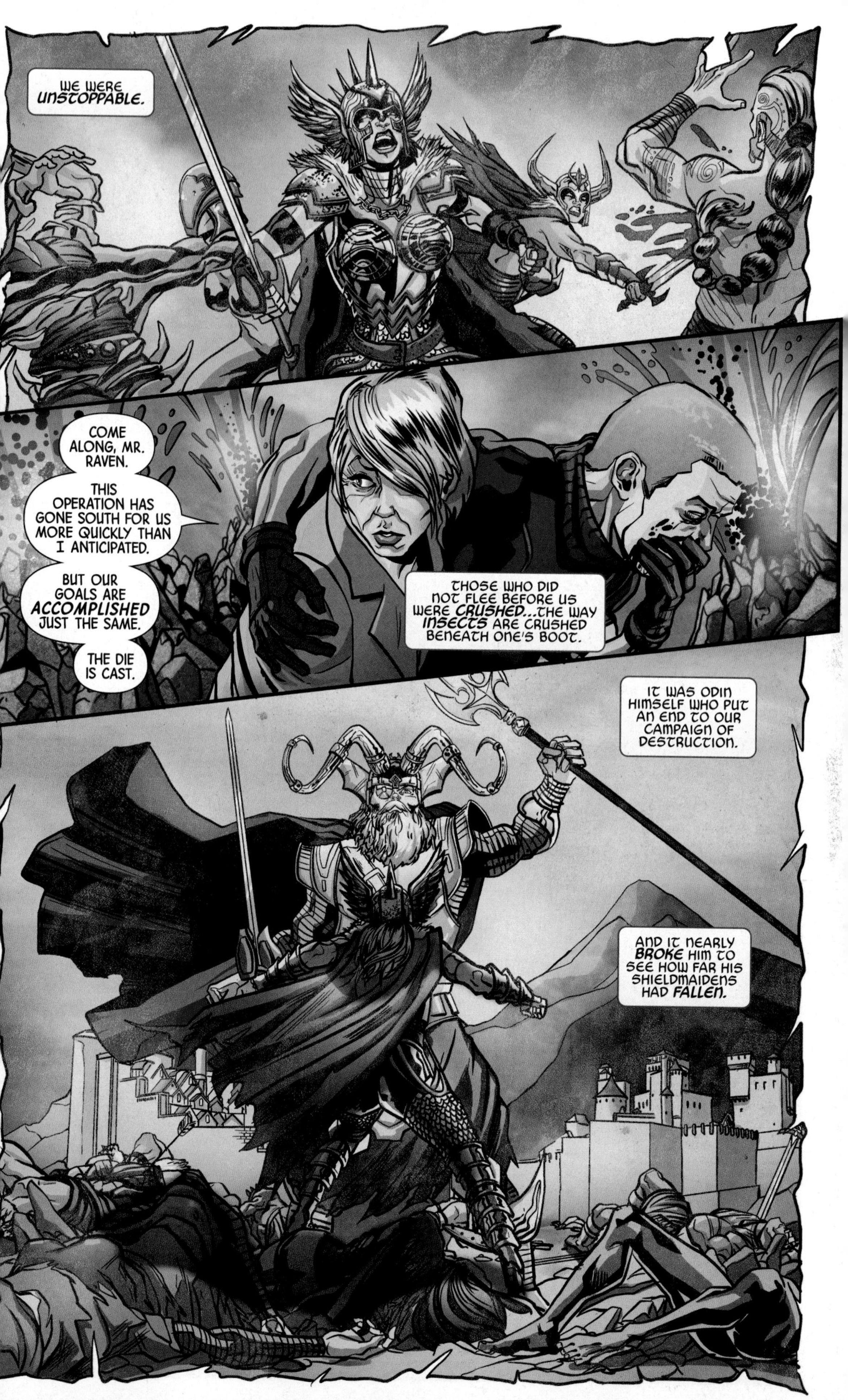

WE WERE UNSTOPPABLE.
COME ALONG, MR. RAVEN.
THIS OPERATION HAS GONE SOUTH FOR US MORE QUICKLY THAN I ANTICIPATED.
BUT OUR GOALS ARE ACCOMPLISHED JUST THE SAME.
THE DIE IS CAST.
THOSE WHO DID NOT FLEE BEFORE US WERE CRUSHED...THE WAY INSECTS ARE CRUSHED BENEATH ONE'S BOOT.
IT WAS ODIN HIMSELF WHO PUT AN END TO OUR CAMPAIGN OF DESTRUCTION.
AND IT NEARLY BROKE HIM TO SEE HOW FAR HIS SHIELDMAIDENS HAD FALLEN.

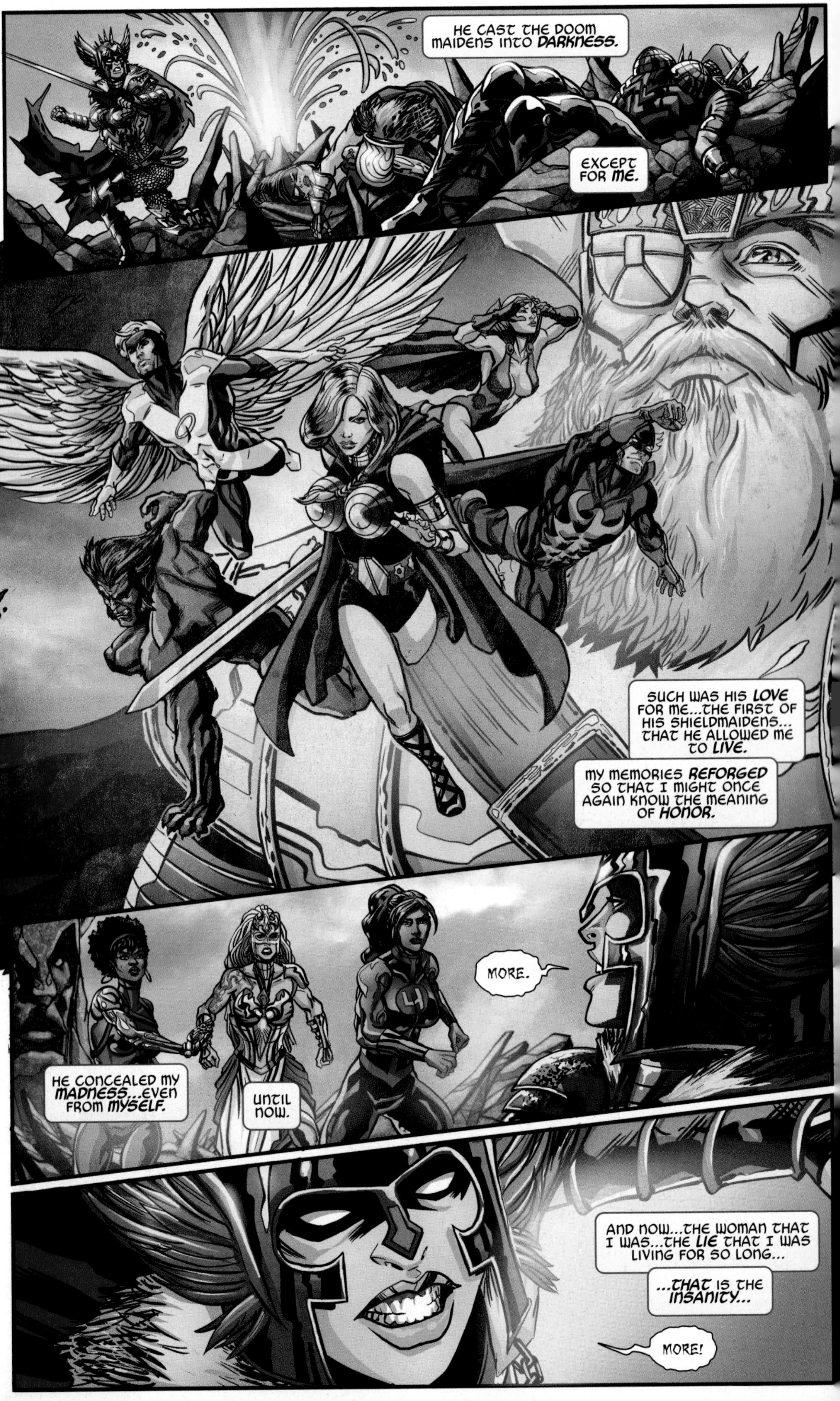
HE CAST THE DOOM MAIDENS INTO DARKNESS.
EXCEPT FOR ME.
SUCH WAS HIS LOVE FOR ME...THE FIRST OF HIS SHIELDMAIDENS... THAT HE ALLOWED ME TO LIVE.
MY MEMORIES REFORGED SO THAT I MIGHT ONCE AGAIN KNOW THE MEANING OF HONOR.
MORE.
HE CONCEALED MY MADNESS...EVEN FROM MYSELF.
UNTIL NOW.
AND NOW...THE WOMAN THAT I WAS...THE LIE THAT I WAS LIVING FOR SO LONG...
...THAT IS THE INSANITY...
MORE!

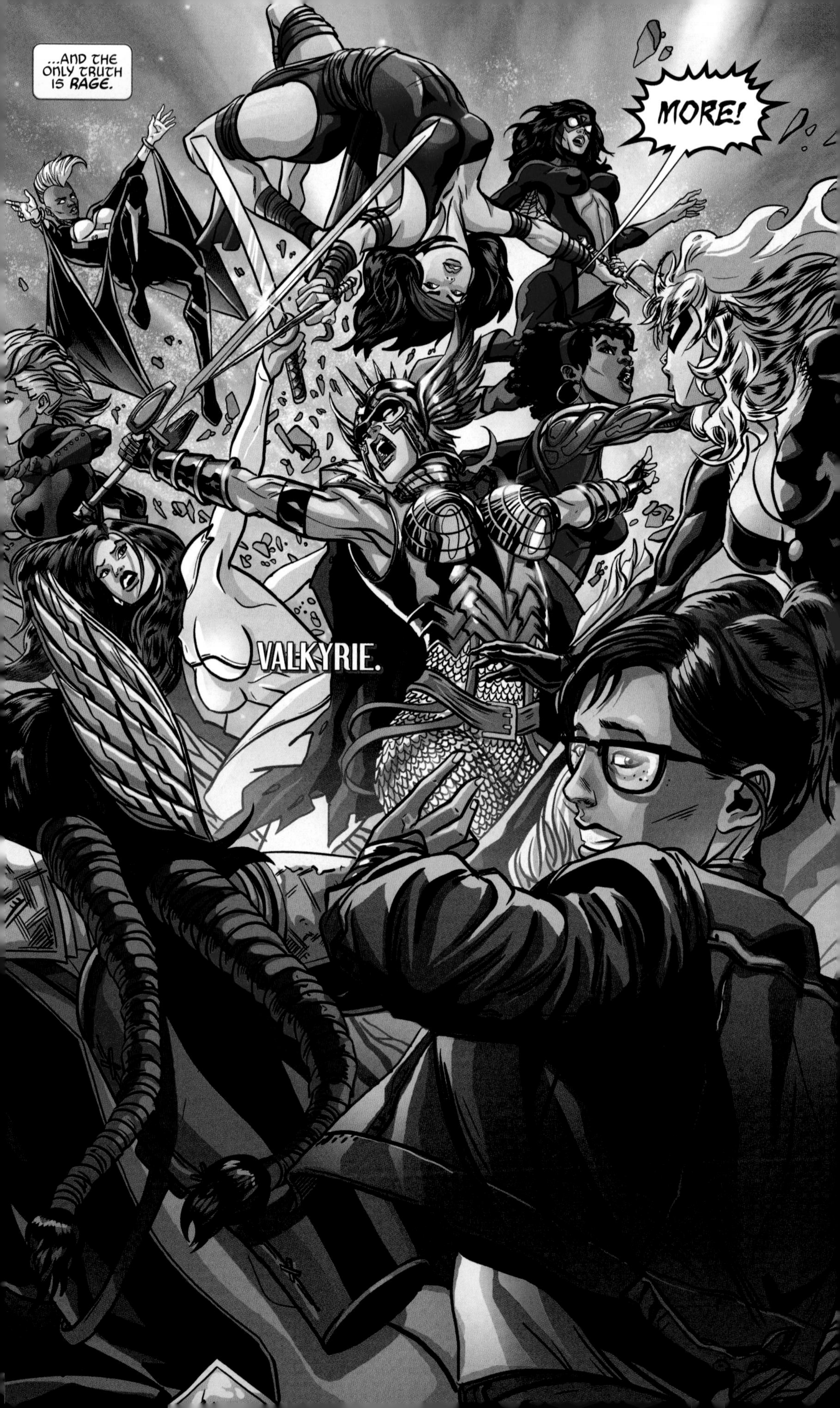
...AND THE ONLY TRUTH IS RAGE.
MORE!
VALKYRIE.

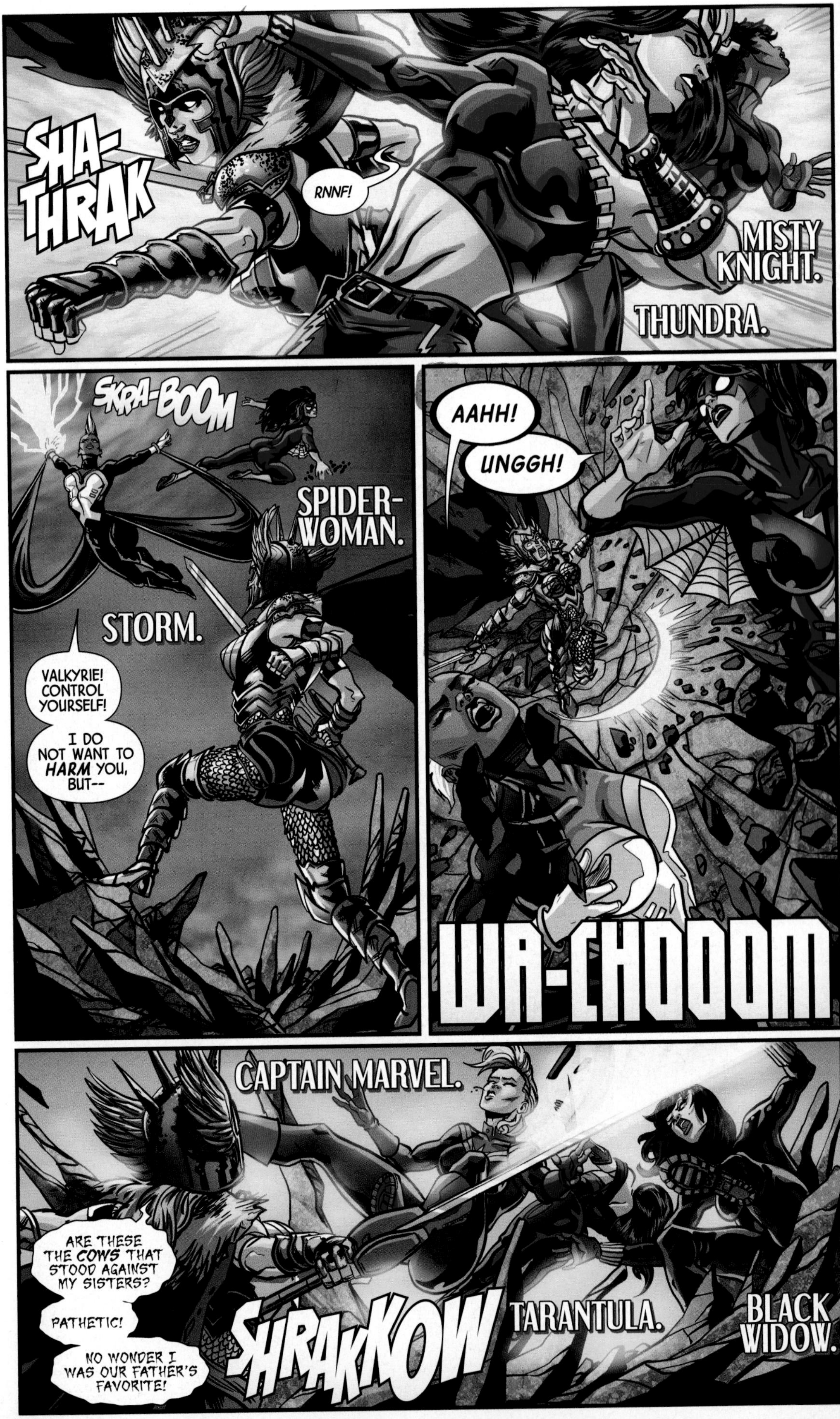
SHA-THRAK
RNNF!
MISTY KNIGHT.
THUNDRA.
SKRA-BOOM
SPIDER-WOMAN.
STORM.
VALKYRIE! CONTROL YOURSELF!
I DO NOT WANT TO HARM YOU, BUT--
AAHH!
UNGGH!
WA-CHOOOM
CAPTAIN MARVEL.
ARE THESE THE COWS THAT STOOD AGAINST MY SISTERS?
PATHETIC!
NO WONDER I WAS OUR FATHER'S FAVORITE!
SHRAKKOW
TARANTULA.
BLACK WIDOW.

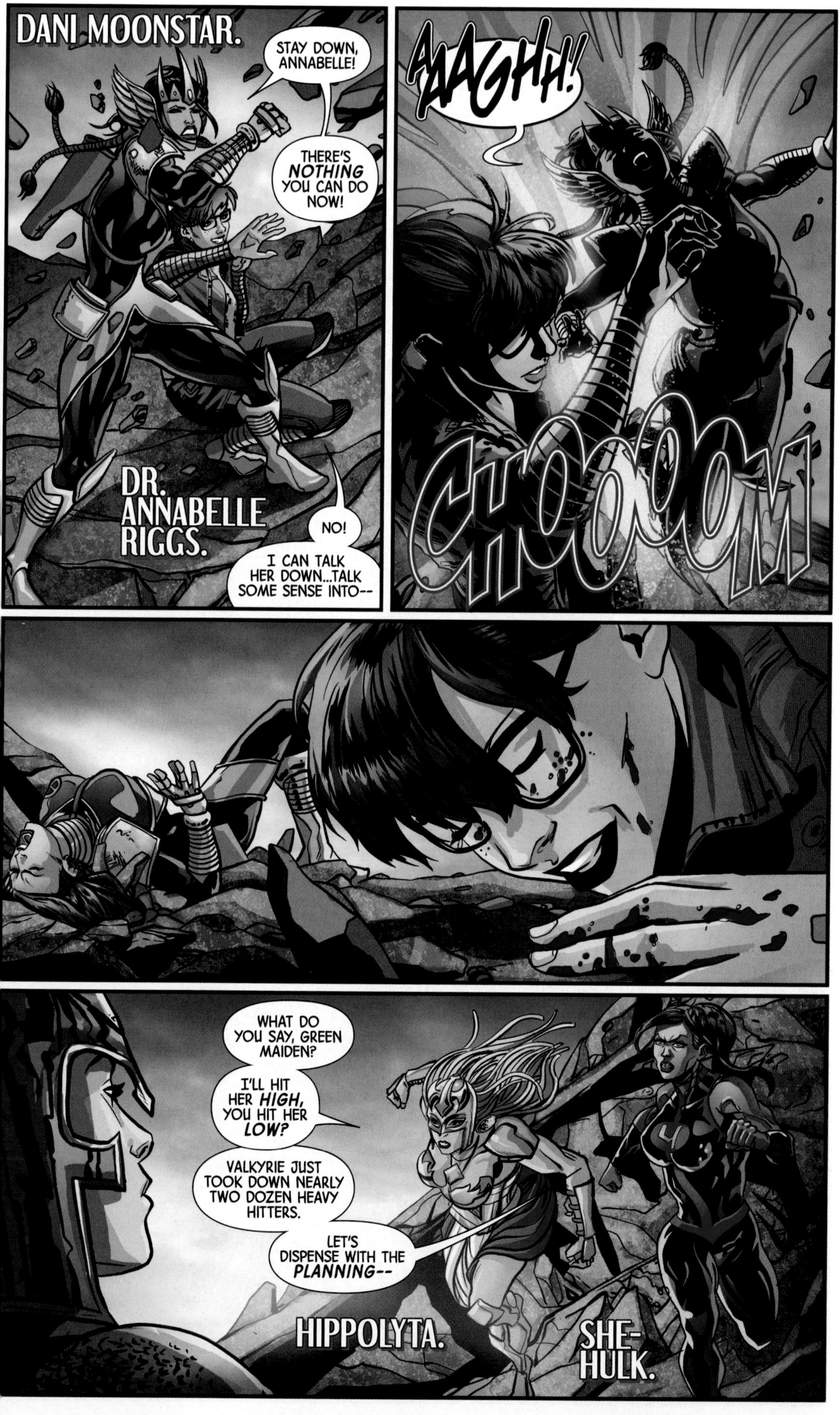
DANI MOONSTAR.
STAY DOWN, ANNABELLE!
THERE'S NOTHING YOU CAN DO NOW!
DR. ANNABELLE RIGGS.
NO!
I CAN TALK HER DOWN...TALK SOME SENSE INTO--
AAAGHH!
CHOOOOOM
WHAT DO YOU SAY, GREEN MAIDEN?
I'LL HIT HER HIGH, YOU HIT HER LOW?
VALKYRIE JUST TOOK DOWN NEARLY TWO DOZEN HEAVY HITTERS.
LET'S DISPENSE WITH THE PLANNING--
HIPPOLYTA.
SHE-HULK.

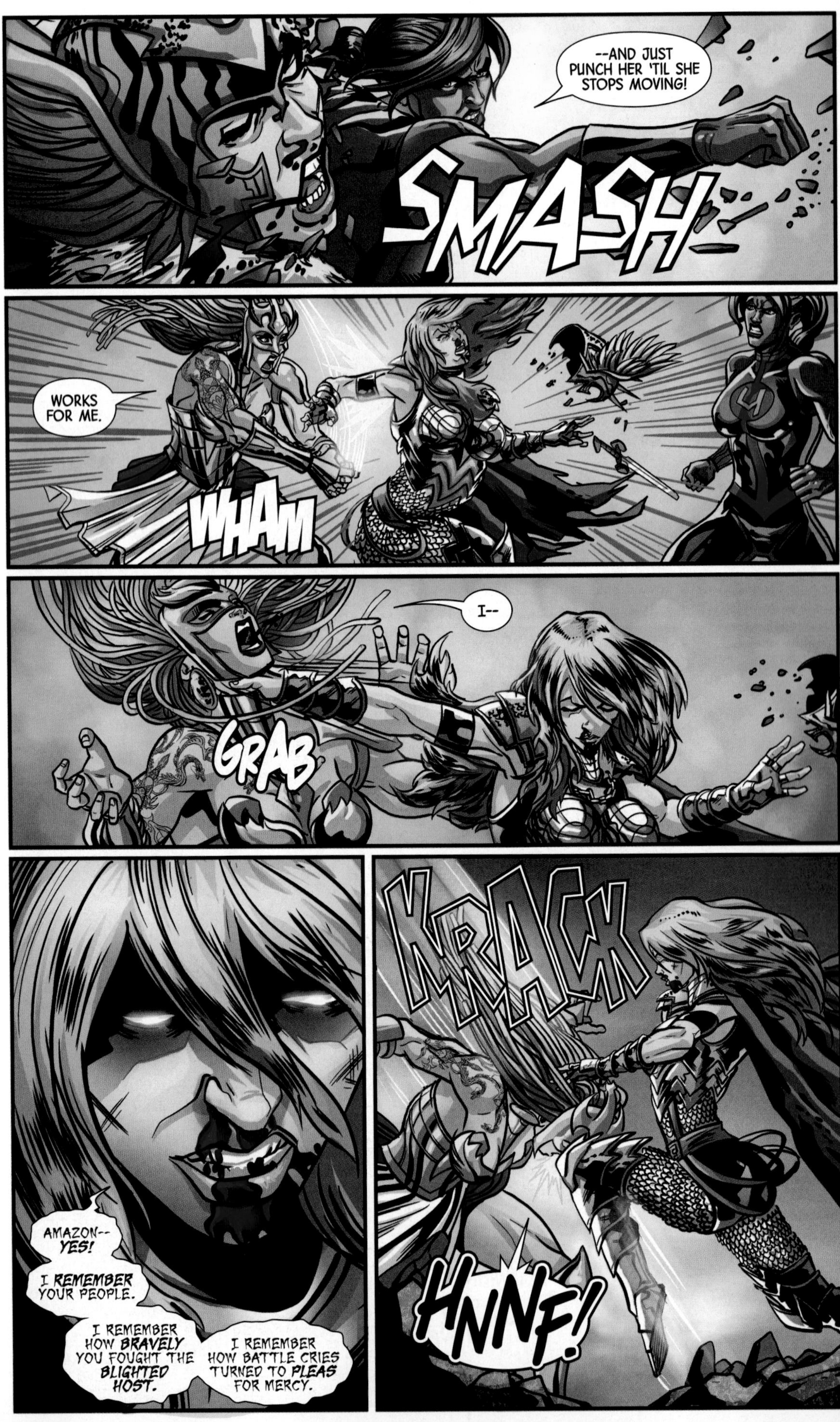
--AND JUST PUNCH HER 'TIL SHE STOPS MOVING!
SMASH
WORKS FOR ME.
WHAM
I--
GRAB
AMAZON-- YES!
I REMEMBER YOUR PEOPLE.
I REMEMBER HOW BRAVELY YOU FOUGHT THE BLIGHTED HOST.
I REMEMBER HOW BATTLE CRIES TURNED TO PLEAS FOR MERCY.
KRACK
HNNF!

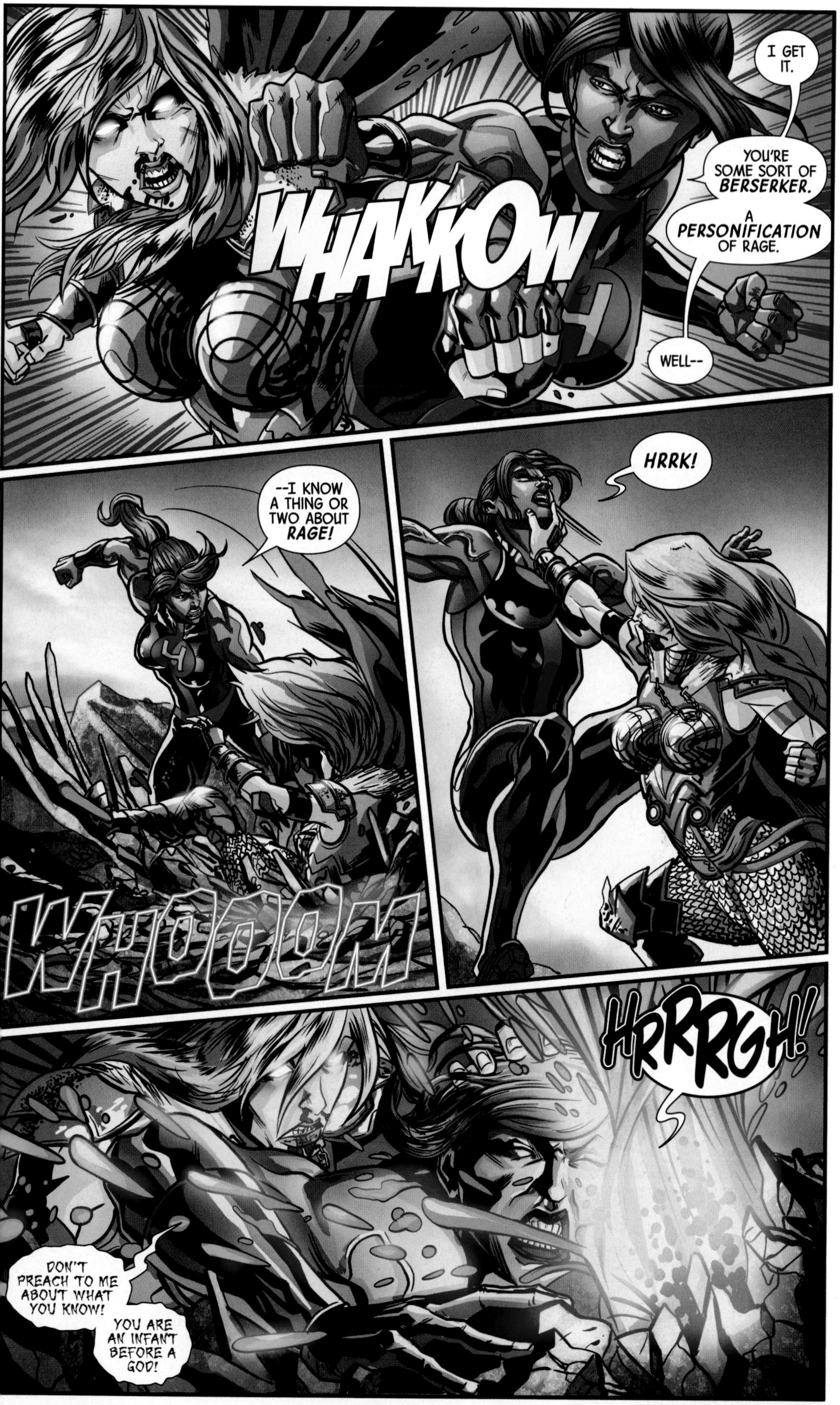

WHAKKOW
I GET IT.
YOU'RE SOME SORT OF BERSERKER.
A PERSONIFICATION OF RAGE.
WELL--
--I KNOW A THING OR TWO ABOUT RAGE!
WHOOOOM
HRRK!
HRRRGH!
DON'T PREACH TO ME ABOUT WHAT YOU KNOW!
YOU ARE AN INFANT BEFORE A GOD!

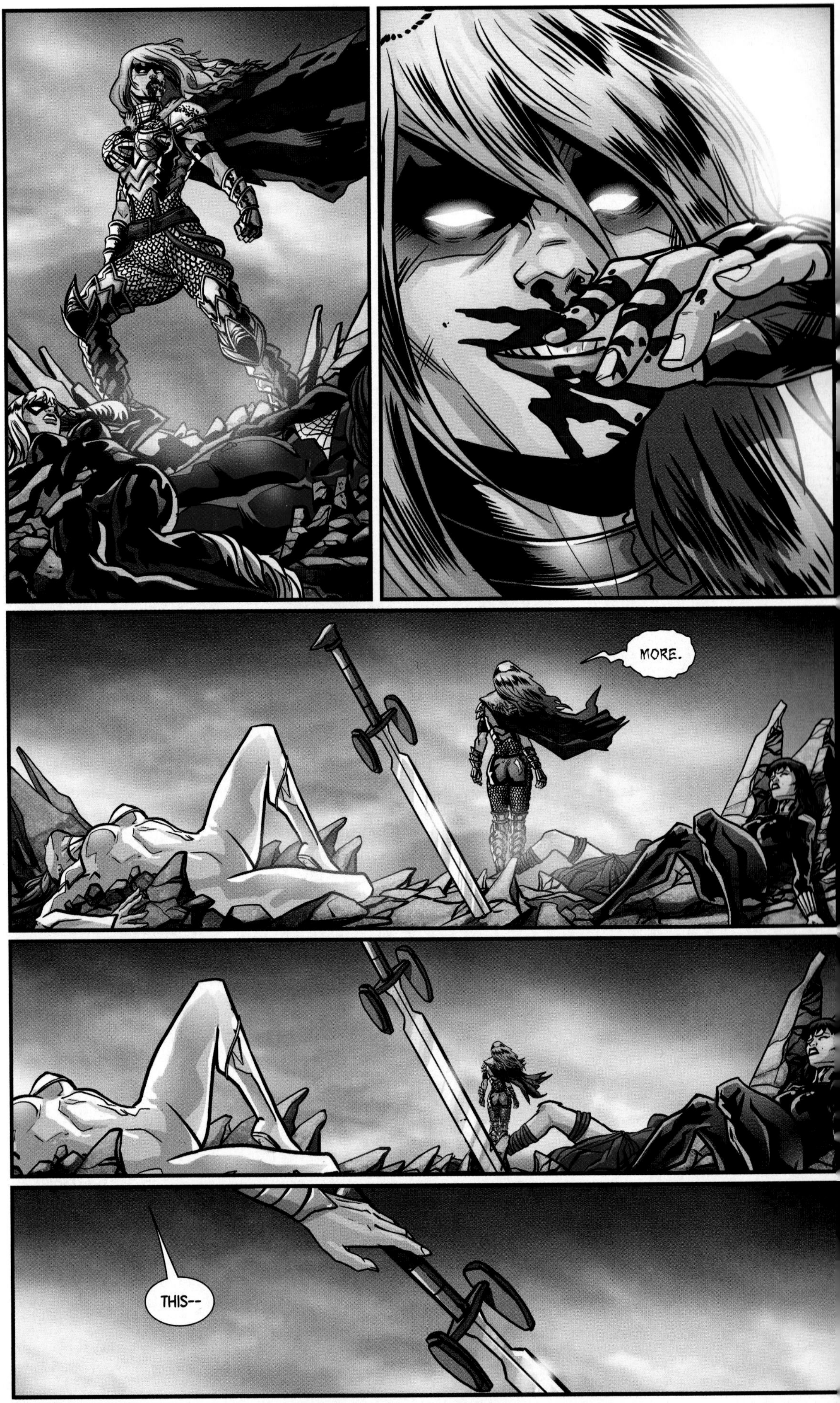
MORE.
THIS--

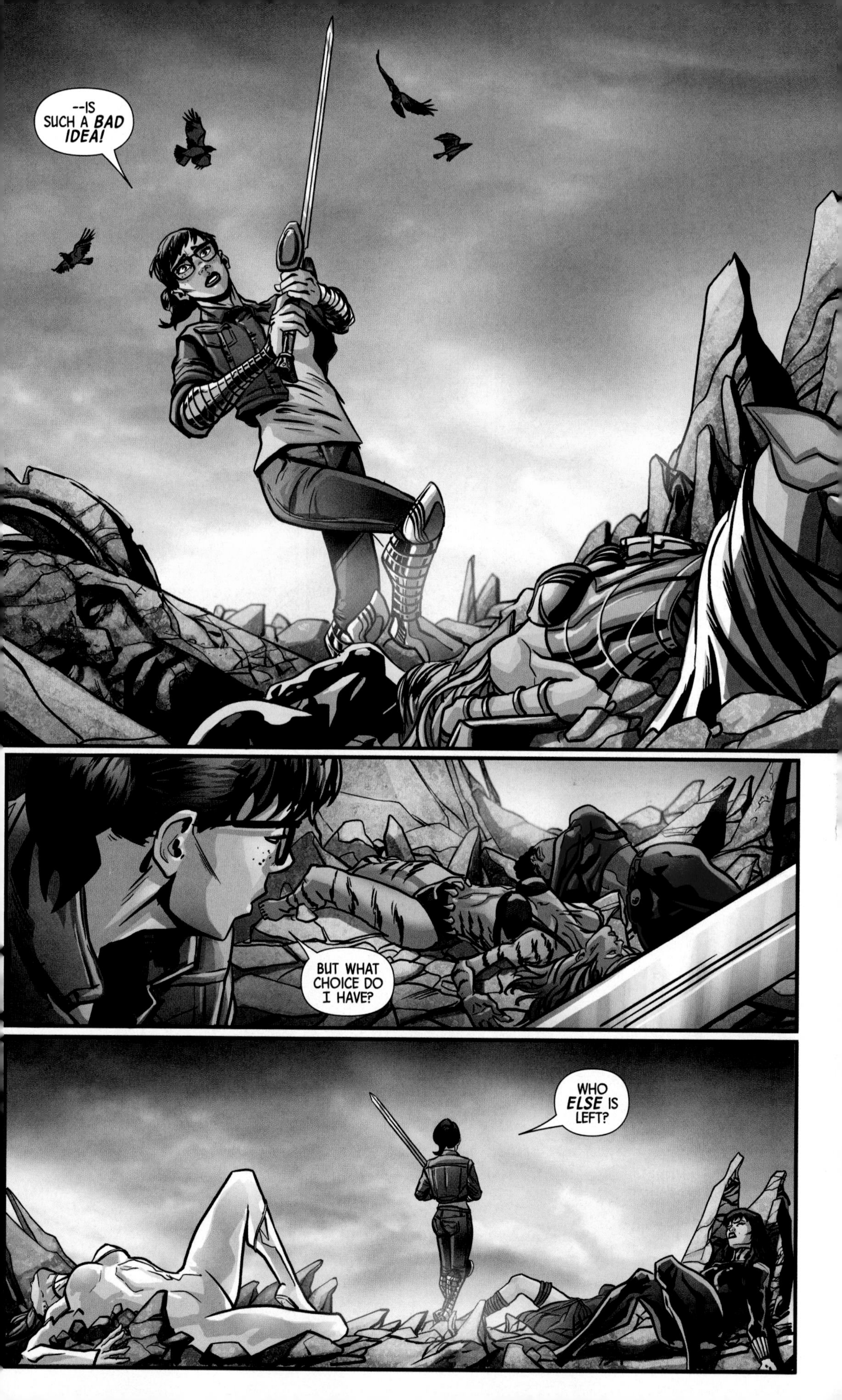
--IS SUCH A BAD IDEA!
BUT WHAT CHOICE DO I HAVE?
WHO ELSE IS LEFT?

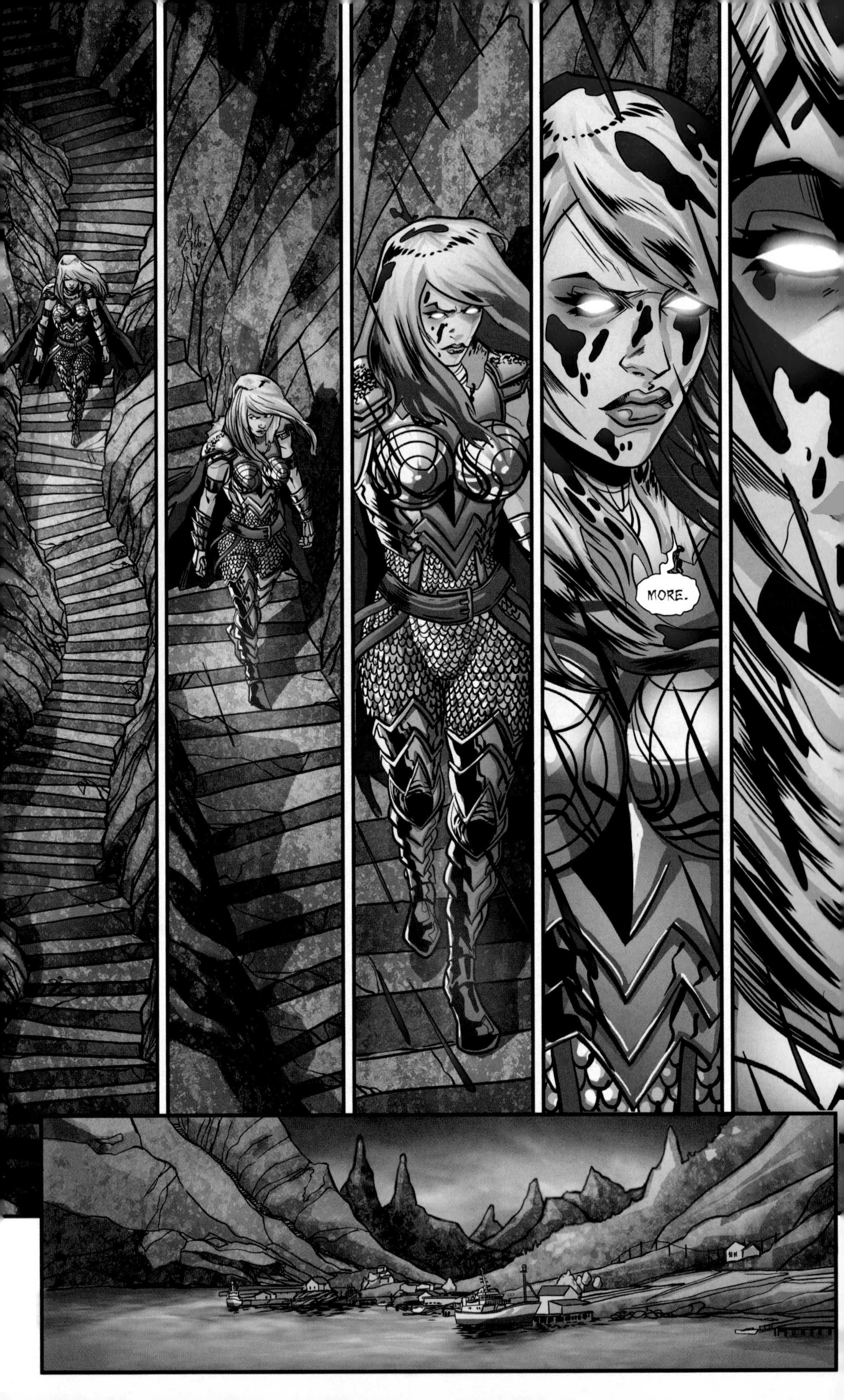
MORE.

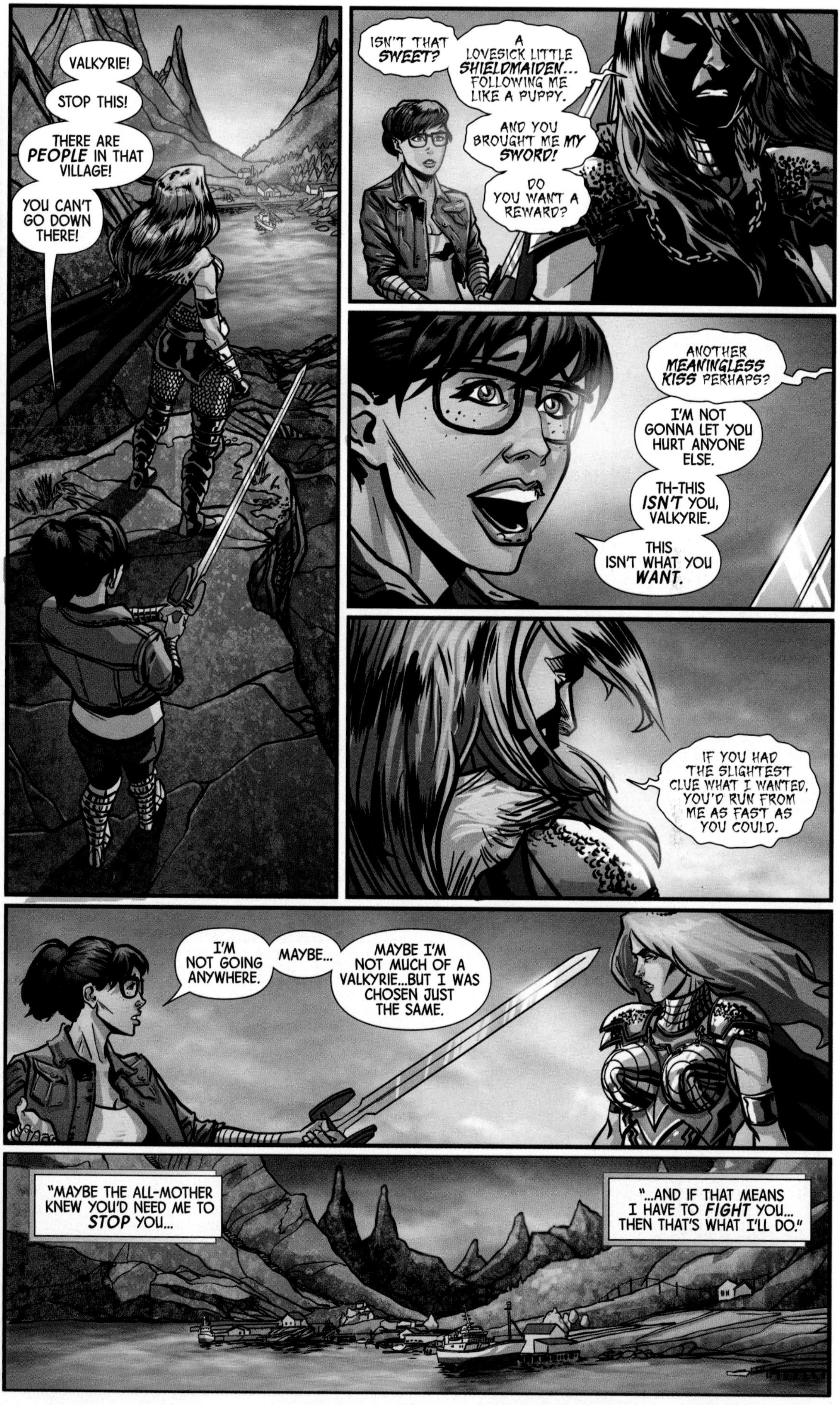

VALKYRIE!
STOP THIS!
THERE ARE PEOPLE IN THAT VILLAGE!
YOU CAN'T GO DOWN THERE!
ISN'T THAT SWEET?
A LOVESICK LITTLE SHIELDMAIDEN... FOLLOWING ME LIKE A PUPPY.
AND YOU BROUGHT ME MY SWORD!
DO YOU WANT A REWARD?
ANOTHER MEANINGLESS KISS PERHAPS?
I'M NOT GONNA LET YOU HURT ANYONE ELSE.
TH-THIS ISN'T YOU, VALKYRIE.
THIS ISN'T WHAT YOU WANT.
IF YOU HAD THE SLIGHTEST CLUE WHAT I WANTED, YOU'D RUN FROM ME AS FAST AS YOU COULD.
I'M NOT GOING ANYWHERE.
MAYBE...
MAYBE I'M NOT MUCH OF A VALKYRIE...BUT I WAS CHOSEN JUST THE SAME.
"MAYBE THE ALL-MOTHER KNEW YOU'D NEED ME TO STOP YOU...
"...AND IF THAT MEANS I HAVE TO FIGHT YOU... THEN THAT'S WHAT I'LL DO."

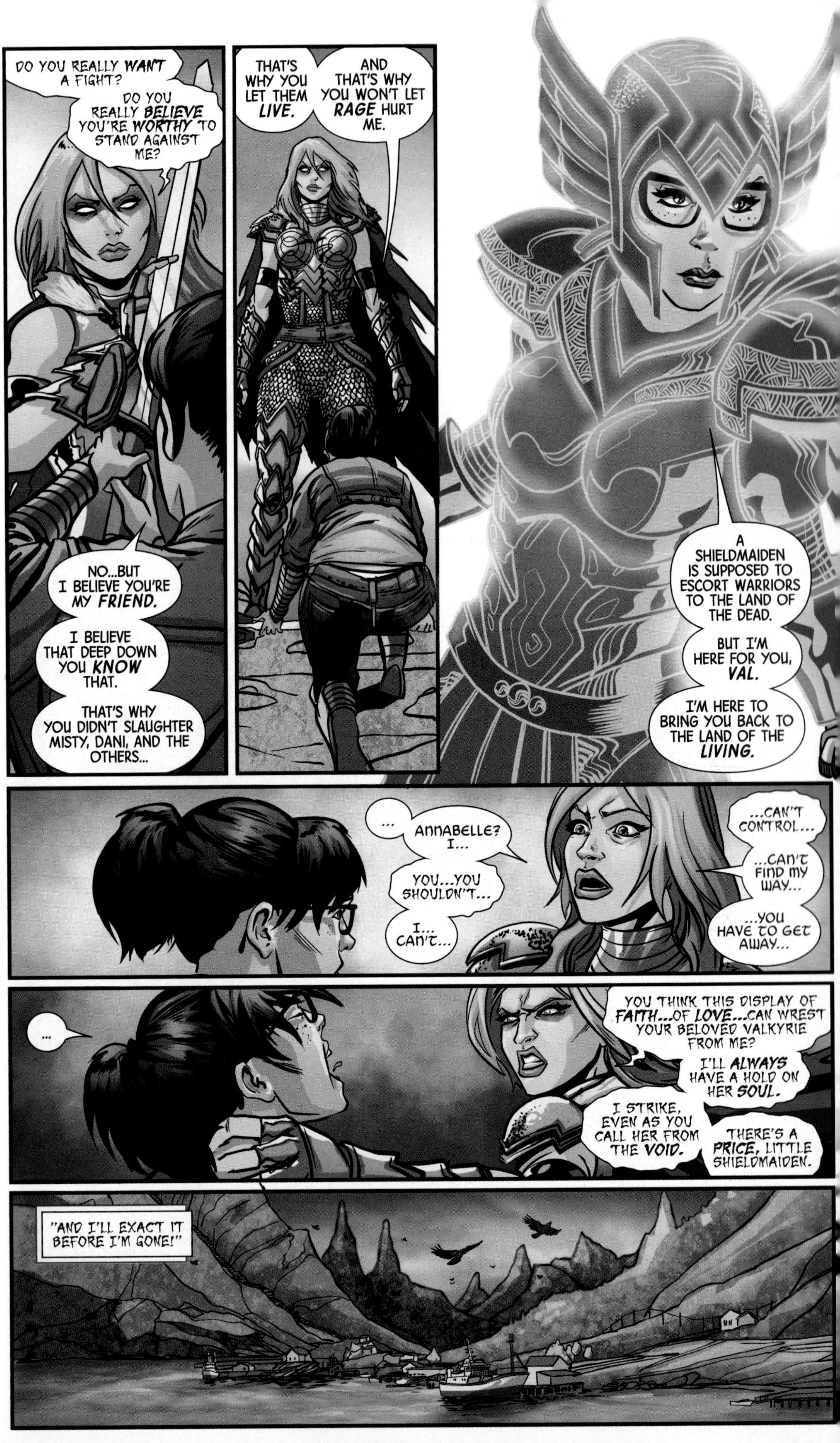

DO YOU REALLY WANT A FIGHT?
DO YOU REALLY BELIEVE YOU'RE WORTHY TO STAND AGAINST ME?
NO...BUT I BELIEVE YOU'RE MY FRIEND.
I BELIEVE THAT DEEP DOWN YOU KNOW THAT.
THAT'S WHY YOU DIDN'T SLAUGHTER MISTY, DANI, AND THE OTHERS...
THAT'S WHY YOU LET THEM LIVE.
AND THAT'S WHY YOU WON'T LET RAGE HURT ME.
A SHIELDMAIDEN IS SUPPOSED TO ESCORT WARRIORS TO THE LAND OF THE DEAD.
BUT I'M HERE FOR YOU, VAL.
I'M HERE TO BRING YOU BACK TO THE LAND OF THE LIVING.
...
ANNABELLE? I...
YOU...YOU SHOULDN'T...
I... CAN'T...
...CAN'T CONTROL...
...CAN'T FIND MY WAY...
...YOU HAVE TO GET AWAY...
...
YOU THINK THIS DISPLAY OF FAITH...OF LOVE...CAN WREST YOUR BELOVED VALKYRIE FROM ME?
I'LL ALWAYS HAVE A HOLD ON HER SOUL.
I STRIKE, EVEN AS YOU CALL HER FROM THE VOID.
THERE'S A PRICE, LITTLE SHIELDMAIDEN.
"AND I'LL EXACT IT BEFORE I'M GONE!"

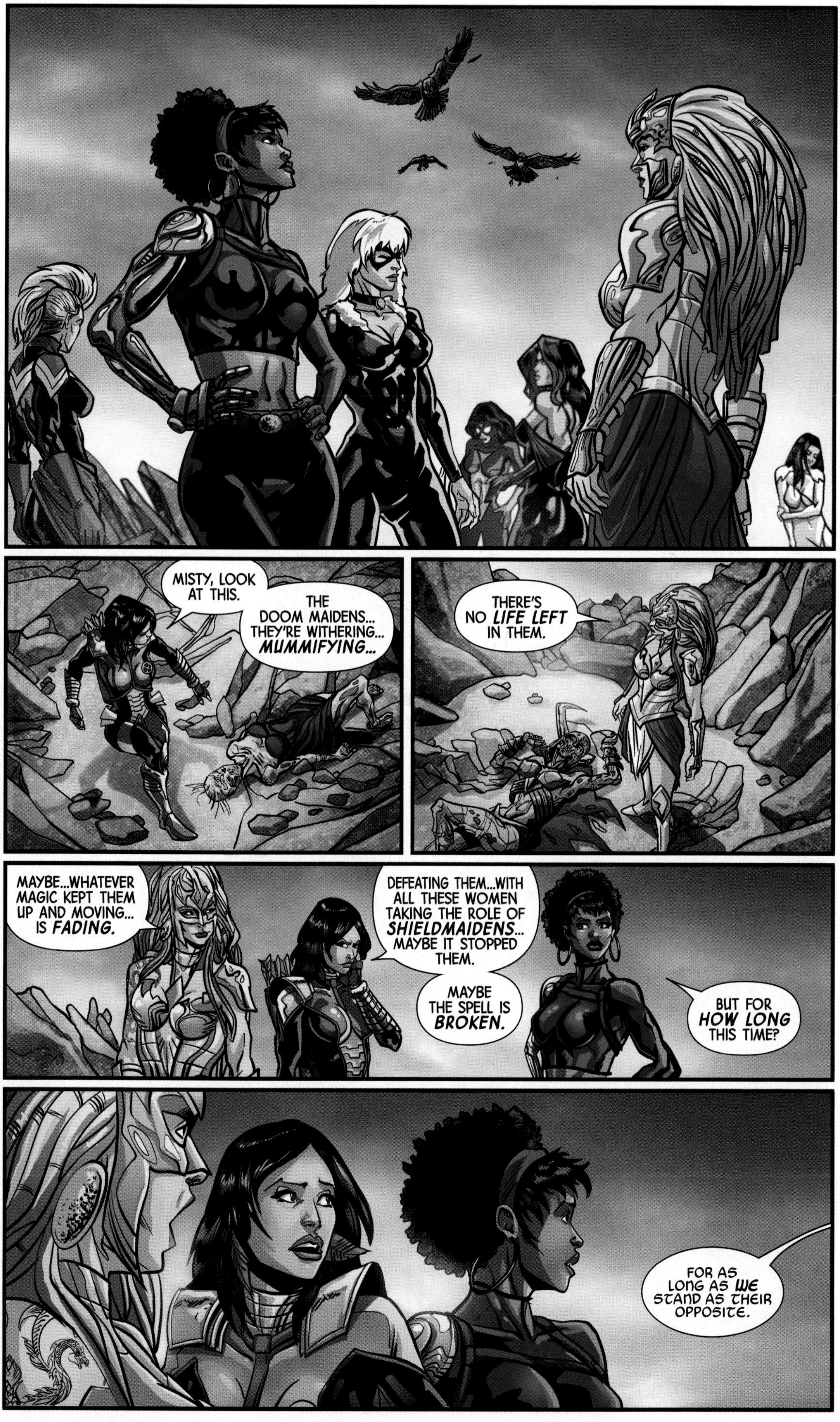

MISTY, LOOK AT THIS.
THE DOOM MAIDENS... THEY'RE WITHERING... MUMMIFYING...
THERE'S NO LIFE LEFT IN THEM.
MAYBE...WHATEVER MAGIC KEPT THEM UP AND MOVING... IS FADING.
DEFEATING THEM...WITH ALL THESE WOMEN TAKING THE ROLE OF SHIELDMAIDENS... MAYBE IT STOPPED THEM.
MAYBE THE SPELL IS BROKEN.
BUT FOR HOW LONG THIS TIME?
FOR AS LONG AS WE STAND AS THEIR OPPOSITE.

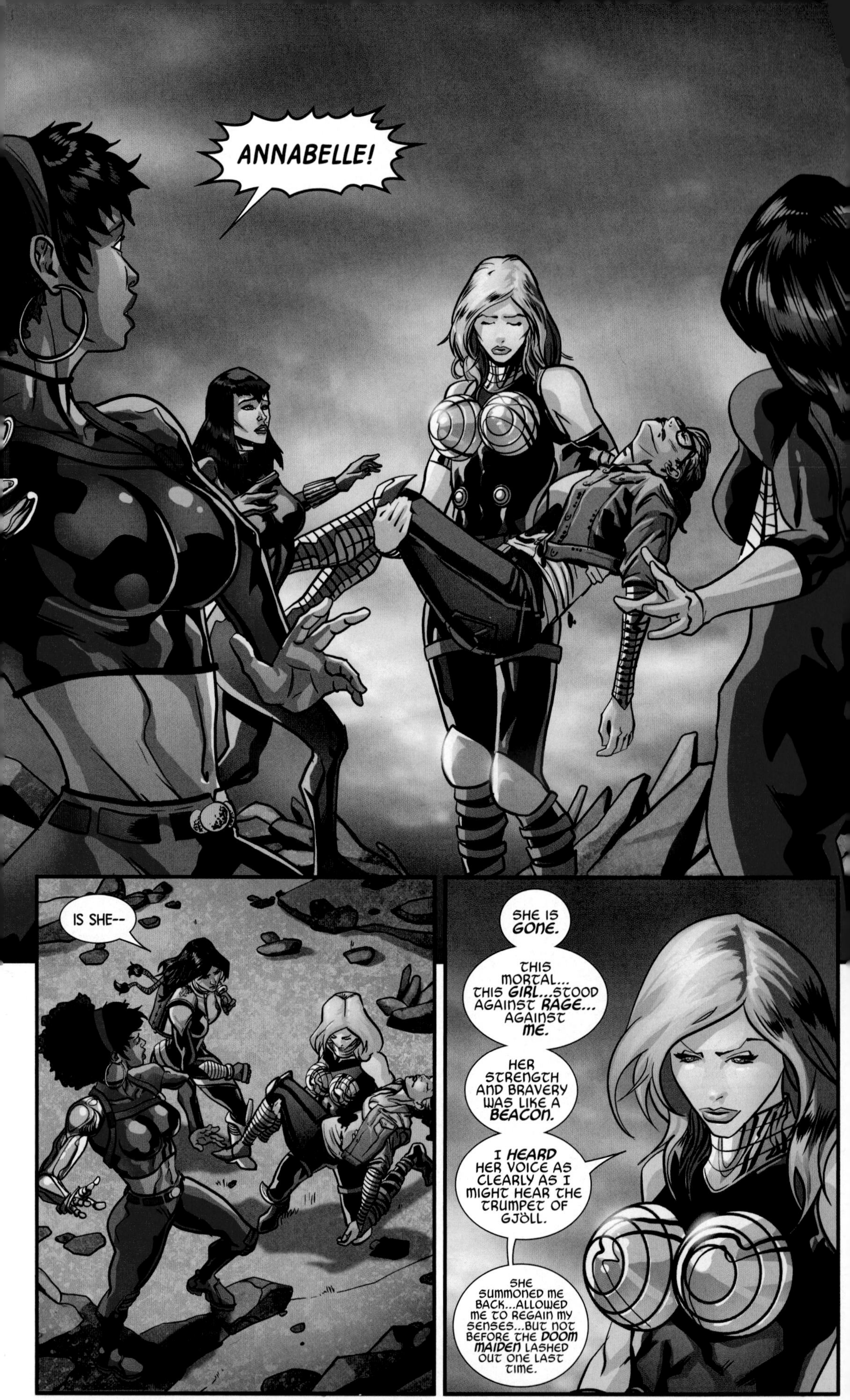
ANNABELLE!
IS SHE--
SHE IS GONE.
THIS MORTAL... THIS GIRL...STOOD AGAINST RAGE... AGAINST ME.
HER STRENGTH AND BRAVERY WAS LIKE A BEACON.
I HEARD HER VOICE AS CLEARLY AS I MIGHT HEAR THE TRUMPET OF GJÖLL.
SHE SUMMONED ME BACK...ALLOWED ME TO REGAIN MY SENSES...BUT NOT BEFORE THE DOOM MAIDEN LASHED OUT ONE LAST TIME.

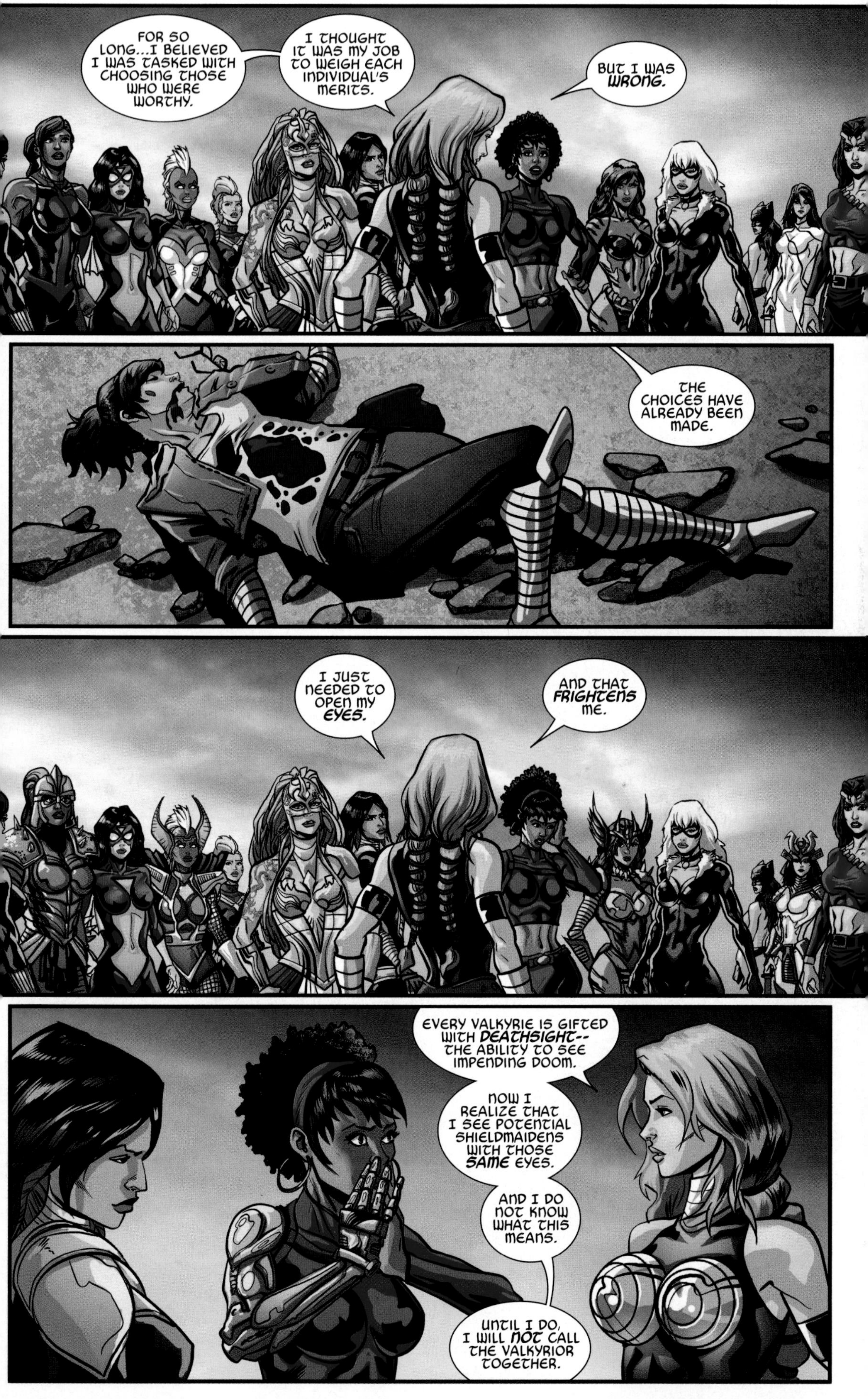
FOR SO LONG...I BELIEVED I WAS TASKED WITH CHOOSING THOSE WHO WERE WORTHY.
I THOUGHT IT WAS MY JOB TO WEIGH EACH INDIVIDUAL'S MERITS.
BUT I WAS WRONG.
THE CHOICES HAVE ALREADY BEEN MADE.
I JUST NEEDED TO OPEN MY EYES.
AND THAT FRIGHTENS ME.
EVERY VALKYRIE IS GIFTED WITH DEATHSIGHT-- THE ABILITY TO SEE IMPENDING DOOM.
NOW I REALIZE THAT I SEE POTENTIAL SHIELDMAIDENS WITH THOSE SAME EYES.
AND I DO NOT KNOW WHAT THIS MEANS.
UNTIL I DO, I WILL NOT CALL THE VALKYRIOR TOGETHER.

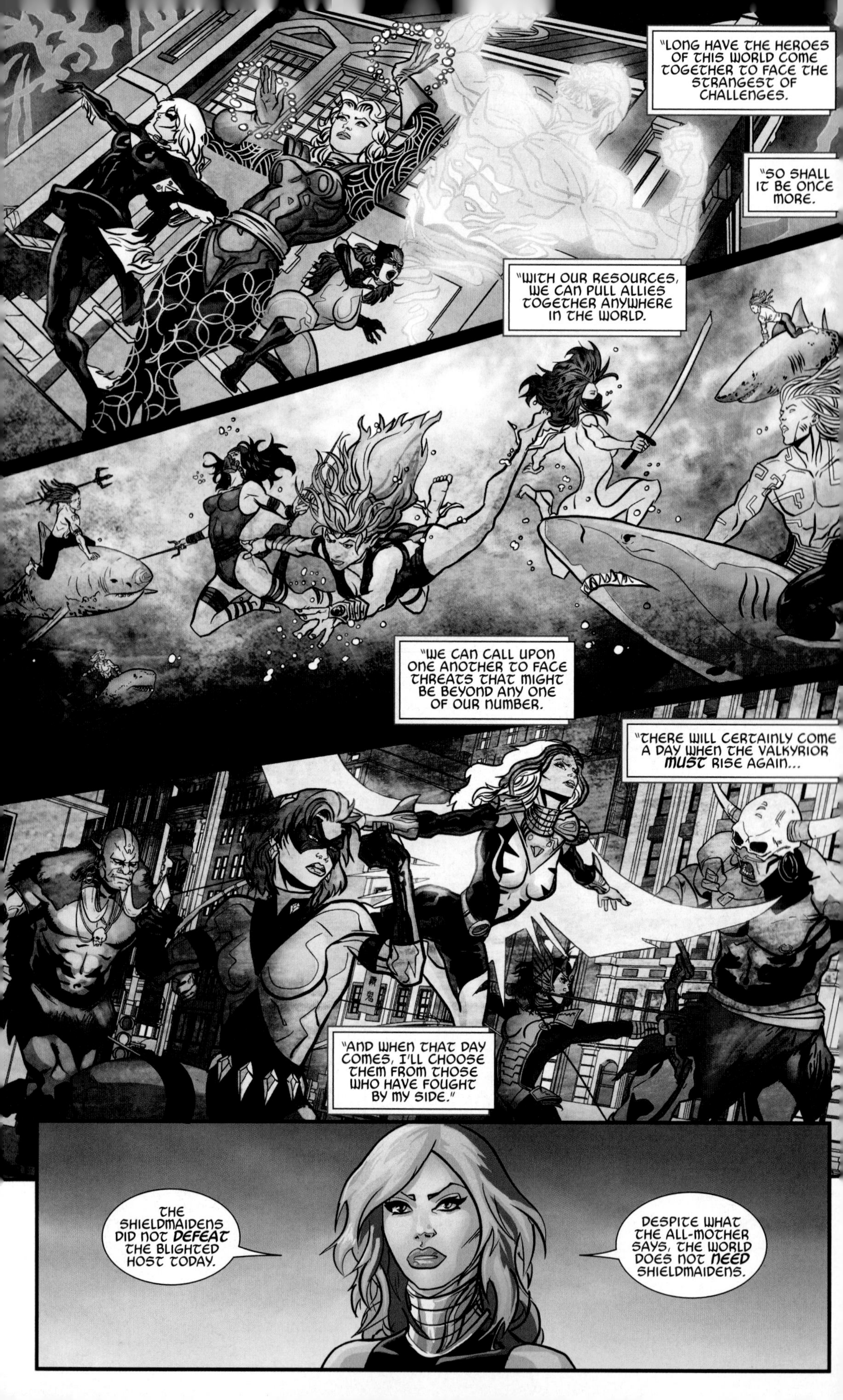
"LONG HAVE THE HEROES OF THIS WORLD COME TOGETHER TO FACE THE STRANGEST OF CHALLENGES.
"SO SHALL IT BE ONCE MORE.
"WITH OUR RESOURCES, WE CAN PULL ALLIES TOGETHER ANYWHERE IN THE WORLD.
"WE CAN CALL UPON ONE ANOTHER TO FACE THREATS THAT MIGHT BE BEYOND ANY ONE OF OUR NUMBER.
"THERE WILL CERTAINLY COME A DAY WHEN THE VALKYRIOR MUST RISE AGAIN...
"AND WHEN THAT DAY COMES, I'LL CHOOSE THEM FROM THOSE WHO HAVE FOUGHT BY MY SIDE."
THE SHIELDMAIDENS DID NOT DEFEAT THE BLIGHTED HOST TODAY.
DESPITE WHAT THE ALL-MOTHER SAYS, THE WORLD DOES NOT NEED SHIELDMAIDENS.

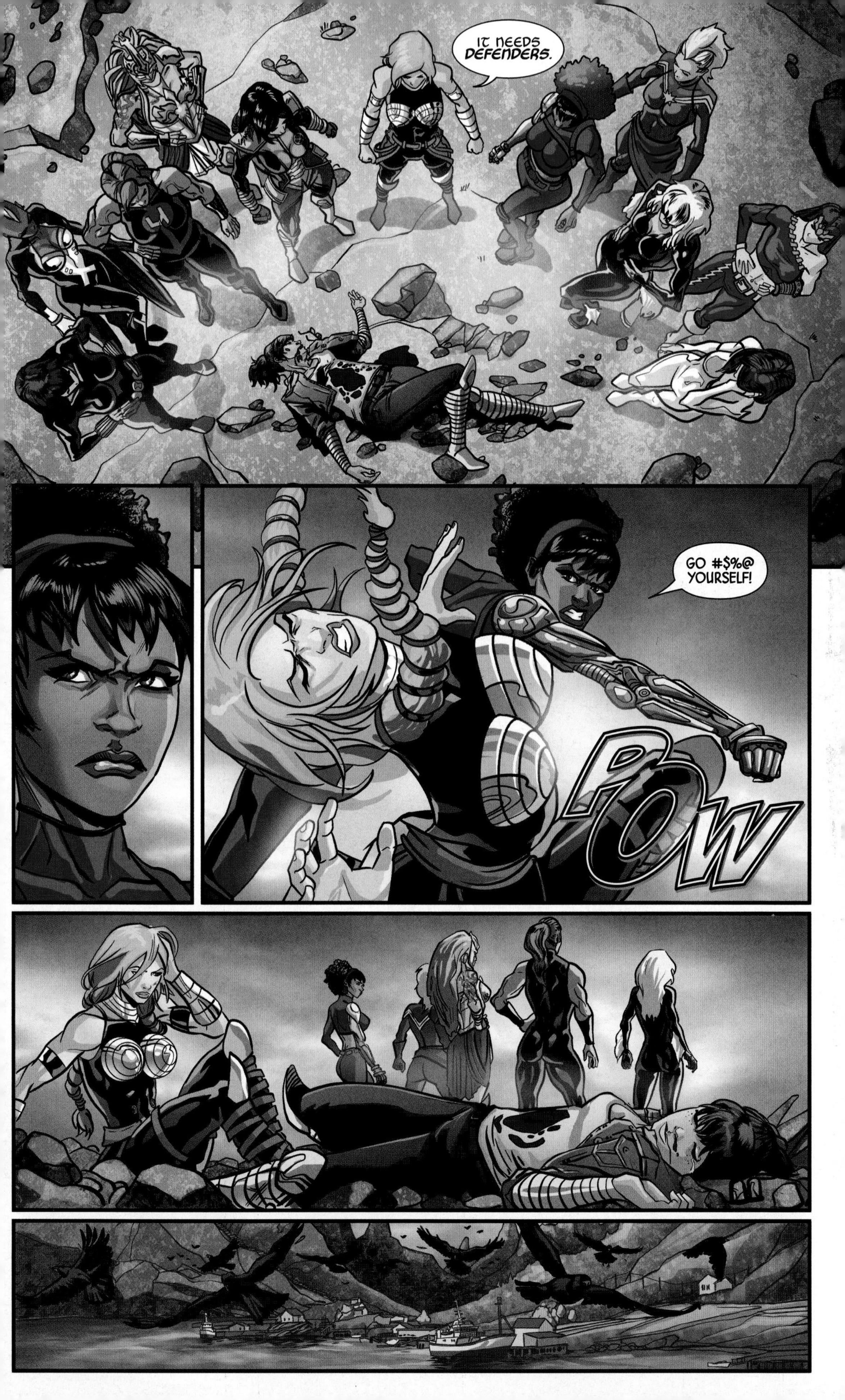
IT NEEDS DEFENDERS.
GO #$%@ YOURSELF!
POW

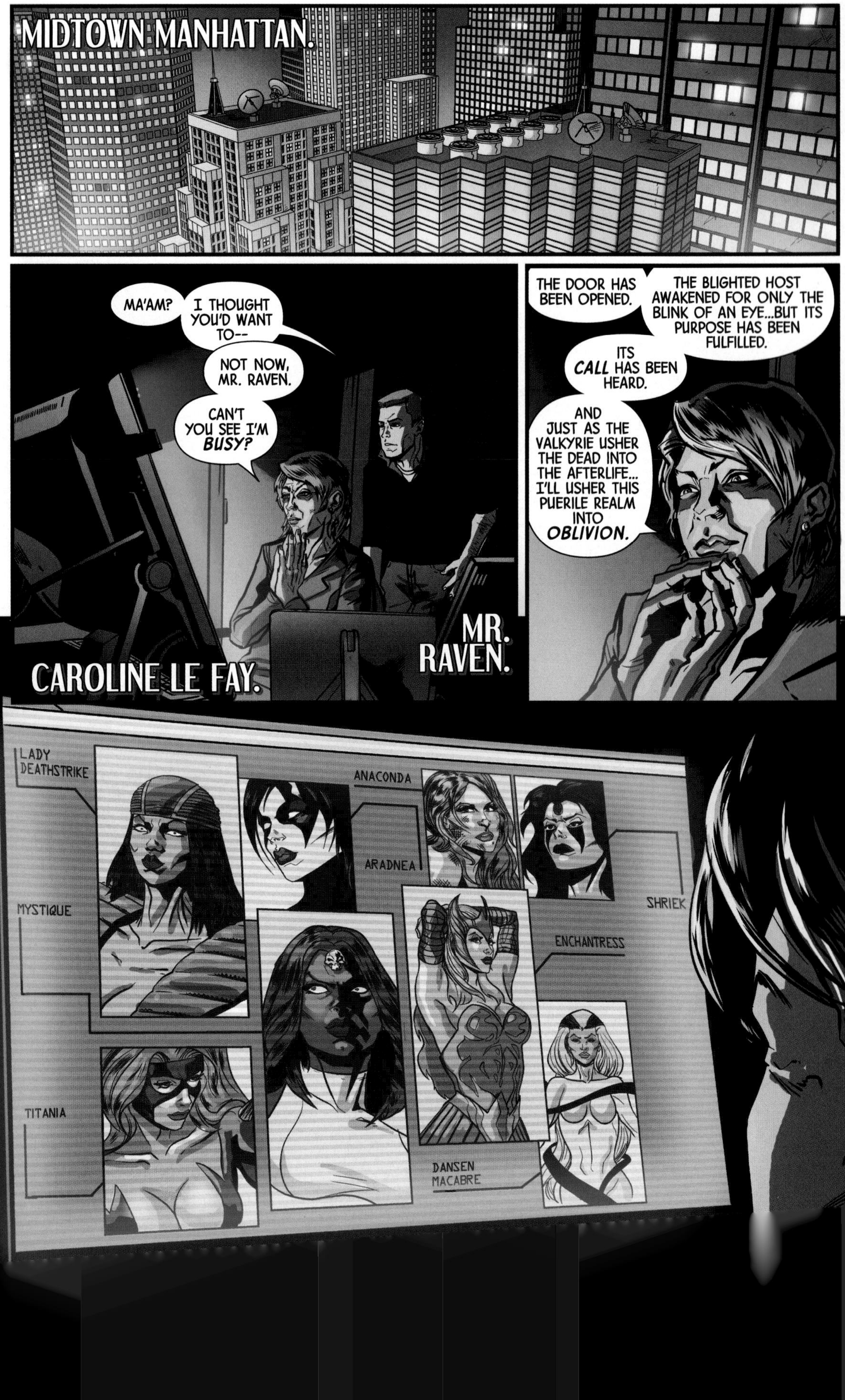
MIDTOWN MANHATTAN.
MA'AM?
I THOUGHT YOU'D WANT TO--
NOT NOW, MR. RAVEN.
CAN'T YOU SEE I'M *BUSY?*
CAROLINE LE FAY.
MR. RAVEN.
THE DOOR HAS BEEN OPENED.
THE BLIGHTED HOST AWAKENED FOR ONLY THE BLINK OF AN EYE...BUT ITS PURPOSE HAS BEEN FULFILLED.
ITS *CALL* HAS BEEN HEARD.
AND JUST AS THE VALKYRIE USHER THE DEAD INTO THE AFTERLIFE... I'LL USHER THIS PUERILE REALM INTO *OBLIVION.*
LADY DEATHSTRIKE
ANACONDA
ARADNEA
MYSTIQUE
SHRIEK
ENCHANTRESS
TITANIA
DANSEN MACABRE

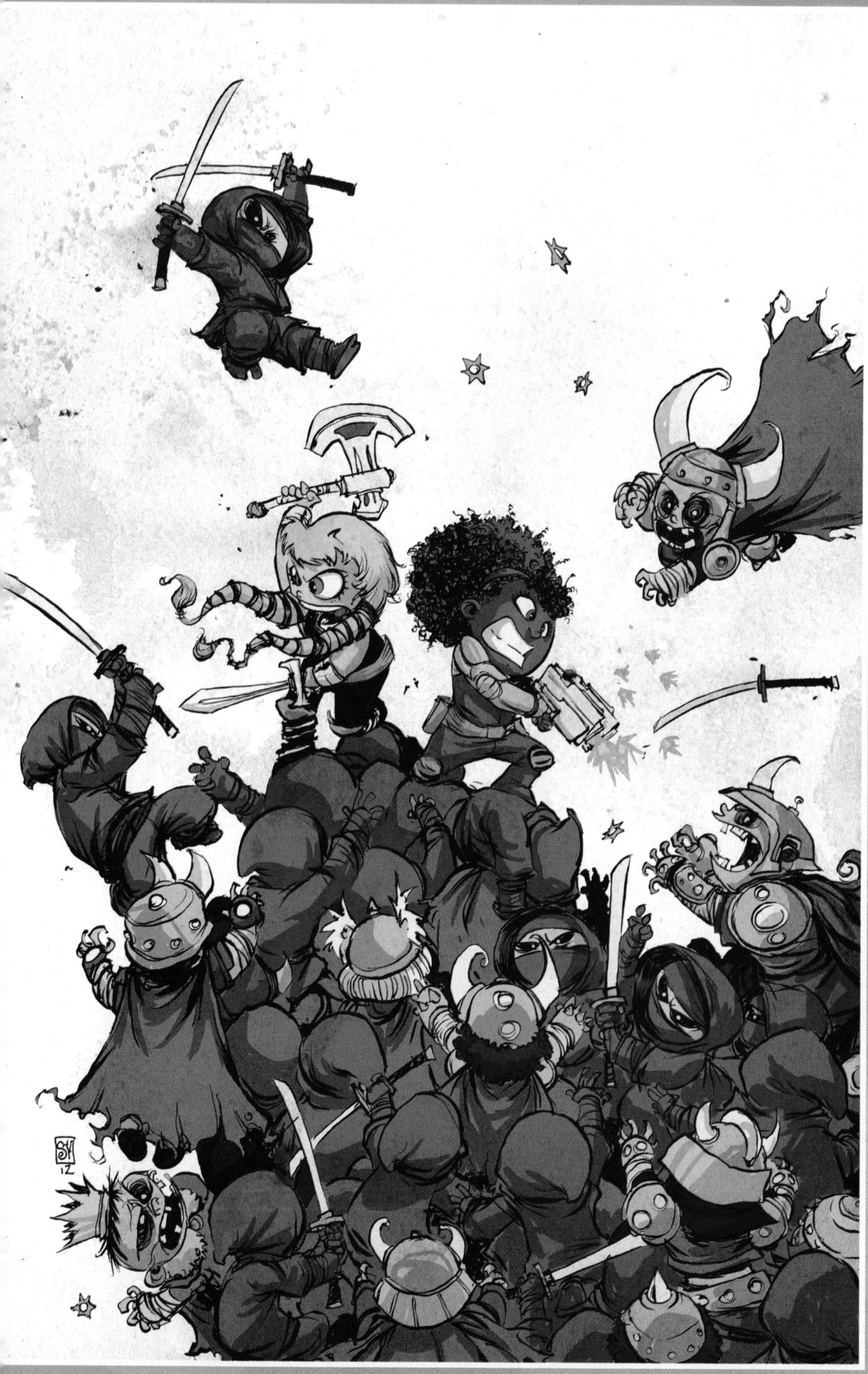

FEARLESS DEFENDERS #1 VARIANT BY SKOTTIE YOUNG

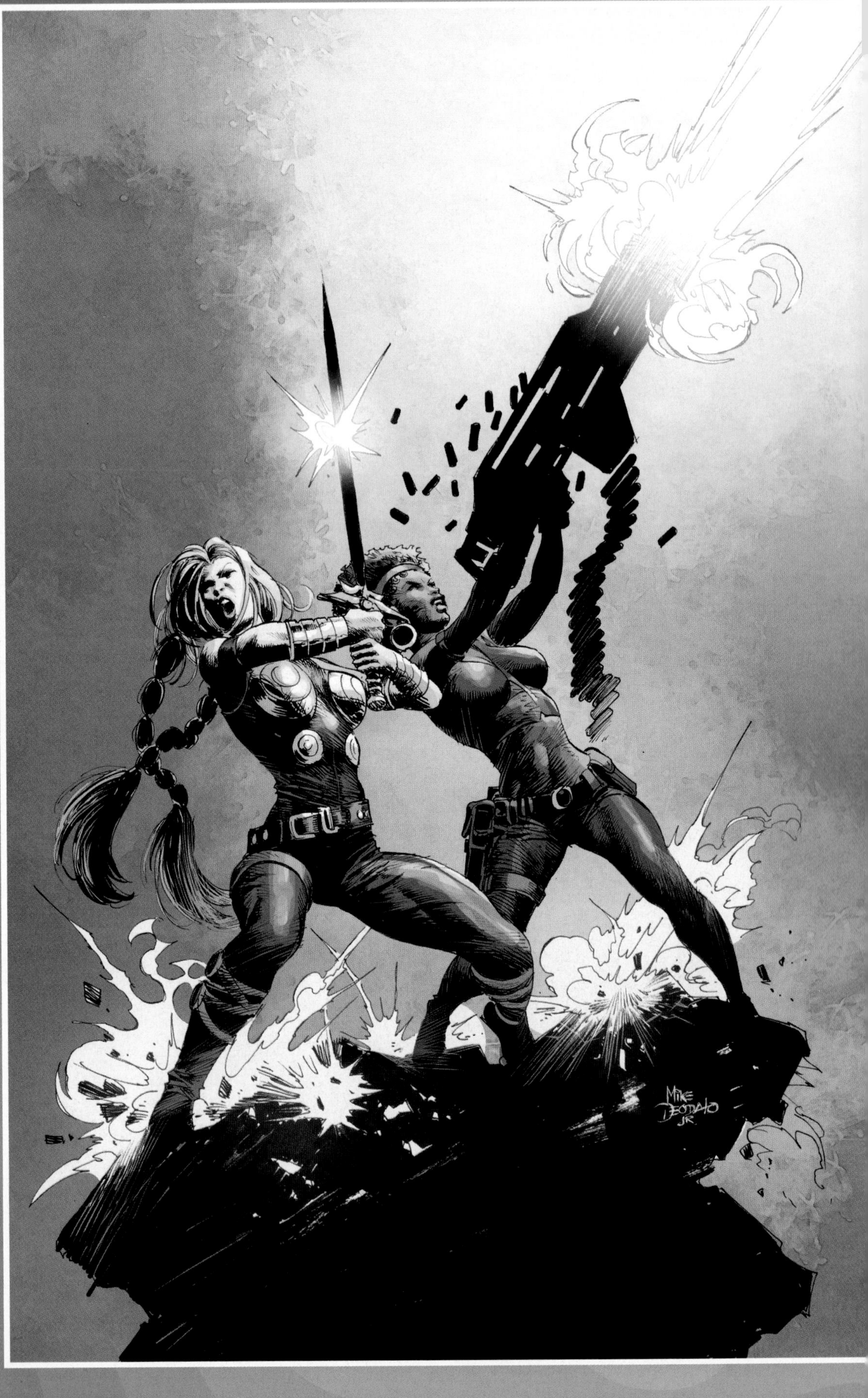
MIKE DEODATO JR

FEARLESS DEFENDERS #1 VARIANT BY MIKE DEODATO & RAIN BEREDO

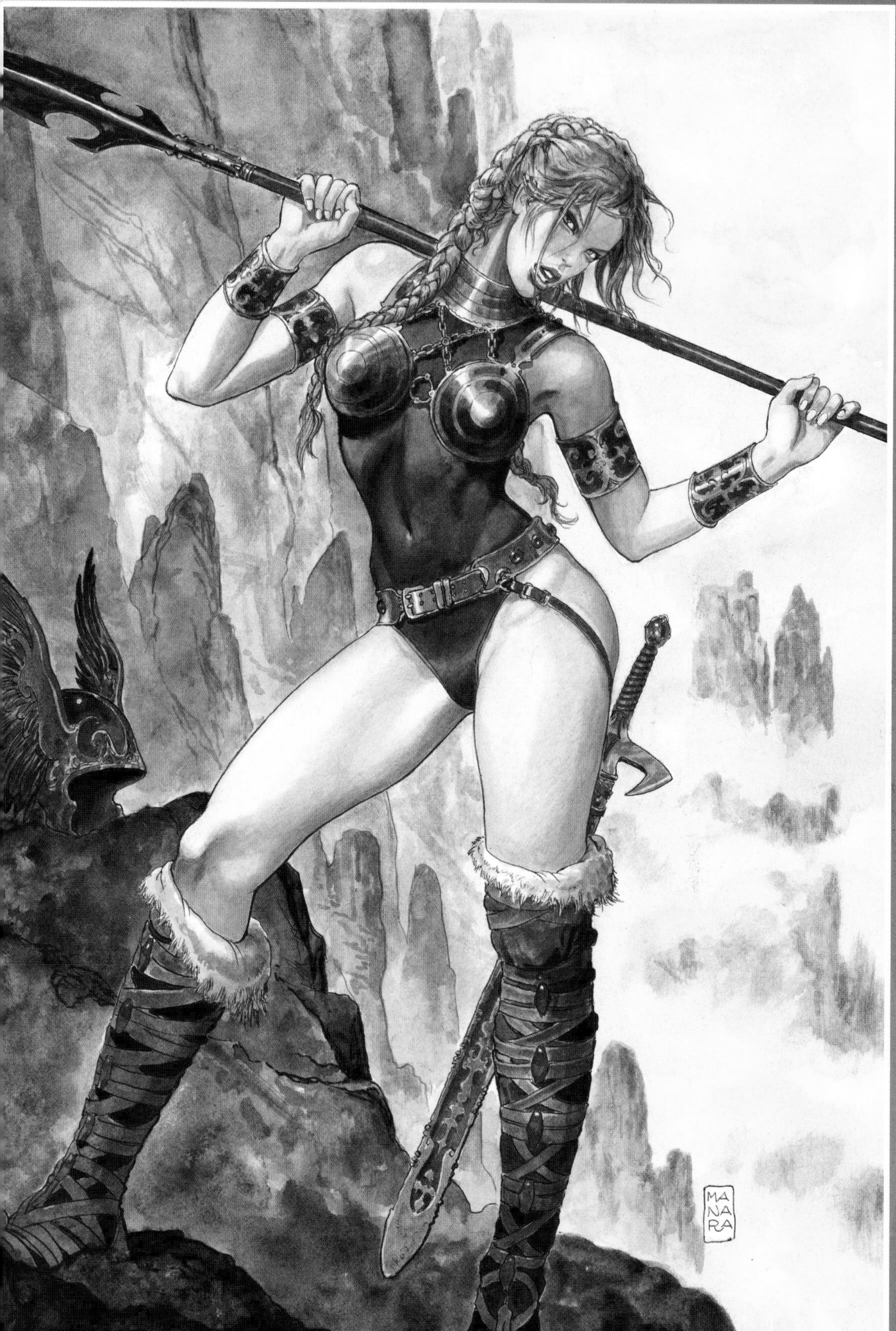
MA
NA
RA

FEARLESS DEFENDERS #1 VARIANT BY MILO MANARA

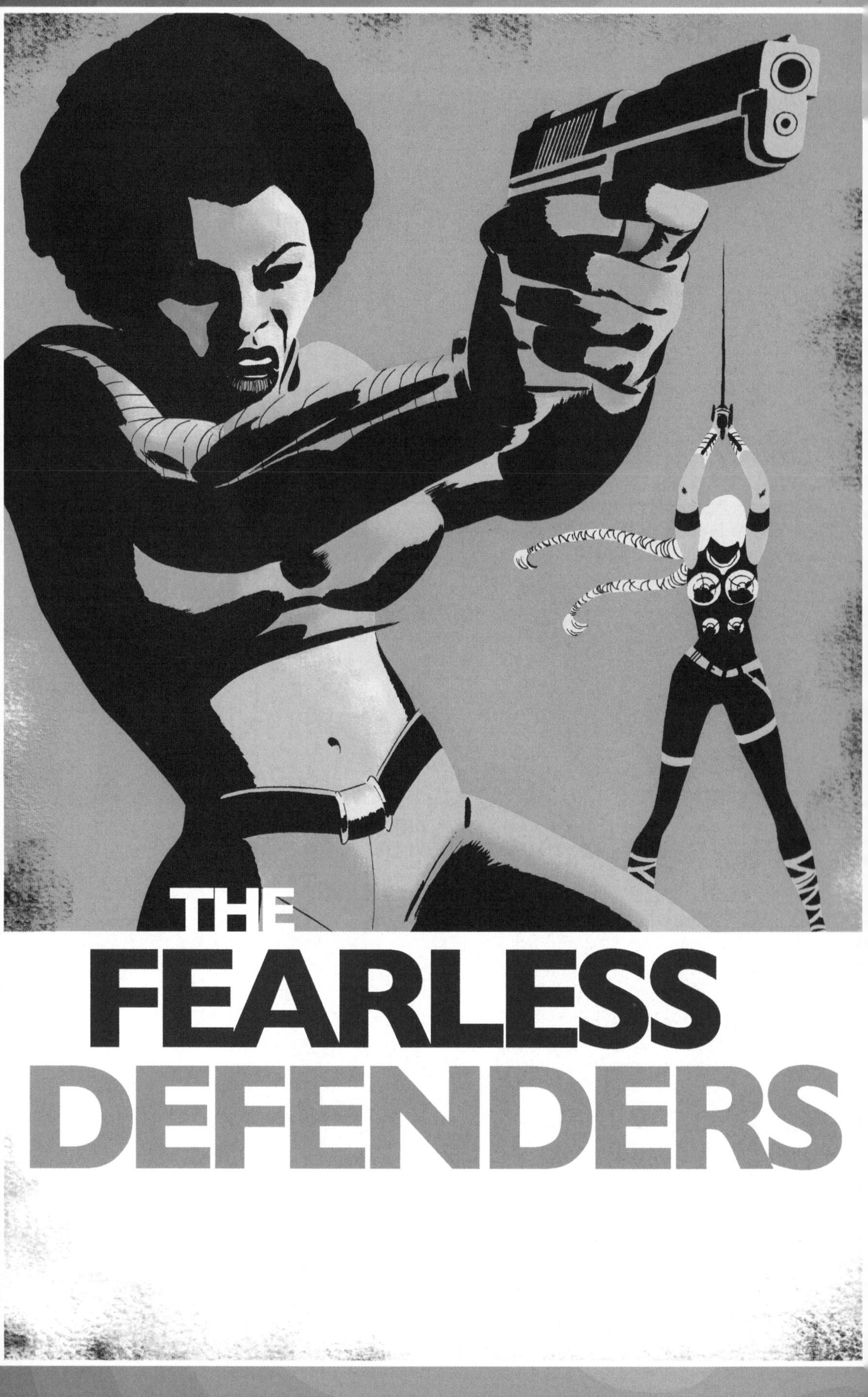
THE
FEARLESS
DEFENDERS

FEARLESS DEFENDERS #2 VARIANT BY MARCOS MARTIN

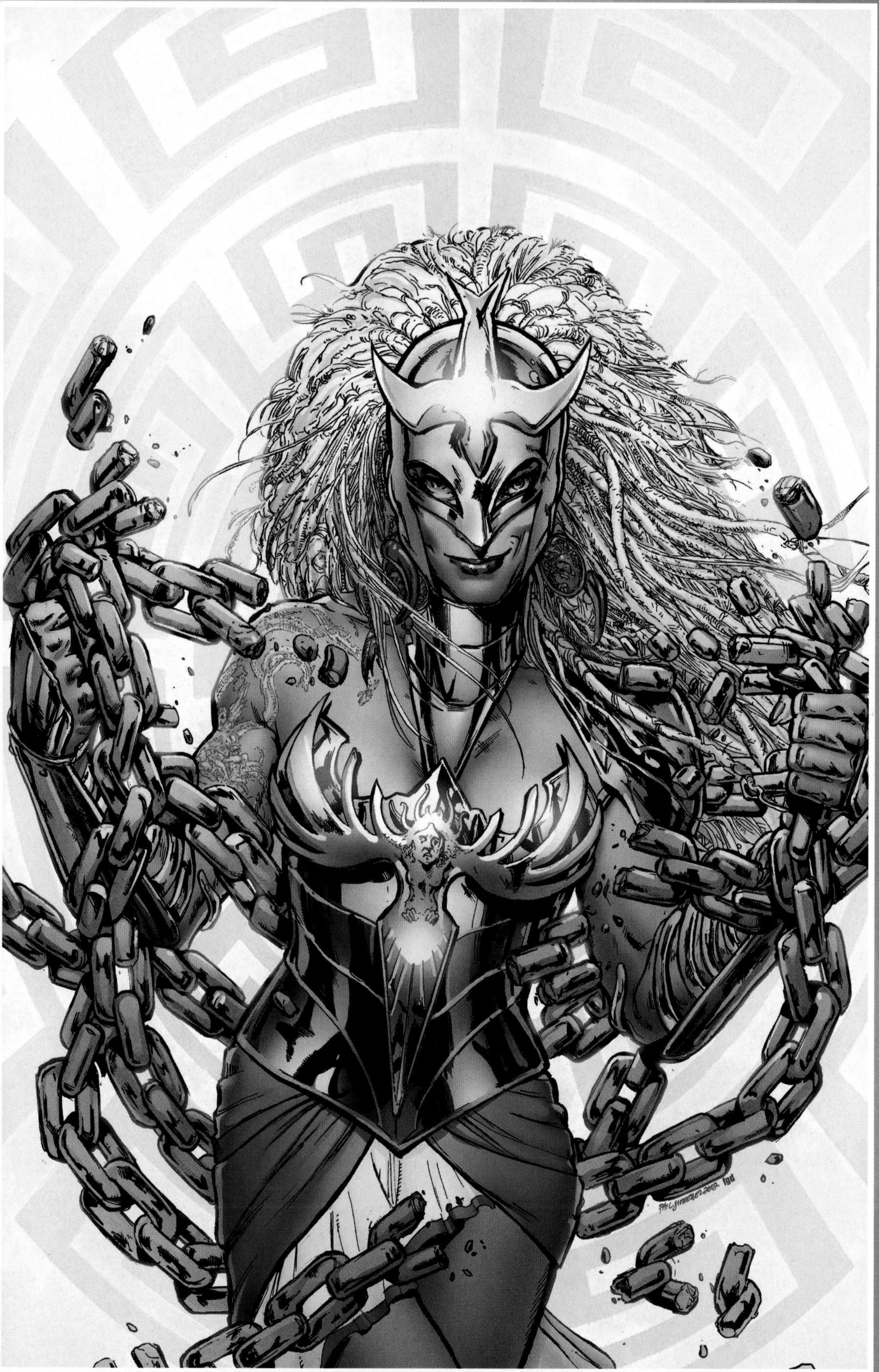

FEARLESS DEFENDERS #3 VARIANT BY PHIL JIMENEZ & FRANK D'ARMATA

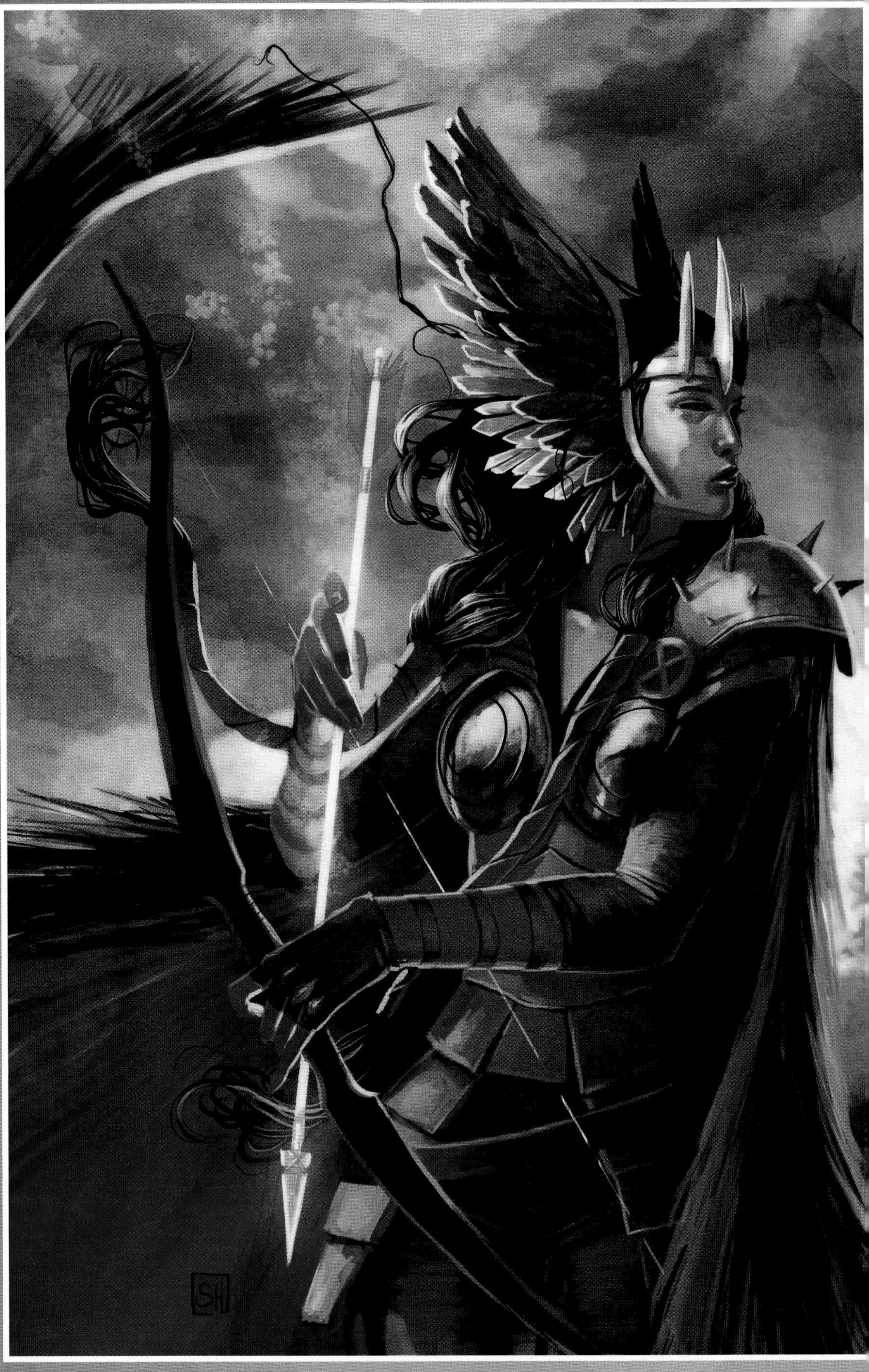

FEARLESS DEFENDERS #4 VARIANT BY STEPHANIE HANS

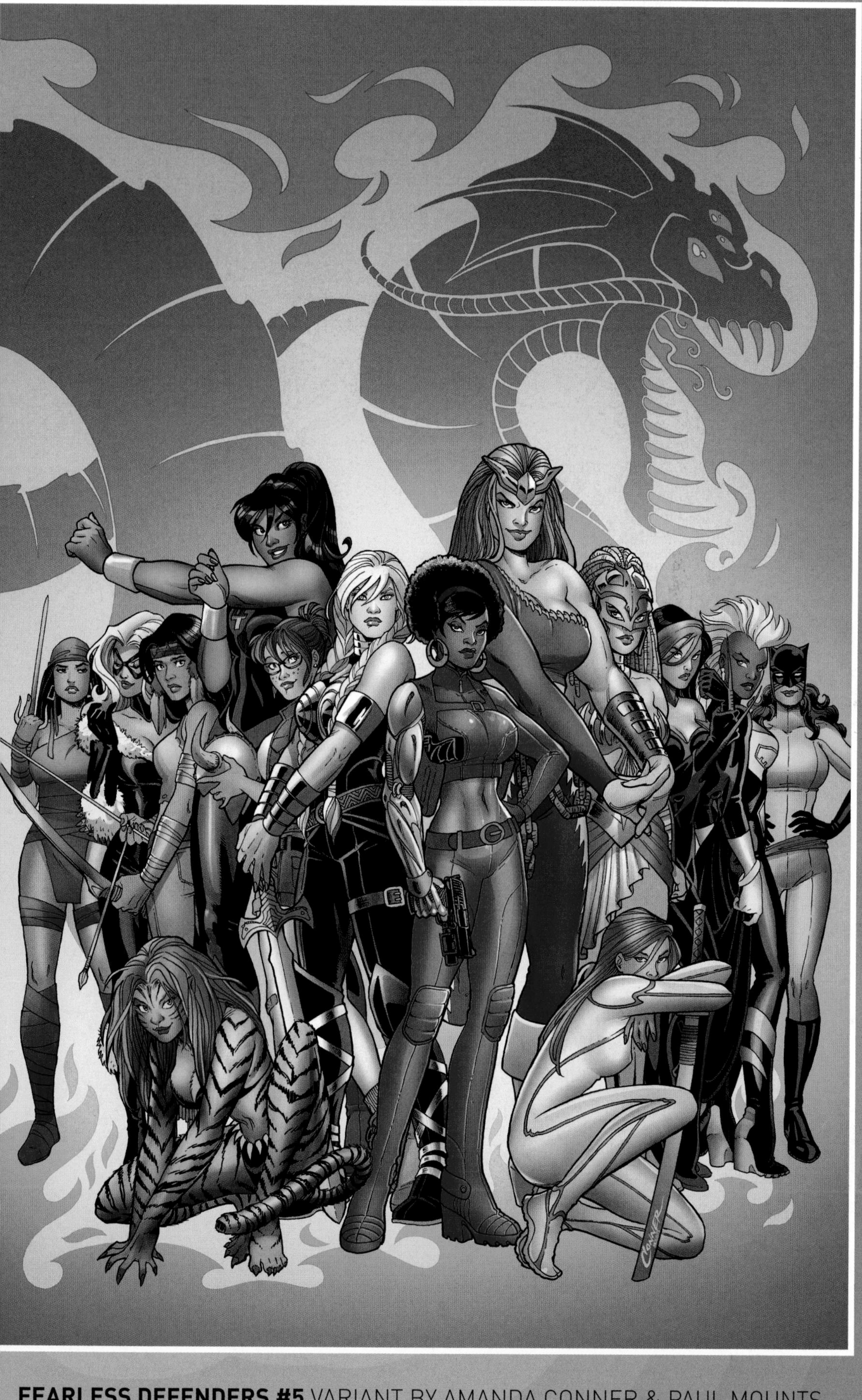
CONNER

FEARLESS DEFENDERS #5 VARIANT BY AMANDA CONNER & PAUL MOUNTS

CHARACTER SKETCHES
BY PHIL JIMENEZ

HIPPOLYTA

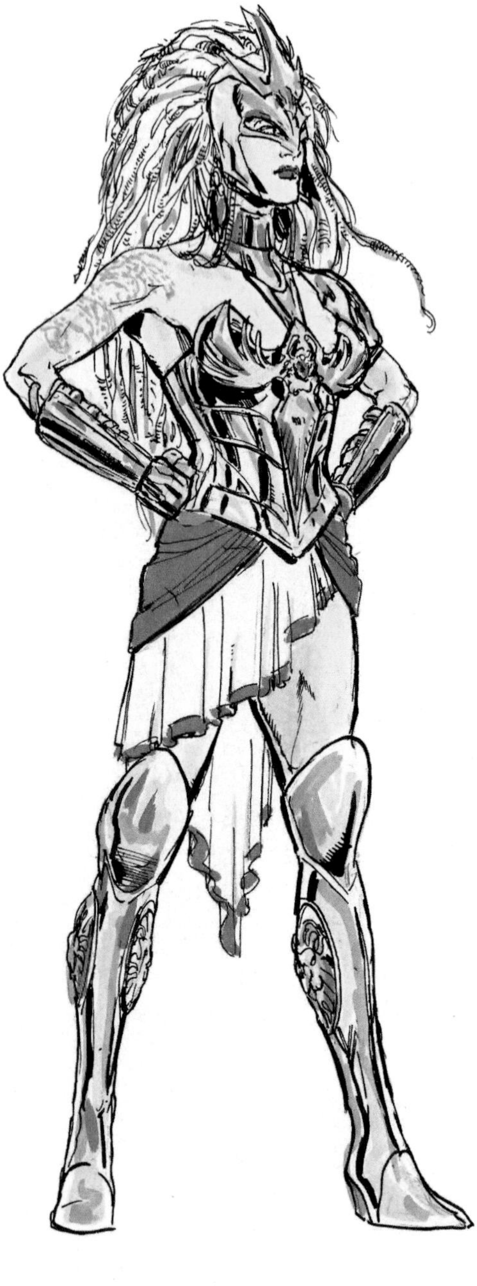

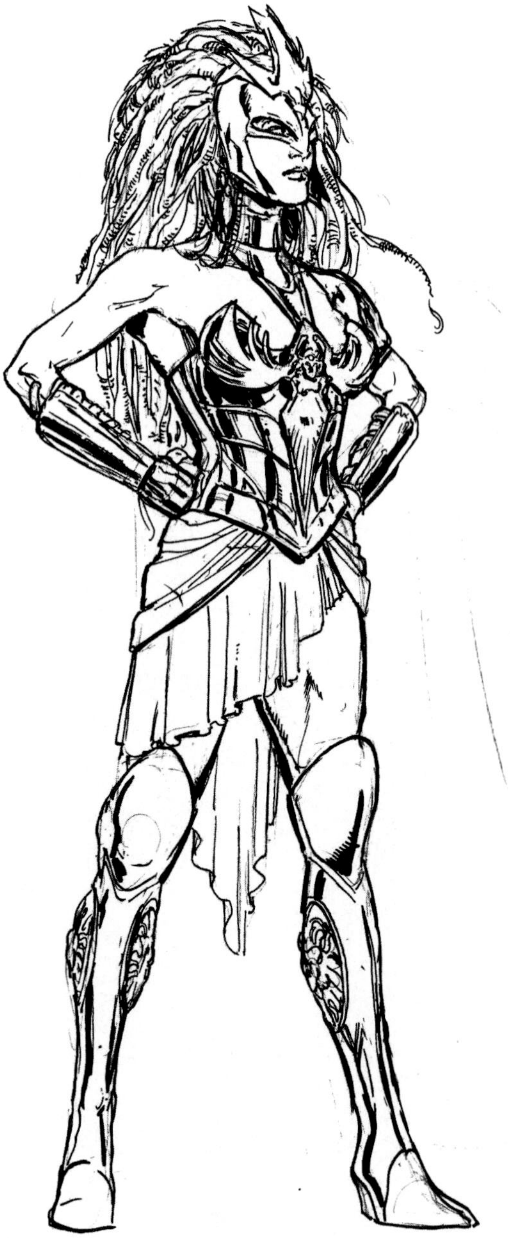

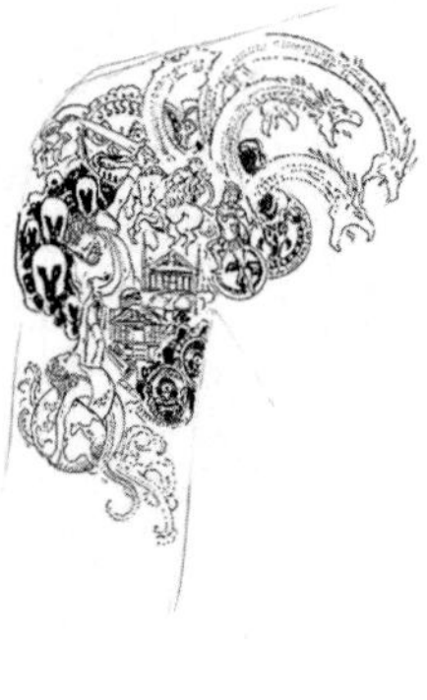

HIPPOLYTA

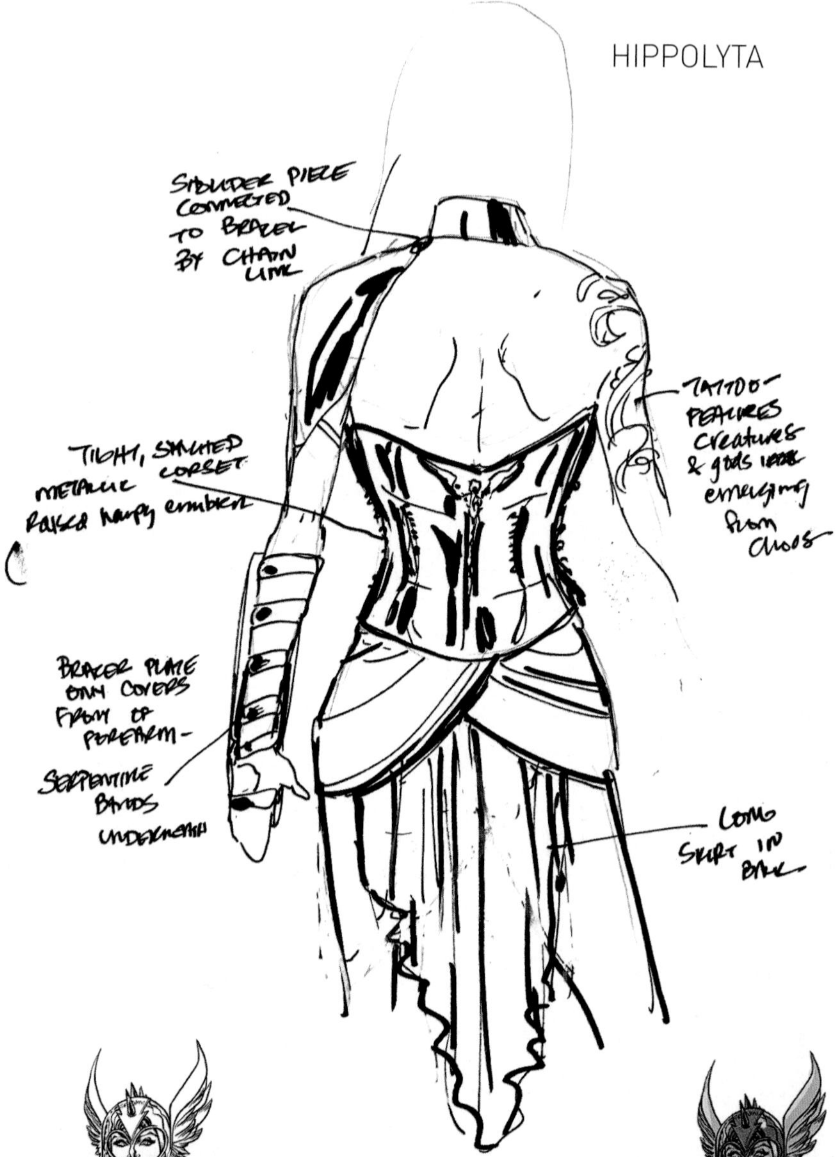

SHOULDER PIECE CONNECTED TO BRACER BY CHAIN LINK
TIGHT, STITCHED METALLIC CORSET
Raised harpy emblem
TATTOO- FEATURES Creatures & gods emerging from chaos
BRACER PLATE ONLY COVERS FRONT OF FOREARM-
SERPENTINE BANDS UNDERNEATH
LONG SKIRT IN BACK

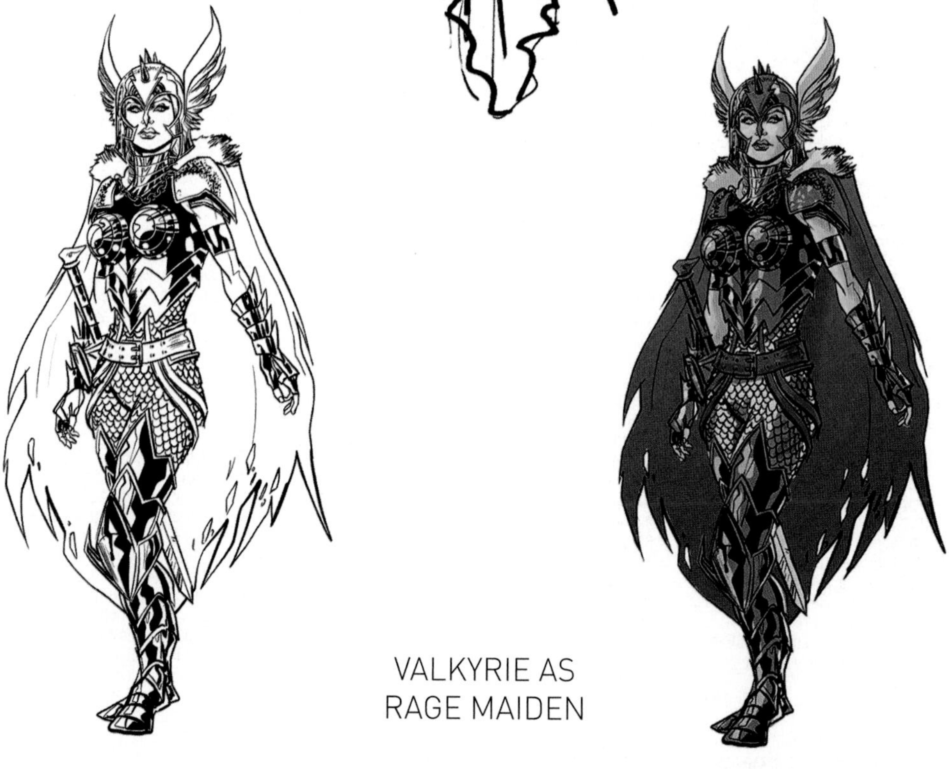

VALKYRIE AS
RAGE MAIDEN

IN OUR DEFENSE

Hello, Fearless readers!

Thank you all for the OVERWHELMING response to this book. Everyone here on the Fearless Defenders team has just loved hearing all of your excitement, glee and support! In fact, we got so many letters in the one week that our first issue has been on sale that I unfortunately cannot print them all. But I'm going to keep my attempts at wit and charm to a minimum in an effort to fit as many onto this page as we possibly can!

First off, I just want to say...WOAH!

I picked up Fearless Defenders because I saw a lot of good buzz about it, and after reading it, I'm glad I did.

Annabelle is awesome! I love that she was inspired by the Indiana Jones movies to become an archaeologist. Because, let's face it, we all would love to be archaeologist like Indy. I really hope she has a big role in the book along with Valkyrie and Misty. I'm not gonna lie...I believe I've developed a slight crush on Annabelle.

Stay Classy,
Hana
Irvine, CA

P.S. Annabelle needs a cool hat. Fedora, possible?

Yes! But... how do you keep a fedora on when teleporting on the back of a flying horse?

You guys!

I am having to restrain myself so much from writing this email in ALL CAPS!!! because I just read Fearless Defenders and I am SO EXCITED. IT WAS SO AWESOME. The writing, the art, the very existence of it at all.

As a female comic book fan, there have been some rough years, but you guys at Marvel are killing it lately. Thank you so much for your continued support of female led books.

FEARLESS DEFENDERS is the BEST THING I HAVE READ SINCE LIKE THE LAST ISSUE OF CAPTAIN MARVEL. I am sooo excited! I would pester you to include Jessica Drew, but I saw Cullen has already mentioned her, so let me say USE HER A LOT IF YOU CAN BUT I TRUST YOU NO MATTER WHAT SO FAR.

Your overly enthusiastic, over affectionate
and very satisfied customer,
Rachael Sherwood

I had to pick up Defenders #1 because it didn't have Spider-Man, Wolverine, Iron Man, Colossus, Black Widow, Captain America, or the many others that populate so many of Marvel's comics. I saw two characters that are not used that much and was very happy to see them. It is refreshing to see some characters that haven't been used that much and now brought to the forefront. I can't wait to see who you bring in to the series. I think Misty is amazing and a fun character to read. I would also like to see a few other female characters that haven't been seen or used for a bit brought in to the series. Why not bring in Dusk, Echo, Hellcat, Dusk, Thor Girl, Ladyhawk, Starlight or even Shamrock....These are a few that would be interesting to see in the series. Some have not been used that much so you can kind of rewrite them.

Thank you for a great new series and PLEASE don't bring in the too much used characters!!

Sean
Bangor, Maine

Don't worry, Sean, while you will be seeing some of Marvel's more familiar faces in the coming months, the focus of this book is absolutely on giving

a home to awesome characters who you won't find in the regular cast of five other books. Thank so much for supporting us in that goal!

Friends,

A while back - and not so long ago, at that - it was an odd, lonely thing to be a woman who loved comics. There were some wonderful female characters in comics, but not a lot of (male) comic book writers who seemed to know what to do with them.

And now, and now... well. You've got me smiling broadly as I finish rereading "Fearless Defenders #1". This is no lip-service, this is an action-adventure story with female heroes and no self-conscious artificiality.

Valkyrie: warrior with a sword. Bring it on.

Misty Knight: Detective? Martial artist? Freelance whatever? She has style.

Dr. Annabelle Riggs: likes girls, and Indiana Jones. I think I'm in love with her, what with the swooning and kissing and the attitude. She's sticking around, right? Right? Please?

Thanks, guys, for a great first issue.

Namaste,
Elizabeth Holden

I am so glad Annabelle has such a fantastic new fan club! Trust me, she won't be going anywhere any time soon!

Ellie & The Fearless Ones,

FEARLESS DEFENDERS #1 is Fabulous! I put it at the top of my monthly stack of Marvel comics. Just finished reading it, and WOW! This book is going places. Beautiful cover by Brooks. Very crisp art by Sliney & Gandini. Action packed plot with lots of character development already in place by Bunn. Excellent lettering by Cowles.

As a long time Defenders reader (since #2, circa Oct. '72), I'm extremely excited about seeing a monthly Defenders book. I loved FEAR ITSELF: THE FEARLESS and am very glad to see the return of the Valkyrie (and Aragorn). Val has always been a great leader with a complex personality. And of course Misty kicks @$$. Seeing them together is a hoot. They will make a great team with their sword-slinging, face crunching and "Why do you talk like that?" dialogue. I can see lots of upcoming moments where these lasses save each other's' hides while getting on each other's' nerves. Dr. Annabelle is also a nice addition for the first arc.

If I'm not mistaken, this might be Marvel's very first all-female monthly book. I applaud this decision and look forward to many more fun issues of these fearless, female, fighting furies!

"In Our Defense" is a very catchy title for the letter column. If you're still looking for new ideas, how about "Fearless Fe-Mail"!

And with regard to other characters joining or visiting the book, consider: Jessica Jones, Doreen Green, Nico Minoru, Molly Hayes, Kate Bishop, Jeanne Foucault, Bobbie Morse, Carol Danvers, Monica Rambeau, Sue Richards, Kismet, Scarlet Witch, She-Hulk, Red She-Hulk, Pepper Potts, Alicia Masters, Mary Jane Watson and Sarah Wolfe. And if you have any male guest stars, how about Doc Strange? Hey, I figure if I suggest a comprehensive list, someone I like is bound to show up in the ranks of the Fearless Defenders. LOL! Looking forward to issue #2 w/Dani Moonstar and #3 w/Hippolyta. Keep up the great work and see you in 30!

Dan Walsh

Thanks, Dan! Believe it or not Fearless Fe-Mail came up in our letter column name discussions but

I'm saving that for a Rescue book someday.

I just read the 1st ish of Fearless Defenders. I love the idea of an all-female super hero group! I always thought Marvel needed that. You all (everyone involved in bringing this book/idea to life) are off to a great start! I can't wait to see Danielle Moonstar in the next ish! How about bringing Hellcat/Patsy Walker back into the fray or even Black Cat? What about Nova (Frankie Raye) to fill the Silver Surfer role or Namora to fill Namor's role? Or, how about bringing Thundra in? My ultimate dream would be to have an all Lesbian super hero group! Can you say Bad-ass, bitches!? Just some thoughts! Also, thank you so much for the shout out (Dr. Riggs kissing Valkyrie & Valkyrie not freaking out! Gays in the house! Yu-yeah!) Thanks for the great work! Make mine Marvel! Excelsior! (I always wanted to say that!) Btw, I've never written to a letters column before & I've been collecting comics since about the early 70's! =)

Paul Cabral
San Francisco, California

Dear Cullen and Will,

Well, I can give the most sincere compliment a new series can get: I'll be getting #2. It was fun and educational, I had no idea you had megaliths in Vermont, until I looked into it. Was there a legal reason for the Indiana Jones comment? I mean, look at Dr. Riggs...and she's literally raiding a tomb when we meet her! I suggest "The Honored Read", or "Black and White and Read" for the letter column title. Great to have Dani Moonstar next issue, any chance of Kate Bishop dropping in? A team, or non-team with an archery section could be fun.

Best
David Morris
Bristol, England

I'll be honest with you, David, the connection between Annabelle Riggs and Indiana Jones was in the very first draft of the script. No other parallel ever really occurred to me because I too watched A LOT of Indiana Jones growing up and that's about as awesome as archeology got until Cullen brought Annabelle into all our lives.

I absolutely LOVE the first issue. Thank you for bringing my girl Misty Knight back! I can't wait to see the dynamics between her and Valkyrie. And I don't blame Dr. Riggs one bit. I'd probably swoon over Valkyrie too, she is bad a$$! :)

A.Z.

The tweets I've been reading suggest that you are not alone in that A.Z., and I love it!

Dear Defenders Team,

Thank you.

Since I jumped into the Marvel Universe last June I have been searching for great female characters. They exist, certainly, but they are spread out and unfocused and not entirely accessible to newer readers. But Fearless Defenders fixes that in wonderful ways.

And thank you for Annabelle. I have been following various boy/ boy couples in the MU because those were the only gay couples I could find since the one girl/ girl couple I knew of are currently in limbo. But when the owner of my local comic store told me about Annabelle, new hope was born. A girl who likes girls and isn't a terrible stereotype or mere fan service.

Thank you.

Holly Hadde
Columbia, S

Dear Ms. Pyle,
I have to admit, I was skeptical about this new series. EFENDERS without Dr. Strange? Blasphemous! But the revious run of DEFENDERS was amazing, so I figured d pick this book up to see if it could carry the torch. liked the first issue a lot. Valkyrie and Misty Knight? 'ersus undead Valkyries? I'm eager to see how this nfolds.
Since you asked, here's who I'd like to see on the am (I am, of course, assuming that since the story was oout Valkyrie gathering a new team of Shieldmaidens, ey should all be female):

• X-23, because she's my favorite character, and ecause I think her personality contrasts with Val and e others' nicely. She seems the type that doesn't aspire join teams but does well when placed on them.
• Colleen Wing, because I like her relationship with listy. Also, the team seems to be going for diversity ith a white woman, black woman and Native American oman, so why not an Asian woman as well?
• Dust, because she hits again on the whole diversity spect of the team. In her case both because of her eritage and her powers, what with Val, Misty and Dani lying mainly on physical prowess.
• And finally, I'd like to see Captain Marvel, because A) d be good to have someone else who was a Defender some point, B) She's a heavy hitter that the team is cking in right now, and C) Um.... I like Captain Marvel :>

As for antagonists, since Val is the central character the book, Loki is an obvious choice. But I don't think no they face is as important as what they face, and in ost Defenders books I've read, what they faced were uge, Avenger-level threats that required the characters work together in the first place. I think as long as ere's something large-scale looming on the horizon at's keeping them together, you can't go wrong.

Can't wait to see Dani next issue!
Brett

Love, love, love issue #1 of Fearless Defenders. Truth told, As a comics fan for almost 40-years, I haven't ught a Marvel book for over two decades. Back when id buy Marvel, the Defenders line up with Valkyrie was e of my fav books. My streak of buying a couple zen books a week was broken last year when your stinguished competition, decided things weren't NU ough. I've dropped all of those books and have looked vain for something to fill the niche for over a year.
This month with FEARLESS DEFENDERS, comics came fun again! I enjoyed the story, it had a great lance of actions, character development and plot. e art was good, but I am hoping with time Sliney will t a better handle on defining the faces more so the aracters are a bit more different from one another. d the page with Misty asking about the giant, flying rse is bound to be considered a classic. Keep up the od work. As a fan of a certain Amazon Princess who n't even stomach her book anymore, I can't wait to see opolyta interact with the team! Now to read "Young engers" and see if they're titanic enough to fill another che.

Thanks for such a great book and keep up the cellent work.

Anthony Lower
Philadelphia, Pa

In my eyes, Marvel can do no wrong these days... a long-time reader (which may or may not be the al demographic you're looking for, but still...), and current crop of Marvel titles is as good as it's been years. I just wanted to say that Fearless Defenders nicely into that description as well, and I'm looking ward to the series as it progresses.
What promoted me to write though is Cullen's ntion of the New Defenders, one of the oddest team oks ever in my opinion, but one I'm quite nostalgic for. love to see one or two (or more) "classic" members out the ranks... Moondragon, Hellcat, maybe Clea... if there's a chance for a male member... Gargoyle! e of the weirdest looking super heroes ever, and such ool concept (sweet elderly man in demon's body) h so much potential. So there's my vote, but looking ward to following this series either way!

PWitham

Marvel-Folks,
Just read Fearless Defenders #1. Looks like a very mising new title. I've always been one for the more scure, less used characters, so when I saw Valkyrie Misty Knight in one book I was intrigued but wasn't sure I'd be adding it to my list.
After reading up further on it, I LOVED the idea of Valkyrie looking for a team of shieldmaidens and readily added it to my sub list. Danielle Moonstar is another great character. Although she's bad ass on her own, I do wish she would get her powers back somehow. I think her fear-projection power would really fit a valkyrie shieldmaiden rather well.
As for who I'd like to see on the team....hmmmm, so many interesting choices. My suggestions would be Moondragon, Mantis, Hellcat....possibly Snowbird, Crystal of The Inhumans, Dagger of Cloak & Dagger, Colleen Wing (since Misty's already there).
I'd love to see a reformed Pavane from Master of Kung Fu (I know it's a long shot, but I always thought she was a cool, underused character with her whip, black panthers and sexy outfit.)
Anyway that's my choices. Look forward to reading more.

Robert

I am absolutely thrilled that our Fearless ladies are inspiring not just letters but fanart and fashion as well!

To the hardworking Fearless Defenders team,
I hope you enjoy this fanart!

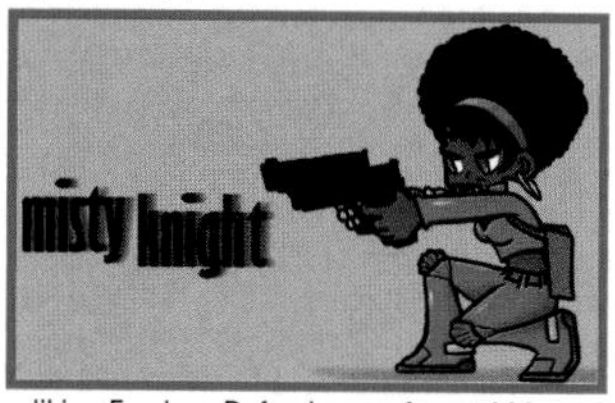
misty knight

I'm liking Fearless Defenders so far, and I hope in the future some former Thunderbolt ladies join the crew! (You can make it work, somehow...) Preferably Troll, but Songbird would be cool, too.

Thank you for your time,
Vivi

Hi Ellie!
We were both so thrilled the minute we heard that Fearless Defenders was going to be a thing that we instantly decided that we had to do character inspired outfits for our geek fashion blog to celebrate the launch of Issue #1! The first issue was a wonderful read and we can't wait to see where the book goes and what other fabulous ladies join the team.

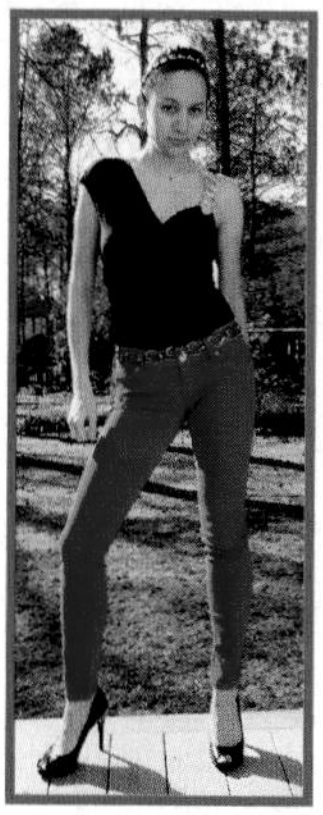

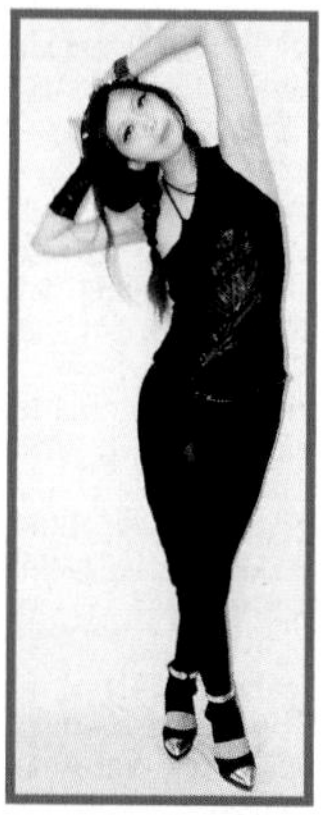

Bria and Lin
Geek Pursuits x Stylish Ladies
whitehotroom.com

Cullen,
This issue started out well enough; simple home invasion at Dani Moonstar's place...maybe too simple. The Dani parts of the issue were fine; she's new here and is a character I've always liked, followed. The rest of the issue, blachh: it was boring, wordy, contrived--! What worked last issue, did not here. As for Valkyrie and her entire origin being a lie? Between that and her usage both here and in SECRET AVENGERS: don't treat Brunhilde like an entirely new character! And don't damage her for all time! I couldn't honestly believe that this was the same creative team from the fun first issue.
Thumbs Way Down, think about changes.

Sincerely,
Andrew J. Shaw

Thanks, Andrew! We who make comics count on you to keep us honest with your constant and consistent feedback. Hopefully this issue help set your concerns about us treating Valkyrie as a new character aside. I'm sure you will let me know.

Hello!
My name's Melita and I'm just writing in to say how much I absolutely love this new series. I read about it on a blog about female super heroes and bought it the next day BECAUSE IT DOES EVERYTHING RIGHT!! Misty is just the coolest lady and I wish I could find more heroes like her (even having these three ladies around when I was a kid would have been the best thing!). Absolutely kudos for making the kiss between Annabelle and Valkyrie not fan service to those who trivialize female sexuality!
I would like to criticize the issue though in the tiniest of ways...I understand, in order to keep creating this amazing (AMAZING!!) series, you need advertisers buuuuut having that stupid Dr. Pepper 10 ad in the middle of one of the most potentially female empowering comics I have EVER read (and will continue to do) was discomforting. It made my joy at finally having a trio of bad-ass women to look up to completely shatter as the ad just reminded me that even today, comic books are still being aimed at that magical demographic of heterosexual men aged 18-34, and not me, a nineteen-year-old still-trying-to-discover-herself girl.
All in all, I've recommended this series TO EVERYONE I know who loves comics (it's a lot of people just FYI) and you all deserve the biggest of high fives for how amazing just the first issue is!
Can't wait for more!

Melita.

Thank you, Melita! Interestingly, you're not the only person to comment on the Dr. Pepper ad but unfortunately I don't have any say on what ads go into the book (only where they end up). My favorite comic when I was a kid was X-Men #28 where Jean Grey fights Sabretooth and wins so I'm just thrilled by the idea that Misty, Valkyrie, Annabelle, Dani and Hippolyta could find an audience with a new generation!
And speaking of how awesome Misty is check out this awesome pinup by Cormac Huges:

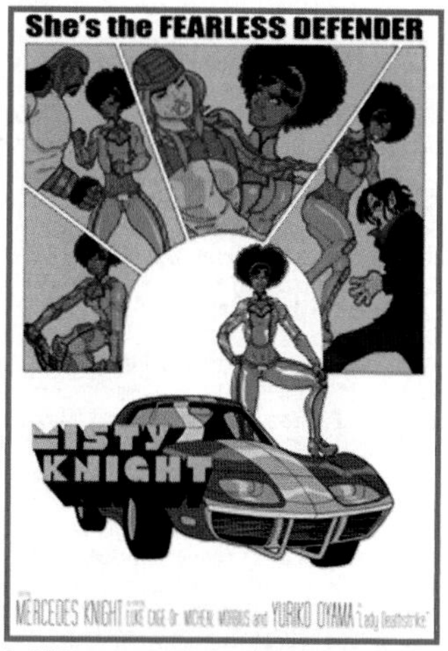
She's the FEARLESS DEFENDER
MISTY KNIGHT

And this gorgeous bit of cosplay by Lady D:

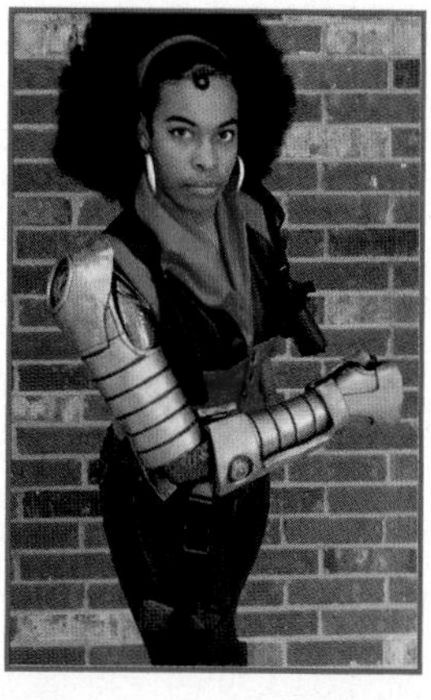

Hello,
My name is Dominique Melder but the cosplay world knows me as Lady D. I am a 22-year-old amateur cosplayer and Theater Arts major. I attend the University of New Orleans. I've been cosplaying for four years now yet my love for the craft grows with each new costume I attempt. I attend anime & comic book conventions annually where I love to showcase new cosplays. To date I have won 2 Best In Show awards, 1 Best Walk On award, and 2 Judges awards. I like to cosplay lesser known characters because I believe those characters too deserve to be showcased center stage for all to appreciate. Above the awards my true goal is to inspire people to discover new titles and new characters in anime or comics. In doing so, I believe I'm doing the character justice which is the number one goal of a cosplayer. To see some of my work please follow me on Twitter @ULP_LadyD.

Hi!
This is Jay Justice, costumer & cosplayer from NYC. Recently I, along with my friend Katie Dee, had the opportunity to attend C2E2 & meet the lovely & talented Ellie Pyle and tell her how much we love FEARLESS DEFENDERS. Oh, and we happened to be dressed as Misty Knight and Valkyrie respectively, at the time. We tell everyone about how amazing this book is, and have gotten quite a few of our friends, acquaintances, local baristas, bank tellers & delivery boys to buy it! Here are a few photos of us in costume together, feel free to print whichever one you like, and we hope to see Cullen, Will, Ellie & the rest of the Fearless Crew at a con in the future! We're building up our roster, Misty, Valkyrie, Dani & Hippolyta will see you at New York Comic Con!

Much love,
Jay Justice & Katie Dee

So yeah, I'll admit it, we here at FEARLESS DEFENDERS love knowing that people are out there reading and caring about this book. We especially love knowing that you're telling your friends, neighbors, acquaintances, co-workers, family, and perhaps even some complete strangers about it. Because honestly? We're making this book for all of you. And the more of you there are, the longer we will get to keep making it!
Another fantastic fan I'd like take a moment to acknowledge is Sherwoode, who is more commonly known to us here at FEARLESS DEFENDERS as @SongbirdDiamond on Twitter and the curator of the [word I can't print but you can all probably figure out what it is]YeahFearlessDefenders Tumblr. Sherwoode has been a constant and outspoken supporter of this book since before it even came out and we definitely appreciate his efforts!

Hello!
Ah hoy hoy!
Just wanted to say how much I am enjoying and continually getting excited for this book. There is an air of unpredictability to it all, with each reveal from the monthly solicits hinting a tiny bit more about what's ahead! I've been excited about this book since the reveal at the end of FEAR ITSELF: THE FEARLESS, and I must say, keep up the good work! I'm on board this train for the long haul!

Sherwoode

P.S. Please have Songbird and Diamondback team up! They don't even have to join the team!

Stay tuned, SD! Here at FEARLESS DEFENDERS, any team-up is possible!
And speaking of more obscure characters:

Team Fearless,
It seems that when Hela called in her favours from the "countless" death gods... she didn't go to any of the many Marvel death gods we've seen before. I understand that she's not exactly friendly with any of them at the moment given the events in X-Factor at the moment - but were we supposed to know who any of those characters were?

- Adrian J. Watts
Melbourne, Australia

Hi Adrian,
Thanks for asking! I think this confusion is a result of the difference between a "death god" and a "hell lord". I have also been reading X-FACTOR and while you are correct that Hela was mixing it up there recently with Mephisto and others, for the purposes of reviving Hippolyta she needed to go to Pluto, the death god of Hippolyta's home pantheon, who first appeared in THOR #127 in 1966. The other death gods she eventually had to call in favors from included Osiris and Seth (Heliopolitans) Ahpuch (Mayan), Yama (Daevas) and others who have appeared in the THOR books and elsewhere in the Marvel Universe. The biggest difference between a Death God and a Hell Lord I would say is that Death Gods are pantheon based where as Hell Lords might not be gods but are rulers of specific hell or demonic dimensions, so it is more of a geography based title. Hela just happens to be the point of overlap between the two.

Ok.
I know...
I know...
Stop screaming.
Stop crying.
Take a breath. Get some water.
Pick the book back up from across the room (where you threw it).
Ok.
An editor's most important job is to be their book's first audience, and as such, I was Annabelle's first fan. And I am overjoyed that she found such a devoted fan base in such a short time. So, I absolutely understand why you are angry at Cullen, and me, and probably even poor Will who just draws what we tell him to (beautifully!) But I am going to ask you to trust us. Stick with us, knowing that we love Annabelle as much as you do, and her death will prove necessary as well as noble.
In fact, when I asked Twitter what you all thought was going to happen this issue, several of you saw this coming:

@pwongview Fearless Defenders #6--Annabelle tragically dies & Valbelle shippers hate Cullen forever.
@MarkKirwan I think Whedon fever has taken over Marvel and Annabelle is going to bite it. #youmonsters

And others of you weren't far off:

@Seccruz Val dies and Annabelle rescues her, becoming full Valkirye in the process... Also the girls kick ass!!!
@LastOneHere182 Valkyrie goes nuts on the Doom Maidens, turns on friends, big fight, Annabelle kisses her to snap her out, & awkwardness.
@SongbirdDiamond Okay. I am going to bet Dani Moonstar sacrifices herself cause she is the battery for the Doom Maidens. And Songbird and Diamondback have their epic team up!!!
@Daversphere I think Dani's going to take control of the power that Le Fey gave her and take those Doom Maidens down. Ok to print
@JESSICADREWSW Spider-Woman will join the Team Kicks butts of Caroline and her mother and save the day and will be a sheildmaiden.

And some were:

@jmartinwrites Basically the ending of Tim Burton's Alice In Wonderland, but with more

Asgardians and shooting.
@ImCVV Invisible Woman has been there all along, just, you know, invisible.
@Paul_Sebert Spider-Girl (Anya Corazon) wi[ll] join the team and everyone will fight robot gorillas barbarians, and a mummy!
@Paul_Sebert The return of Nomad: Gir[l] Without of World. Guest starring Blink & Nev[?] Exiles. Plus who are the YOUNG THUNDERBOLTS?
@angrysunbird Squirrel Girl and Pixie save the[?] day.
@ChrisEliopoulos The Pet Avengers save th[e] day.
@ChrisOHalloran It's all a dream in purgatory and they're still on the island.

See? I was thinking ahead, knowing you woul[d] all need a laugh after this issue.
But back on a more somber/ominous note[?] check out this fan art by James Murphy:

And now the sheer joy of this amazin[g] Hippolyta cosplay by Caitlin Rhyne of Contagiou[s] Costuming! (picture courtesy of Pat Loika)

It's going to be ok, my fearless friends. B[ut] until you know that for sure, send me all yo[ur] Annabelle fan art, thoughts, feelings and outrag[e] Want to have a conversation about female deat[h] and/or sexuality in comic books? Let's do it! [I] will devote next issue's letter page entirely [to] Annabelle in memoriam if we get enough stuff.
And speaking of next issue, don't forg[et] we double-ship this month! (Planning ahea[d] So I will see you back here in two (very long[?]) weeks when Stephanie Hans will give us a Ve[ry] Asgardian Look at How ALL of this is A part of t[he] plan.

Said with a smil[e]
Ellie Py[le]

TO ACCESS THE FREE *MARVEL AUGMENTED REALITY APP* THAT ENHANCES AND CHANGES THE WAY YOU EXPERIENCE COMICS:

1. Download the app for free via marvel.com/ARapp
2. Launch the app on your camera-enabled Apple iOS® or Android™ device*

3. Hold your mobile device's camera over any cover or panel with the **AR** graphic.
4. Sit back and see the future of comics in action!

*Available on most camera-enabled Apple iOS® and Android™ devices. Content subject to change and availability.

THE FEARLESS
DEFENDERS
AR INDEX